Adulting

Also by Kelly Williams Brown

Gracious: A Practical Primer on Charm, Tact, and
Unsinkable Strength

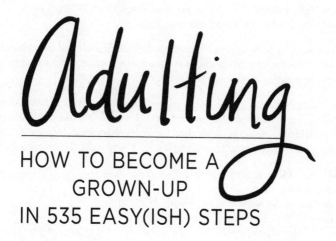

HOW TO BECOME A
GROWN-UP
IN 535 EASY(ISH) STEPS

Kelly Williams Brown

GRAND CENTRAL

Life & Style

NEW YORK · BOSTON

Grand Central Life & Style
Hachette Book Group
1290 Avenue of the Americas, New York, NY 10104
grandcentrallifeandstyle.com
twitter.com/grandcentralpub

Originally published in hardcover and ebook by Grand Central Publishing in May 2013.

First Revised Edition: March 2018

Grand Central Life & Style is an imprint of Grand Central Publishing. The Grand Central Life & Style name and logo are trademarks of Hachette Book Group, Inc.

The publisher is not responsible for websites (or their content) that are not owned by the publisher.

The Hachette Speakers Bureau provides a wide range of authors for speaking events. To find out more, go to www.hachettespeakersbureau.com or call (866) 376-6591.

All line drawings by the author.

Library of Congress Control Number: 2017959713

ISBNs: 978-1-5387-2913-7 (revised trade pbk.), 978-1-4555-1689-6 (ebook)

Printed in the United States of America

LSC-C

10 9 8 7 6 5 4 3 2 1

To Barbara, Joel, and Barbara

Contents

A NOTE ON THE
Second Edition

Dear Reader,

Feel free to skip this part. Any of the book, really, but this little section especially, because it has just one concrete, useful life strategy, and here it is: Pour liquids from one container into the other over the sink; pour solids over a garbage can. Assuming the solid in question is, say, sugar and not your collection of loose sapphires, in which case, maybe just pour over a big empty bowl.

So here is a story: When I was twenty-six, I was a reporter in Salem, Oregon, which is my real-life Pawnee. My beat was events and music and nightlife and any of the things human beings do, not because they have to but because they want to. I also wrote a weekly column of whatever nonsense I came up with, like crowning the cutest baby animal at the Polk County Fair, or writing a musical about the time everyone thought we were finally getting a Trader Joe's but it was a mean trick, or spending an afternoon "solving" "mysteries."

Sample Mystery: Wait, we have an *entire* store dedicated to clocks? What? *Findings:* Yeah, we do, and it has a *whole bunch of clocks.* These clocks are all going their own way in terms of ticking and chiming; they were supervised by an intense owner who answered all my questions with one word, then watched me as I moved among his precious time-pieces. In fact, this experience introduced more questions than answers, but they remain unanswered; I couldn't spend more than twenty minutes there. It is alarming to step out of your *Parks and Rec* life and into a David Lynch movie.

People—again, not just my mother!—asked me if I "was ever going to write a book," which is sort of like asking an aspiring actor if they were "ever going to star in a movie." Plus, I had no idea what I could possibly write a book about. I lack the focus to write the kind of dense nonfiction that takes a decade of research (*A Cohort of Scoundrels, Scholars, and Princes: How Truman's Forestry Department Changed Everything and Everyone, Forever [and What It Tells Us about Sexuality and the American Dream]*. I lack the creativity to write fiction; every time I do, I end up just telling one of my own anecdotes with my name changed to Betsy. The world does not need my memoir. Plus, at the time, I did not have a computer, nor the money to buy one. Challenges!

One afternoon, in an attempt to get the community to basically write my column for me, I posed a question on Facebook: What concrete, tangible skills should you have by the age of thirty? There were a lot of very thoughtful replies, though, sadly, not enough to make a column out of. Then, a little while later, a friend complimented me on giving good advice and said maybe I should write an advice book. I felt, based on the way my fridge smelled at that very moment, that I was in no place to tell anyone anything about how to live.

When I was twenty-two, my friend Rachel (who, at the time, was twenty-seven and capable and wise and generous and lived in a *tasteful* apartment with *actual furniture*) gave me a wonderful gift. We were driving back to the newsroom of the small Mississippi town where we were both reporters, and... well, now, I can't remember what problem I was crying about. There were a lot of possibilities.

Maybe I was lamenting that I had no real furniture, as mine was made of particleboard and had literally dissolved when I moved during a rainstorm. Maybe I was sobbing because I was only a few months into my first grown-up job and, while I was doing what I had always dreamed of doing, I was also consistently screwing *every single last thing up*, and felt like I had tricked my editor into hiring me, and any moment I would be caught and exposed for the fraud I was. Maybe I was agonizing over my long-term relationship with a truly wonderful guy who, I knew, was not right for me and vice versa. Maybe she had just treated me to a Sonic Cherry Limeade because my take-home pay was $610 every two weeks and I had student loans and my post–Hurricane Katrina rent was a bargain at $450, which meant I was always overdrawing my bank account and relied on what I called the Walmart Check-Bouncin' Grift. In short, I was twenty-two and my life was nothing but chaos and shambles, and it showed no signs of ever being otherwise.

"You know, no one tells you this, but the first year out of college or on your own is *really, really hard,*" Rachel said. "Before then, your life progresses in an orderly way—you finish one grade and then you go to another. You are constantly getting feedback and you know what's expected of you. And then it's just... all open-ended, and confusing."

Having someone say this to me—*Yes, this is* really *hard. You're not an idiot because there are things you don't know and can't do right now. It's okay, and it will get better*—for the first time was... whatever the opposite feeling is of exchanging pleasantries with the Walmart clerk as she copies down your driver's license number on a check you know is no good.

Five years later, I thought: Maybe, perhaps, I can write a book that not only would have been useful to my very confused and sad past self, but also could give someone the comfort that Rachel gave me that day.

Around that time, I was sitting with a friend in her fifties at a bar. Lovely Jessica Maxwell lived the life that I wanted—she'd been a longtime travel writer for all sorts of schmancy magazines and had published many books, and also her house is so pretty that I am sort of afraid of it. She was talking about the importance of a good title, and I blurted out the word "adulting," and she clapped her hands and said that was *perfect*, and then bartender Rob came over and wondered if that sounded too much like adultery? But *Adulting* it was.[1]

I tackled it like a reporting project: Find someone who can speak authoritatively about, say, how bleach works or how to have a cute living room. Interview them for a long, long time. Print out said interview, then highlight and cross-reference and fact-check and weave the information into a readable narrative and blah blah blah. Eventually, hey! You have a book!

My mom and dad, for my twenty-seventh birthday, sent me to the Willamette Writers Conference to pitch the book to agents and editors. For the record, writers conferences are a *great* way to get that precious, precious face-to-face time with someone who can actually make a book happen, but you have to pay for it. This conference was, I think, pretty normal, pricewise, but it may as well have been $100,000 for all I could afford at the time.

Then I got struck by metaphorical lightning, and life became very strange and terrifying. Agents at the conference were *very* into it, and approaching *me* to ask about it, and then on the second day a TV producer wanted to ask if I'd considered making it into a sitcom. So within three weeks—I am not kidding—I had gone from having my debit card declined at Popeyes to trying to act like it was *nooooo biiiig deal, who caaaaaares?* while Skyping with executives from FOX and Warner Bros.

Then, the book came out and people liked it and oh, man, I am *so happy they did*. I really hope you do, too.

For those of you who were wondering what might happen if you, too, decided to write a how-to reference on being a grown-up, here's what you can expect:

o Every time you do anything—even something totally understandable, like show up a few minutes late to a coffee date or fall asleep cradling a bag of Haribo

---

1. Yes, yes: *I originated the term.* Look, don't be intimidated! It's okay. And I understand how this can be a deeply irritating word. Heck, it irritated me the first time I said it! But this is my very, very tiny claim to fame and you can tear it from my cold, dead, word-inventing hands.

Gold-Bears and then wake up in the morning and wander around for a few minutes before you notice a pineapple bear is stuck to your tummy—your friend (or sexfriend) will smirk and say something like, "Didn't you write a book on this?" and you will smile a not-real smile and say "Ha!" and then wander out of view so you can eat the bear. Pineapple is the best flavor and there's only ever four of them.

○ Every time someone else just, like, exists as a human being, they will apologize constantly to you for transgressions such as not having a special guest towel or only making four delicious courses instead of seven. You'll say it's fine, *seriously,* and then you try to put them at ease by telling them the story about the gummy bear to make them feel better. This, instead, makes everything worse.

○ Sometimes, someone will introduce you and then note that you're very famous (even though you are *not*), and the person you're meeting looks excitedly to you to see what a famous person will say. That clacking noise in your head is the roller coaster cranking up to the top of the hill, except it is not a loop-de-loop ahead; it is their disappointment and your social anxiety that's about to wash over everyone.

○ Your mom will be very, very proud!

○ Word will get out that you're an expert on many things that you are not, like adulthood or millennials or car maintenance, and journalists will call you to ask you questions you cannot answer with any authority, and you can sense, so clearly, them thinking, *Didn't you write a book on this?*

These interviews begin with the same question, every last time—"So what *is* a grown-up? When *are* you an adult?" This ding-dang question! I've been thinking about it for six years now, and hooooo boy, I wish I had an answer! I wish there *were* an answer. I would trot it out at every interview:

"Well, Ellen, first, thank you *so* much for having me on and also telling me that I am a good, super-funny person that you want to go with on a friend-vacation to Dollywood. I *cannot* wait. Anyway, Science Peer-Reviewed Research has shown that you are officially an adult at ten thousand days, which happens a few months into your twenty-seventh year. On that day, you wake up and your life is just *together*, Ellen, it *really is*.

"Your career will be fulfilling, lucrative, and unlimited, complimentary coconut water is available. Friends, family, significant others—to each one, you will be loving, giving them always what they need and deserve while respecting your own boundaries. Your counters are never sticky; there are never little dried spider corpses in your bedside drawer. It's great!"

I do have my talking point for when they ask me the question. Being a grown-up means treating others and yourself with decency and compassion, figuring out what needs to be done and then doing it with minimal fuss or self-pity.

Here, though, is the other, uglier truth: Being an adult—heck, being a human—is hard. No one feels like they're doing it correctly (or, if they do, they feel very sure that others *aren't* doing it right, an opinion that they will often voice or vote for). There is nothing I can give you in this book that will allow you to protect and cushion yourself, not against the million tiny insults or few truly life-altering traumas that we all go through.

But I can say this: You get better at it, the same way you are better at a job after a year and way, way better after five. With every experience, every heartbreak, every month, and every year, you grow better and more capable at the very real work of living in your own skin.

I wrote the first edition of this book when I was twenty-seven. I am now thirty-two, and those five years have been both wonderful and awful. I published a book (this one!). I worked in advertising and did some real neat things. I mourned my beloved Grannybarb, to whom this book is dedicated, and, last week, Marigny Treme Brown-Gervais, the cat I adopted within a week of getting my first apartment. I wrote another book. I did not have to worry about money for the first time in my post-pubescent life. I got married and then unmarried, the second being the most wrenching and awful thing imaginable. I got a 1994 Miata (as all divorcées must—and, for the record, money cannot buy happiness, but if you have $3,500, then it *can* buy fun). I made peace with the idea that I would never have another romantic relationship; then I found someone incredible. Donald Trump was elected. You get the idea. Highs 'n' lows!

The world changed, too, in ways good and bad. I'm so grateful that this second edition exists, that I can go through this and take out things that are irrelevant or thoughtless or, in one case that gave me multiple panic attacks right before publication, incorrect. I'm sure, also, that there are things I'm writing now that, in five years, I will look at and wish I hadn't etched into the stone that is a Final Manuscript. But, of course, the only way to ensure that you don't make a mistake is to not do or say anything in the first place. In this, like everything, I remember my Grannybarb's mantra: Everyone does their best, and some people's best is shitty. What is more important is how you correct the error, and what you do going forward to be different.

I still fall asleep with bags of gummy bears, my kitchen is still messy, and I should probably change my sheets soon. And this, like me, is okay. It's not great, but it's *fucking fine.* You, dear reader, whoever you are—you are much, much more okay than you know. You are way more capable than you know. While many things are terrifying and out of your control, I've found again and again that doing the small things in my own life with competence is the best, and perhaps only, comfort. When I feel afraid, there are small things that I can do to make sure that at least I am not getting a thirty-five-dollar late fee from Giant Bank. I can go wipe my counter. I can make my bed, and then, at the end of a day when nothing has been okay, at least I can slip into clean cotton and not get tangled in a top sheet. These little things help me feel sane in the face of a world that is often not.

Sometimes, you'll screw up or just not have a single bit of effort left in you, and that's okay, too.

You can do it. I promise.

Love,
Kelly
September 2017

Adulting

INTRODUCTION

What's that you say? You're a colossal sham who will never have your life in order? One who eats microwave taquitos in lieu of breakfast? One who has many dead bugs trapped between the windowpanes in your bedroom, which doesn't make sense, because *how did they even get there?* One who, much of the time, could best be described as "anxious," "terrified," and/or "sticky?" One whose actions do not reflect the fact that they, chronologically and/or legally, are absolutely, completely, and undeniably an adult?

Yes. Of course you think that. Everyone does. There is not one adult on this earth who has not felt the deep, unsettling feeling that their life is wobbly and unmanageable, no matter how diligently they sort the recycling and iron their sensible slacks. This is supported by the popular, though incorrect, perception that you're surrounded by people who have it together while you flop around like a fish who can't remember to pay her water bill.

We look jealously around at others, noting their lack of grubby visible bra straps or crusty under-eye mascara sprinkles,[1] and it's hard

I swear I paid this.

not to be resentful. *Why you and not me?* you think, squinting angrily at this person who probably has a beautiful apartment and an actual career and a boyfriend who never uses a skateboard to go from place to place.

But perhaps he has $12.37 in

---
1. Or, as I call them, "Failure Flakes."

his checking account, or she has no idea how to cook anything, or he slowly lets his car rot from inside rather than pony up the thirty bucks to get the oil changed. Chances are good that person is looking at you the same way.

Figure 1:

Failure Flakes
(also- WHY WHY WHYYYY
is there mascara
on my eyelid?)

We all sense our own dysfunction so clearly. And because we can't do that one thing—whether it be keeping a clean house, not feeling shy and awkward at work, or having a credit score of 750—we assign it a high priority on our own personal Things That You Must Be Good At If You Wish To Be A Functional Adult list. We don't remember the fourteen things we do reasonably well; we remember our one arena of miserable failure.

It might be tidiness. It might be money. It might be the capacity to have a normal, low-stakes conversation with a stranger where you don't mention intestinal parasites in *any* context. In this vulnerable arena, we assume that, through the awesome power of being really frustrated and angry with ourselves, we will somehow magically evolve into someone else, someone who *isn't* afraid to log on to online banking. When this strategy fails (spoiler alert: it *does, every time*), we just feel worse.

There are certain parts of being a grown-up that come easily to us, and some that...don't. When I asked people what advice they have, they'd say, "Well, this probably seems really obvious, but [thing that was not at all obvious but afterward *did*, in fact, seem obvious and a little embarrassing that someone had to tell a twenty-seven-year-old]."

For example, I am really, really bad at keeping my house clean. I am good at lots of things, but noticing dirt in crevices is not one of them. In fact, I do not even see the crevice itself. It *may as well not exist.* So while I don't need to worry about, say, honing my thank-you-note-writing skills, I do need to figure out how to see the crevices that others do. Then I have to remind myself of those crevices, at least once a week. Since my brain doesn't do this naturally, that means developing some sort of strategy, perhaps involving phone reminders and/or a Post-it that just has an arrow and a :(, guiding me to the crevice in question.

It is these small discoveries and decisions that, in the end, allow you to behave like an adult. It's developing those good habits; it's having toast with peanut butter instead of cigarettes for breakfast. It's not always, or even usually, fun. But it has perks—personal pride, financial security, and the feeling of accomplishment and control that comes when you just swap in a new toilet paper roll rather than resorting to Kleenex, then fast-food napkins, then paper towels.[2]

You can't control the economy, or whether you're single, or when your cat decides to vomit neon orange tummy contents onto your white rug. *What is she even eating that is that color?* But there are lots of things you can control, and lots of decisions are up to you.

It feels like there are all these things that People Should Know, and if you don't know them, it means you're stupid. You're not. Not knowing how to sew on a button isn't the end of the world. Just figure out *how* to sew it on rather than obsessing about *why* you don't know, then tumbling down into the Why Am I Like This Canyon. Fill that gap, and then not only will you know how to sew on that button, but you will also feel all grown-up and powerful. So go forth, perform these steps (if you want!), check them all off, and feel smug at your newfound adult skills.

Here is what I'm trying to tell you: *Adult* isn't a noun; it's a verb. It's the act of making correctly those small decisions that fill our day. It is something that you can practice and that can be done in concrete steps. And if you slip up and have Diet Coke for breakfast, no one busts in and snatches away your Adult card. Just move forward and have milk tomorrow.

QUESTIONS... AND *ANSWERS*

Q: What is adulting? Does it have anything to do with adultery?
A: It does not. The word *adulting* is taking a noun, *adult*, and making it a verb. Actually, this strategy works with many

---

2. Please do not do this. It's very, very bad for your plumbing.

nouns (sandwiching, Nashvilling, bridesmaiding, et cetera). But point being, adult isn't something you are; it's something you do. You are a grown-ass man, or grown-ass woman, and you can act like it even if you don't feel like it on the inside.

Q: Who are you to tell anyone how to be a grown-up?

A: I'm Kelly. I'm a reporter for a newspaper who has red hair. You should know this important thing about me: I'm not a super-great grown-up. I'm *okay* at it, and improving steadily, but I'm in no way a model of what adulthood looks like. I am not the Martha Stewart of basic human competence. Lots of times, Comcast has to call and ask nicely, then not-nicely, for me to pay my cable bill. Or my sink is full of gross dishes, which languish as a tomato-sauce-encrusted monument to my shortcomings.

A while ago, I was talking to my beloved friend Ruth, who suggested I write an advice book, perhaps as a way of extricating herself from the bossy advice monologue I was in the middle of. My mind flashed to the dishes, and my disorganization, and all the things that make me fall into I'm-not-a-grown-up anguish, and I felt I was in no position to tell people how to conduct their lives.

But I decided, since I am a reporter whose job is to go find people who are smart and ask them about things and distill what they tell me into something readable, maybe I could treat this as a reporting project.

This is the result. I definitely threw in things I've learned in my six years of being on my own, but most of this is from others. Lots of times, I've identified them by name and quoted them; others just wanted to share their ideas without their names getting in print. Sometimes, it was just someone saying something really smart to me in a bar. I included those tips, too, even though I didn't know their names. Wise random strangers at bars are modern-day Oracles of Delphi, except drunk and sometimes leaving abruptly when it's their turn for karaoke.

Q: Do I have to do all these steps? At once? They're a lot. It's kind of overwhelming.

A: Nope. You do not have to do a single one of them. Ever! It's not a moral judgment—you're not a better or worse person if you have a soup ladle, for example. If you don't want to do a step in this book, if it doesn't make sense in your life, then don't—none of the steps is of "Don't commit genocide!" importance.

Nor should you feel like all these things can or should happen overnight. There are lots of steps you've already done, and some you will never do. The point of this book is not to induce guilt about things you can't do or haven't done. Give yourself credit for the things you do, fix the small things you can, accept that some things won't come easy or may never come. The point of this book is that even though things seem—and are—complicated and difficult, we have control over ourselves. Someone is a grown-up by virtue of acting like one. And no matter who you are, you can be a grown-up.

A SPECIAL NOTE TO MALE AND NON-BINARY READERS

Hello! I am so glad you're here. Most of the stuff in this book is for everyone. But watch out! Some specific advice is more geared

toward the ladies. If you read something and think, *Huh, I don't really have any bras to store,* then you're probably right. I don't want you to feel left out. There are lots and lots and lots of things written about and for you, including maybe 85 percent of this book. So if you get to a step that doesn't apply, go ahead and skip it, maybe doodling a masculine doodle of a race car or a wizard over the text. Or be transgressive and read it for super-secret insights into us ladyfolk (spoiler alert: *urinary tract infections!*).

DISCUSSION QUESTIONS

1. Which is a better name for mascara sprinkles: Satan's Pepper or Failure Flakes?
2. What is something that other people notice and you never do, even when it's pointed out to you, at which point you act like you knew that all along even though it still isn't totally clear?
3. What is your biggest adult failure to date? Be honest. Did it involve coconut-flavored rum? It did, didn't it? Oh, coconut rum.

Chapter 1
GET YOUR MIND RIGHT

The vast majority of this book is full of practical, interacting-with-the-world sorts of steps—wiping your counters or breaking up with your surly boyfriend or whatever. Most of being an adult is not up in your head; it's in your actions. In fact, let's get this out of the way now: Intentions are nice, but ultimately intentions don't really matter because they only exist inside you. Meaning to send a thank-you note but then not doing it is exactly the same as never thinking to send one—that person is still receiving zero thank-you notes.

So, yes. Actions are greater than intentions. But before we get to those actions, there are just a few things you should know.

Step 1: Accept that you are *not* that *special*

This is the most difficult and important thing to accept if you wish to be a grown-up: You are not a ~~Special Snowflake~~ Singular Seahorse.[1]

Step 2: Appreciate those who disagree with step 1

Well, you are to some people. Your parents, presumably, love you very much and think you are perhaps the most adorable, talented thing ever to prance upon this earth. Your friends agree with them, as do your favorite teachers, as does your significant other. When there is a You Parade, these people will be the flag bearers, the drum majors

---

1. Here lies the phrase "Special Snowflake," 1996–2016. Alas, I first wrote this in 2012. 'Twas a simpler time!

and majorettes, so make sure you are always flag bearing and drum majoring for them, too. These people who think so highly of us are very special and precious, and we must treasure them. Because here is the truth: Most of the world doesn't give a flying fuck about you.

Step 3: Don't get hurt when the world doesn't care about you

It's not as depressing as it sounds. It's not as though the world *hates* you—it just has no idea who you are. It is, at best, indifferent to your wants and needs, your preferences, your pet peeves, and so on. When you walk into a new office, new city, new country, whatever, you are starting from scratch and cannot call upon that loving capital that your friends and family have for you. You sometimes find patches of immediately friendly people, but that won't be the rule. It is now up to you to find and surround yourself with people for whom you feel affection and respect.

People will come to care about you, but only if you give them a valid reason. Don't assume they'll give you love like your parents, emotional support like your best friend, and cheerful feedback like a soccer coach for seven-year-olds. Because they won't, unless you give them good reason to. And even then, they still probably won't.

Step 4: It is nearly always easier to adjust your expectations than it is to change the world; your comfort and well-being are up to you

The lowest-stakes example is this: I always carry earbuds in my Pouch of Necessities,[2] because the world is *chock-full* of noises that irritate me. I have no control over whether the man behind me is having a loud, gross discussion, but guess what? I don't have to listen to it . . . if I have my earbuds with me. Sure, I can glare at that guy all I want, but it probably won't change much. A much better strategy is to focus on how I can make myself comfortable in a world that is not.

---

2. Other things in there: a spare phone charger, Band-Aids, Super Glue, tampons, a little tin with three days' worth of my medication and some ibuprofen, a twenty-dollar bill, a nail-polish remover wipe, matches, travel-size toothpaste, mascara, lipstick, and a teeny Vaseline for chapped lips and hands.

I wish, really and truly, that we had a world that wasn't always so...well, so much itself. But, thus far, it has yet to ask me about my preferences, and I don't think it will ask you about yours, either. It does not care what upsets or offends or hurts us; it will not shield us from these things but instead seems to delight in enthusiastically hurling them at us in the same manner a ten-year-old enthusiastically hurls a basketball toward his little sister's head.

So it is up to us to figure out what our metaphorical earbuds are and to let go of a lot of our expectations, particularly those that have little to no relation to reality. This can, and should, happen on the personal level, too: "I will not get upset when my friend is dating someone who doesn't treat them well, because they have *never* dated someone who treats them well. They know I feel this way, but it hasn't made a difference. I don't like the choices they make in their dating life, but I can love them anyway."

By all means, work for what you believe in, and live a life where your values and actions are in line. But also work on your own resiliency—the ability to let things go or, if you just can't do that, then your ability to turn your attention elsewhere. Because it doesn't particularly matter what you *think* of something; your emotional reaction only exists inside of you, and feeling helpless and terrified only prevents you from taking whatever small action you can—either to change the world or protect yourself. **Note:** "Taking action," in this case, almost *never* involves calling someone out on the internet; see step 155.

Step 5: Accept that right now, you are small-time

Before you go out into the world to seek your fortune, you make a lot of assumptions about how easy things will be or how quickly you'll rocket to the top. You might hit this wall, hard, when the *New York Times* doesn't beat a path to your door, but instead it is time for you to go be a reporter in rural Mississippi. Or you graduate law school with glorious visions of the important work you'll do for the Southern Poverty Law Center, but find yourself photocopying briefs in Shreveport. Whatever happens immediately post-graduation, chances are good that it will be at least a little disappointing.

So for right now, being a small-time whatever is your position. It's not shameful and it doesn't mean you're a failure. It means you're embarking on adulthood and starting from the beginning, just like every other person in the world must do. When you begin at the beginning, any progress you make is yours. From now on, it doesn't matter who your parents are or how much money they make. It's time to make your own money. You are the captain of your own destiny, even if it isn't all that glamorous or fabulous at the moment.

Step 6: Set reasonable goals for yourself

There will never be a time when every item in my house is meticulously organized in cute storage solutions. It will just never, ever happen. So looking at a bunch of organization blogs and despairing that my living space doesn't look like theirs is not a healthy thing for me to do.

A big part of being a well-adjusted person is accepting that you can't be good at everything. Some things will always be hard. Decide what you *can* do in those arenas, without making yourself crazy or setting unreasonably high expectations, then feel proud when you do it.

Step 7: Stop enjoying things ironically. Just enjoy them

Know what? I love Britney Spears and Forever 21. And I could pretend like it's this whole meta thing where I'm not actually enjoying it but rather just making this esoteric statement on lowbrow culture, but (*insert hand-job motion here*).

The truth is that I love trashy dance pop and the garments that are its clothing equivalent. You don't need to make your tastes a self-conscious statement about who you are. Just unapologetically like the things you like.

The *Shame* BOOMERANG

Hiii! Hello!! It's me, and I'm BACK, and I've got a LOT MORE to say about you and that *TERRIBLE**THING* you did! So, first, remember when you...

Step 8: Avoid shame boomerangs

I'm just going with *shame* because it would be too cumbersome to call them "Shame, Anxiety, Remorse, Dread, And Any Number of Ugly Emotions Boomerangs."

Here's how that process works:

inciting shame incident → bad feelings → forgetting and/or getting distracted for a little while → shame boomerang returns → bad feelings *the sequel*, et cetera, *all damn day*

This is the excellent strategy put forth by my internet friend Emily:

Step 1. Acknowledge the problem, and take any possible steps to correct it.

Step 2. Figure out how you will avoid making this same mistake again.

Step 3. Decide on a coping mechanism mantra that you will repeat when the shame boomerang returns ("It's done, and I won't do it again") and then play a diverting mental game, like thinking up what you would name a trio of Siamese kittens.

She didn't put this in, so I will:

Step 4. Really try not to make the mistake again. If the mistake happens again and again, then take a hard look at what you are doing and why.

Step 9: Remember your circle of concern versus your circle of action

Grief counselor Susan Gelberg was the one who told me about this and said it's helpful for people who are experiencing anxiety and anguish.

There is a big circle, one that contains all of your concerns, ranging from the super mundane ("Why can I never get the stupid wispy sides of my bangs straight? What if they're somehow made of a lost colony of pubic hair?") to the overwhelming ("I live in a world that also contains war, genocide, global warming, and tapeworms and *there is nothing I can do about any of them*."). But there's a smaller circle inside that circle, which is your circle of action. Inside that circle are the things you can actually effect change on. Work on those things. Those are the things that will help you feel as in control as any one person has the ability to be.

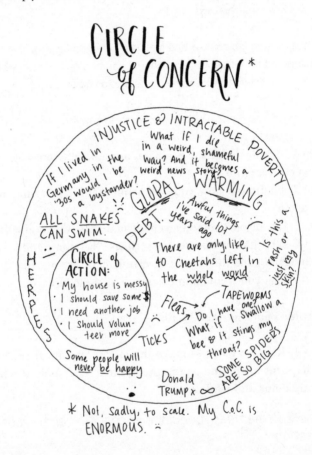

CIRCLE of CONCERN *

INJUSTICE & INTRACTABLE POVERTY

If I lived in Germany in the '30s would I be a bystander?

What if I die in a weird, shameful way? And it becomes a weird news story?

GLOBAL WARMING

ALL SNAKES CAN SWIM.

DEBT.

Awful things I've said 10+ years ago

Is this a rash or just my skin?

CIRCLE of ACTION:
· My house is messy
· I should save some $
· I need another job
· I should volunteer more

There are only, like, 40 cheetahs left in the whole world

HERPES

Fleas → TAPEWORMS
Do I have one? What if I swallow a bee & it stings my throat?

TICKS

Some people will never be happy

Donald Trump x ∞

SOME SPIDERS ARE SO BIG

* Not, sadly, to scale. My C.o.C. is ENORMOUS. :|

Step 10: Begin to separate, in your mind, things that are a Valid Long-Term Plan versus Not A Valid Long-Term Plan

Lots of things are NAVLTP. That is a fun word to try to pronounce out loud, but a bad thing to have in our lives. Common NAVLTPs include:

• Boyfriends you really love but know you don't want to spend your life with.

• Smoking.

• Jobs with little to no possibility for advancement. Not that you need to be the ruthless climbing-the-ladder type, but most people want, eventually, to have a job that is slightly more challenging and lucrative than their current position.

• If you have a drinking or substance abuse problem, you need to deal with that sooner rather than later. One caveat here is that many people who drink a lot in their early twenties do, in fact, kind of naturally taper off as time goes on and hangovers become tougher to deal with. This will happen almost overnight, and it is God's way of preventing thirty-nine-year-olds from drinking until 3 AM and making bad life choices. But if you find yourself drinking more, not less, as you age, that is something to consider, and there are *so many* resources out there—AA is almost everywhere and has helped so many people, and many meetings you are welcome to just go to (and will not be forced to talk). There are lots of online support groups if you're feeling shy or scared. You might also want to read some addiction memoirs and see if you relate a little too much to their story.

Step 11: Be okay with being alone

Lunch, the bus stop, shopping, parties—all these situations and more, you should feel fine being alone in. Here is what *you* think others are thinking when they look at you:

Oh my God, that girl has no friends and no significant other. Wow. How has she made it through life this far without finding a single solitary person to care about her?

Here is what they are actually thinking:

I wonder if I remembered to turn off my hair straightener? Where is Laura? She was supposed to be here by now. Ugh, I hate PT Cruisers so much; how do people not understand that those cars look like giant ugly eggplants? ... [other thoughts completely unrelated to you because no one notices or cares that you're by yourself] ...

You, meanwhile, will be with yourself for the rest of your life, so you'd best learn to enjoy your own company.

Look comfortable alone. You are not itchy, you are not fidgety, you are not looking around desperately for whoever will rescue you from the terrible fate of not being engaged in boring small talk. You're *fine*.

Step 12: Recognize six-month problems

When you get really upset about something, ask yourself if this is something you will remember in six months. Most things aren't. Most things are six-day problems, or six-minute problems. If the answer is *No, I will not remember this*, then you need to try to do your best to move on. If the answer's yes, you *also* need to do your best to move on, but at least a *no* answer puts you in the proper frame of mind.

Step 13: Distinguish between horses and zebras

I am constantly seeing medical dangers and significance everywhere. I don't have a head cold; I have meningococcal meningitis! And will soon die! I start thinking about how tragic this will be for everyone I know, and how sad they will be when they hear how this bright young life was snuffed out so needlessly. What will they say at my funeral? Et cetera . . . and then I get over whatever extremely minor ailment it is and forget all the dreadful predictions I made. Until the next time I get sick, and it isn't a headache; *it's brain cancer!* Or maybe *a tapeworm has gotten in my head!*

Once, I had a mosquito bite on my arm, and it was infected, so *obviously* it was the same antibiotic-resistant flesh-eating bacteria I saw a story on CNN about. I called my godfather (who is also a doctor) to confirm my suspicions that I should head to the emergency room.

Luckily, my brilliant godmother (and intermediary to my godfather) answered and gave me the best quote ever. She was saying it in the context of medical maladies, but I believe it can apply to many other things, too:

"If it's making a galloping noise, it's probably a horse, not a zebra."

In other words, the simplest explanation is probably—not always, but probably—the correct one.

So when you are unreasonably fretting about something and coming up with zebra explanations ("My boss is quiet this morning, so I'll bet she's going to fire me!"), try to steer yourself back toward horse-thinking ("She's probably tired or busy").

Step 14: Your brain is very important, so take care of it, and when it's sick or just not doing well, find someone who can help it out

Brains, man! *What a thing!* It is astonishing that there's a bunch of matter up in my skull that does everything from reminding me to breathe to physically storing every memory *I've ever had.* All our brains are great, and each one can do lots of things well. For example, mine is good at writing *and* making modular origami *and* coming up with ideas like gluing googly eyes over many items in my friend Molly's apartment for her birthday.

But there are some things my brain isn't great at. Serotonin—it doesn't make as much as I need! A lot of times, it doesn't really distinguish between active threats and all the things in my Circle of Concern. It spends a *lot* of time constantly urging me to do something—anything!—other than what I am supposed to be doing.

I can't pretend that I don't have depression (or anxiety, or ADHD)—it's a feature of who I am, and no amount of feeling ashamed or guilty or incompetent will change it. I cannot bully my brain into being other than what it is.

If your brain needs a little extra help to make it through the day, that's okay. It just requires a little bit more of your attention and patience and—this is the really tough part—the should-be-easy-but-instead-seems-insurmountably-difficult task of scheduling an appointment with your doctor or a therapist (for more information on finding low-cost mental health resources, see step 463).

Some people need medication. If you think that might be the case for you, be specific with your doctor: "Lately, I've noticed I'm showing signs of depression [elaborate with examples here], and I think an antidepressant might be a good idea for me. Can we talk about that as well as non-medication possibilities?"

Know, going into the situation, that it will almost certainly require some time and experimentation to find the right medications and amounts right for you. When you're on the meds, *take them exactly as prescribed.* Read the information from the pharmacy ahead of time, and ask the pharmacist specifically what side effects you should be watching for and what you should do if you notice any.

There are also the more mundane but still critically important things we can do. Think of them as mental health hygiene. Almost all of us feel better when we're regularly exercising and practicing mindfulness meditation. Helping other people (or animals!) is a wonderful way to get out of your own head for a bit and feel connected to the world in a positive way.

Treat yourself so, so gently. Ask yourself: If a friend were going through this, what would I say to them? What would I be willing to help them with? Then try to extend that same courtesy to yourself... or, if you just can't, reach out to a friend and tell them what's going on, because I promise they would want to know and help you. You can say, "Hey, so I've been feeling really depressed lately but every time I try to find a therapist I get super discouraged and go binge reality TV instead. Can you help me look around for someone?" (Also, definitely support them in their mental health—for more on this, see step 341).

Finally, know that talking about it can be so ding-dang liberating, and you will find a lot of people out there who are in the same neuroatypical boat.

Step 15: Pay attention to natural consequences, then learn to anticipate them

Natural consequences is actually a parenting concept, but one I use on myself, because sometimes my ability to thoughtfully reflect on a difficult situation is in line with a four-year-old's.

A natural consequence is, essentially, a situation where a parent doesn't have to punish a child for wrongdoing because the universe sort of takes care of that. A natural consequence of splurging when you don't have the money to do it is that you can't go out with friends. A natural consequence of hooking up with someone at work is that you then get to remember it in all its Technicolor, bodily fluids glory every time you sit across from them in a meeting. And so on.

I have taken to whispering, to myself, *Natural consequenceeeeessssss!* when I am experiencing one, to give myself a little Pavlovian incentive not to do it next time.

Step 16: Remember that, for better or for worse, you are in control of your physical self and surroundings

You can make your bed (see step 36) or not make your bed. You can buy paper towels or not buy paper towels. Neither makes you a better or worse person, but you should accept that if you want your bed to be made, there is but one person in the world who is going to do it and that person is you. Extrapolate this principle to many, many other things, because more often than not, it applies.

Step 17: When necessary, look at yourself in the mirror and give yourself some Real Talk

Are you familiar with the concept of Real Talk as popularized by R. Kelly?[3] It means just what it sounds like. We all need a little Real Talk in our lives.

Yes, if someone were to watch you doing this, it would be really embarrassing, so make sure you're by yourself, then look yourself in the eye in the mirror and say it aloud. It makes whatever you are trying so hard to mentally avoid into something that exists in the real world. It reminds you that the lies, or truths, you tell yourself are as significant as the lies and truths you tell others.

"This relationship is over, and you need to end it."

"Right now is not the right time to be crying at work. You are a grown-ass woman, and you're going to splash cold water on your face, take a minute to compose yourself, and then go slay it out there."

"Your needs are not more important than other people's needs."

Please note: There is a big, big difference between berating yourself and Real-Talking yourself.

---

3. Look: R. Kelly is not a good dude. I am *not* here to defend R. Kelly, just the idea of Real Talk.

Step 18: When something bad happens to you, do not rush immediately to figure out why it wasn't your fault

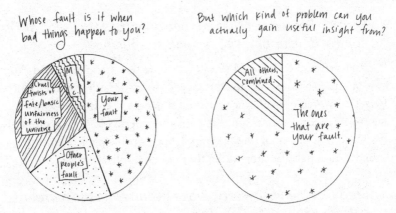

Whose fault is it when bad things happen to you?

But which kind of problem can you actually gain useful insight from?

Cruel twists of fate/basic unfairness of the universe

MISC

Your fault

Other people's fault

All others, combined.

The ones that are your fault.

Point being: before you rush, internally, to deflect blame, figure out what lesson you could/should be learning here.

Step 19: Get used to giving more than you get

A natural transition, as we go from being kids to adults, is going from being self-oriented to other-oriented. When we're little, all this love flows to us, and none is expected back. That ratio has now changed, and if you don't acknowledge it, you will not be a pleasant person to be around.

Discussion Questions

1. What is your worst-ever shame boomerang?
2. Who is the least-special ~~Special Snowflake~~ (*siiiiiigh*) Singular Seahorse you know?
3. If you had a pet zebra, what would you name him? Here's a few to get you started: Edwin Brewster, Señor Stripes, Karen, Pickles, Trotters.

Chapter 2
DOMESTICITY

One of the most jolting days of adulthood comes the first time you run out of toilet paper. Toilet paper, up until this point, always just *existed*. And now it's a finite resource, constantly in danger of extinction, that must be carefully tracked and monitored, like pandas?

It's not just the toilet paper. There are so many endless tiny details to attend to. Food does not spontaneously manifest itself in the fridge. Surfaces become increasingly sticky and dust-covered if not wiped. Disgusting things, like overflowing toilets and dead squirrels your cat leaves on the bedroom floor, are on your shoulders. No one else will remove that spider biding its time in the shower until it can lay eggs in your ears. No friendly stranger will knock on your door to ask if any ketchup has spilled in your fridge and hardened into indelible red paste, then offer to scrape it up. Half-empty beer cans will release foul, regret-scented gases until you empty and recycle them.

But now, the good news: Billions and billions of people around the world manage to live in a home without directly killing themselves or others via their irresponsibility, and chances are very good you are one of them. There is a 98.5 percent chance that you will manage to keep toilet paper stocked regularly, especially if you . . .

Step 20: Buy toilet paper in bulk

Sure, this is a specific rather than general step, but it can be extrapolated to this whole chapter. You see, toilet paper is something that you will always, always need. Let's look at this graph illustrating that very principle:

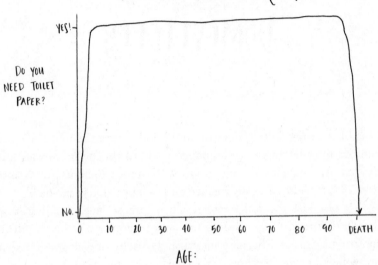

TOILET PAPER NEED OVER TIME:

Do you need toilet paper? — YES! / NO.

AGE: 0, 10, 20, 30, 40, 50, 60, 70, 80, 90, DEATH

Because toilet paper is non-perishable (thank God; that would be disgusting), you may as well go ahead and buy a whole bunch of it at once. It saves you money, cuts down on future toilet-paper-purchase expeditions, and guarantees you will never, ever have to leave your house at 5 AM with a digestive system that is on the march. It's not as though the grocery store clerk will look at this large purchase and assume you poop a lot, so just go ahead and do it.

All right. Now that the most important step is out of the way, let's start with searching for a place to call your own, then on to decorating, cleaning, and showing off your domesticity.

Step 21: Find the right place for you

People who live in New York or San Francisco may as well skip this step, since you're lucky to find someone willing to rent you a closet without putting down first and last years' rent. But for those with a little more choice in their real estate, here are some great things to look for in an apartment:

- **Hot water:** Go turn on the shower and make sure there is sufficient water pressure and it's nice and strong and not, as my mom once memorably said of my shower, like having an eighty-three-year-old man pee on you. Also, does the water get hot in a reasonable amount of time? Is it the either-scalding-or-frigid kind of shower? That's nice to know.
- **Safety:** Come back by the area at night, during the day, on the weekend, and so on. Make sure you feel reasonably safe at all these times.
- **Volume:** Consider whether there is something very loud nearby, like a fire station or train tracks or a high school with a substandard but enthusiastic marching band. Will this make you crazy?
- **Management:** Does the landlord seem at least semi-reasonable? Landlords are tightly wound people, generally speaking, so you have to give them a little leniency, but make sure they set off no Alarming Person Bells (see Warning Signs, page 109). It's okay to ask to chat with another tenant and see what kind of person you are entering into a long-term legal contract with. Because chances are that if you are in a conflict with them, they will win. They have money and lawyers. They're businesspeople. Make sure they're the kind you want to be in business with.
- **Electricity:** Be sure to check all the light switches and, if you can, the electrical outlets, perhaps by taking along your cell phone charger. Otherwise, you could end up like my friend who had fourteen decorative outlets and two that actually powered things. It's also useful to check on how many and how well placed they are. If you like to blow-dry your hair, look for an outlet in the bathroom. It's nice to have several in your bedroom so you're not constantly tripping over your bedside lamp's cord that must stretch taut through the air. And so on.[1]
- **Closets and storage:** Do they exist? Some old houses had bedrooms without closets. Having at least one big non-bedroom closet

---

1. If you do find yourself tragically short on outlets, I suggest investing in some non-shady extension cords and power strips, coupled with those things that plug into your outlet and have three outlets plus a few USB ports.

is a lifesaver, so long as you do not follow my example and allow it to become a dangerous and unstable mess, like a tiny geopolitical conflict right there in your apartment. Is there a pantry, or at least some big cupboards?

• **Appliances:** Is there a dishwasher, or a washer and dryer? These things are luxurious, but if there is nothing you hate in the world more than hand-washing dishes, then you might make that a condition of your search. Also, if there are washer and dryer hookups, do not kid yourself into thinking you're actually going to buy a washer and dryer unless you are so grown-up as to be way beyond this book. A garbage disposal is, in my mind, just about the most luxurious thing in the world, because then I don't have to worry about carefully removing every single sad soggy food bit that may get into the sink.

• **Accessibility:** Can your furniture logically get up the stairs and into the apartment? It's a good plan, if you have really large and/or awkwardly shaped things, to measure them in advance, so take a tape measure along with you.

• **Pets:** If you have a pet, can they live here with you? The lure of a nice apartment is not justification for dropping your pet off at the shelter. **Note:** This is something important to consider when you first adopt a pet, *particularly* if you live in a tight rental market. Sometimes, landlords will make an exception for cats (especially if your previous landlord is willing to vouch for their non-destructiveness), but dogs over twenty-five pounds are notoriously difficult to find housing for. Having a pet in an apartment that doesn't allow pets is a *super-bad idea*, so if you're wanting to adopt, make sure you can find an apartment that will allow that.

• **Paint:** Can you paint the walls? What if you agree to paint them back to the original, sanitarium white when you leave?

Normally, you can expect to pay first and last months' rent, plus a deposit. Be sure to first read carefully—you can, and should, ask questions if anything feels strange to you—and then keep copies of everything you sign. Find out what the policy is to give notice when you're ready to move out. Most require thirty days' written notice, and no, calling them thirty days ahead of time will not cut it.

Step 22: Be a good tenant

Ninety percent of this is paying your rent on time, but also be sure to alert landlords right away when there is a problem, particularly if it has to do with mold, plumbing, or other issues that could seriously ruin their property. It is their property, even if you pay dearly to use it, and you need to respect it as such.

This also means being gentle with hardwood floors, and knowing how to patch any nail holes you might put in the walls. So a couple quick strategies to make sure you can eventually get your deposit back:

Step 23: Learn how to patch nail holes

This is surprisingly easy, although it's for use on drywall, not plaster. If you have plaster, then for God's sake be careful because it is *complicated*. YouTube is your friend. But for drywall: Go to a hardware store and get a putty knife, sandpaper, and some spackle (for smaller jobs) or joint compound (also known as drywall mud). Put a little bit of the compound into a ziplock bag, then cut a corner out so you have a way to pipe it into the hole. Use the putty knife to smooth it out and get off the excess. Wait for it to dry per the instructions, then sand it so it's smooth. A little paint, and it's like the hole was never there.

Step 24: If you need to match paint, chip off a paint sample

This should happen in a discreet area, but take a screwdriver and get a little paint chip off the wall. Then, when you take it to the home-improvement store, they can scan it and match the shade perfectly.

DECORATING

So now you have a place. A big, empty place.

I spent my first few months of living on my own with a decoration scheme that would befit a very casual junkie (casual about home decor, not heroin use). I eschewed traditions like dressers, instead opting to leave my clothes in piles on the floor that in a pinch could double as a couch, since I didn't have an actual couch. If you closed your eyes and also were very high, I imagine it would have been like sitting on a very flat beanbag chair.

Needless to say, this setup made me feel batshit insane and like a complete failure at life. So soon enough, I bribed a co-worker who had a pickup truck with a six-pack of beer and got a bunch of Goodwill furniture. It is embarrassing, now, to recall how proud I was when someone came over and I was able to offer the luxury of sitting on an *actual couch*.

Here is what I'd consider the bare minimum, furniture-wise:

- **Kitchen:** A small table and at least two chairs
- **Living room:** A couch, a bookcase or shelving, and a coffee table
- **Bedroom:** A bed, a nightstand, a dresser

Here are some things that can be nice to acquire once you are no longer offering sweater piles for your guests to sit on:

- **Living room:** A desk, a love seat or occasional chair, side tables, something to set your TV upon that isn't the box it came in
- **Bedroom:** An additional dresser, if necessary; a vanity; a hamper
- **Bathroom:** A storage option of some sort if your bathroom doesn't have any; an additional hamper, space permitting

Step 25: Find furniture on the cheap

Goodwill, Craigslist, garage sales, and your parents' friends are all your friends, although you should make sure ahead of time that you have some way to get your inherited goods and purchases home.[2] IKEA, of course, is the poor twentysomething's wonderland, so long as you don't mind having the same dresser as all your friends, which I most certainly do not.

A couple notes of caution: When looking for old furniture, quality counts. Be sure to jiggle it to make sure it's sturdy. Particleboard is no

---

2. Driving a U-Haul is not as scary as it may seem! Okay, it actually is. But just go slowly and do it anyway, and don't forget to check to make sure your auto insurance will pay for any damage.

good, at least not used. The heavier, the better, if it's made of wood. Use your measuring tape to make sure whatever item this is can fit through your door and won't look ridiculously large in your space. Also, if you live in a bedbug-prone area, just skip secondhand uphol- stered stuff. It's not worth the risk.

I have a deep and abiding love for spray-painting furniture, and it truly opened up my world. You don't have to worry about whether that dresser is a weird, sad wood color, because guess what—it can be any color you want! Just look at the lines of it.

Also, knobs! Tiny, easily attached game changers!

How to decorate

If you have absolutely no idea of what you want your house to look like, look in your closet. My friend Carol, who has the most beauti- ful home of anyone I know, said she thinks that people should sort of match their houses. So do you like to wear a lot of bold, primary colors? Are you more a neutral person? Is your stuff old-fashioned and ornately detailed, or minimalist? Chances are if you like it on your person, you'll like it in home decor.

Another good first step can be to start with a single object that you just really, really like. My little sister found an antique water mister, the kind that an eccentric old lady would use to spritz her orchids in the 1950s, and whenever she wanted to add something to her room, she made sure it would match the spritzer.

Painting walls does make a huge difference. If you don't want to commit to painting the whole apartment, painting just one wall can do a lot, even if it's one of the very short ones.

It's worth it to get a couple samples of the paint and test them on your wall first, to confirm you actually like them and to make sure they look the same in your apartment as they do on the tiny swatch. When you go to buy paint, describe the wall surface to the paint store people— they can tell you if you need primer or not.

Before you begin, put masking tape along the edges of the wall and over anything that shouldn't be painted, like baseboards and trim. Unscrew light switch and outlet covers, then cover the floor with a tarp or a *lot* of newspaper. Go crazy on that last step and be extra, extra cautious so you don't drip paint everywhere. You'll also need a paint pan, a smaller brush, and a roller for covering larger areas.

Step 26: Frames, not posters

Oh, college. There are so many reasons we are all nostalgic for you, but interior decor isn't one of them. Frames don't have to be expensive, either—every time I go to Goodwill, I see thousands of frames for fifty cents or a dollar apiece. If you want to be all Rockefeller about it, IKEA has them for five to thirty dollars.

Again, spray paint is your friend here; I have a wall with all sorts of mismatched frames (some super ornate, some simple) that all look good together because I spray-painted them all gold.

Lots of times, you can find precut mats in standard photo sizes at art stores or go into your local framing shop to see if they have extras or remainders. Use your local Kinko's or printing shop to make big copies of photos you love.

Art is something you can slowly but surely acquire. It doesn't have to be insanely expensive—prints from local artists, small bits of wall art, and stuff from especially talented friends and family members are all wonderful. But treat 'em right, and get 'em framed.

Step 27: You can be poor and still have a really cute apartment

It just takes extra effort and creativity. My friend Ariella had the amazing idea of putting pages from vintage children's books up on her wall, an idea I promptly stole. Vintage postcards are also great for this. Most knickknacks and decor items you find at Goodwill are hideous, but some are adorable and cost fifty cents.

Step 28: Get a nice, actual bed

Once you turn twenty-three, there is a steep drop-off on the acceptability level of a mattress on the floor. But do not let external judgment be the thing that steers you to an actual bed. No. You owe it to yourself.

If you're like most people, your bed is the physical object in the world that you will touch the most. You spend a third of your life in full-body contact with that thing! It should be comfy. If you can scrape together five hundred dollars—maybe, say, from a tax return, or maybe put away forty dollars each month—you can sleep like a king for years and you will never, ever regret it.

Step 1. A nice mattress. Go to several mattress stores. Try all the different ones out, and don't feel uncomfortable about rolling around, getting your significant other to come along and lie down with you, and so on. You can also get mattresses on Amazon and through mattress-specific online shops, but definitely look for free return shipping, because what if you don't like it?

Step 2. Know that mattress stores are weirdly into haggling, so start by really lowballing them, then go from there. What are they going to do, kick you out of the mattress store?

Step 3. Figure out what this nice mattress will sit upon. Box springs aren't totally necessary, especially if you plan on a platform bed. On the other hand, the very cheapest bed solution (and the one I use) is a Hollywood bed frame, which does require a box spring. These frames can almost always be found at Goodwill or garage sales. If you do this, you will also want to buy a bed skirt, and perhaps even a headboard. Again, lots of these are available at thrift stores.

Step 29: Create a correspondence drawer

This can be done for twenty-five dollars or less. Pick a drawer—hopefully that flat, long one in the middle of your desk—and put the following things in it:

- One book of stamps, to be replaced as needed
- A checkbook
- Business envelopes
- Two nice-ish pens, one blue and one black

- Plain card stock and envelopes that you can then doodle something on before sending as a thank-you note or a just-because letter
- Address labels, if for some reason some company has sent them to you
- If you're advanced, a little address book

Then, on the rare occasion when you do need to send a letter (or, um, a rent check), it'll be smooth, capable, responsible sailing.

Step 30: Lean into storage solutions

It's a dumb cliché that is also 100 percent true: Everything you own should have a specific place it lives in your house. Do not be like me and make that specific place for extra keys in, say, the drawer that is also home to crusty old makeup, crumpled up receipts, and all the junk mail you received in 2014. You can make your own little drawer dividers out of small boxes and cardboard; get a pretty vintage tumbler to store your pencils in; look for nice, sturdy gift boxes. Seriously, gift-box technology has come a long, long way—I ended up making one into a jewelry box with plastic trays I got off Amazon.

The fewer items you can visually see when you scan a room, the tidier it will look. It's really, really nice and good for mental health to have a tidy space and, as Carol always tells me, the eye needs places to rest.

Step 31: Buy tools. Five should be sufficient, for now

If you don't already have a big toolbox of tools, chances are you are not the kind of person who needs a big toolbox of tools. But really, for a person of negligible-to-average handiness, these five things suggested by Ben, the handiest dude ever, will take you far:

1. **Hammer:** For the hammerin'. You'll also probably want to get an assortment of nails—home improvement and hardware stores sell small boxes that contain several different types.
2. **Adjustable screwdriver set:** It's a single screwdriver handle with different-size bits you can pop in and out. "It's much cheaper and

handier than a full screwdriver set," Ben said, "and while it's not optimal for major projects, it's more than enough for small projects."

3. **Crescent wrench:** A crescent wrench can be adjusted to any size by using the little dial to increase or shrink the width of the jaws to match the bolt you're tightening/loosening.

4. **Tape measure:** Good for so many things: measuring distance to center a portrait on the wall, placing furniture, figuring out whether your furniture will even fit up the stairs, and so on. Also, as Ben noted, it's fun to push the button and suck the tape back into the device, no matter how old you get.

5. **Cordless drill:** "Hanging drapes? Hanging a heavy mirror? Without a cordless drill, these will be a huge pain in the ass," Ben said. "Manually turning a screwdriver into the wall so you can hang your drapes is torture." Plus, unlike your screwdriver set but like your tape measure, a cordless drill is sort of fun.

It might be easiest to keep your eye out for a little set that all live together in a tidy box.

Step 32: Get a step stool (and use it to check your smoke detector)

Another non-fun, non-glamorous, but super-useful purchase. You know when you're guaranteed to use it? When you check the batteries in your smoke detector once a month, as grown-ups who do not wish to perish in a fire should make a habit of doing. It's nice to do this on the day you send your rent check in (or that it's withdrawn from your bank account).

Step 33: Make two copies of your keys, then give one to a friend and hide one somewhere near your house

Sooner or later, you will lock yourself out of your house. It's just unavoidable.

So make and give a copy of your key to a friend. Ideally, this friend lives very close to your apartment, and super ideally, they are your awesome neighbor who will come over and pet-sit when necessary. Anyway, give them a copy pretty much as soon as you move in, then hide another copy (unlabeled!) within a couple blocks of your house.

CLEANING

Full disclosure: Cleanliness is my Everest.

Even when my house is clean—say, if company is coming over, which is pretty much the only time my house is really, really clean—it's still obviously a recent and temporary effort, like a five-year-old dressed up in a tiny ill-fitting blazer.

But while my house will never be one that gleams with tidiness, I can still keep it from falling into the unlivable hellhole territory that it was in for much of my early twenties.

Step 34: If you are really terrible at cleaning, it may be worth it to hire a cleaner, and ask if they can tutor you while they clean

Ask in advance, since of course what most housekeepers are signing up for is cleaning, not teaching the terribly incompetent how to wipe. But I did this and found Karen, whose wonderful advice is peppered throughout this chapter. She, without judgment, did everything from changing my hand-washing routine to explaining what spring cleaning is all about. Plus, I find it much easier to maintain cleanliness than to get it to that state in the first place.

Step 35: Do some cleaning daily

Here's a list of things that should take you no more than fifteen minutes, but if you do them each day, your habitat will never sink into unbearable filth.

- Do the dishes (for more on this, see the Cooking chapter).
- Take the time to put things away where they go. Hang up your clothes, put the others in the laundry, put away any new purchases, and so on.

See? You can do that. You can even sing yourself a happy little cleaning song of your own invention when you do it.

Step 36: Make your bed, every morning

People go back and forth about whether making your bed is a colossal waste of your rare and precious minutes. But to me, it's worth it, because then no matter what, there is a small, tiny space in the world that I know is orderly, which is more than worth the forty-five seconds it takes me to get it into that condition.

As soon as I get out of bed, I tuck the top sheet back in, smooth out the blanket, and fluff the pillows a tiny bit. Then there is this nice clean plane that I can lay an outfit out on, plus the whole room looks neater (fact: It's impossible for a room to look clean with an unmade bed). Each night, when you come home tired and ready to relax, you'll walk in and your bed will be made, a small testament to control over your universe.

Plus, it's way nicer to get into a made bed. Not like when all the sheets are bunched up and you get tangled in them and feel more like a complete failure at life than the situation really warrants.

The longest sheets should go without washing is two weeks; wash them in warm water by themselves, using half the usual amount of your detergent. Try to have at least three sets of sheets. For more on laundry, see steps 280–286 in the Maintenance chapter.

Step 37: Get in the habit of mindlessly tidying

Some excellent times to tidy:

- While you are on the phone, wander around straightening things up.
- If you've just put something in the microwave or under the broiler, spend those three minutes wiping counters or doing dishes.
- While waiting for the bath to fill or the shower water to heat, wipe down the sink and the outside of the toilet.

Tidying is so very simple: Pick up an item, then put it in its home. Repeat twelve thousand times. Once an object is in your hand, it should go directly to where it lives, whether that be the lowest kitchen drawer or the recycling bin. If it doesn't have a home, figure out what that home could be. If you really, really can't think of one, then thank it for its service and donate, recycle, or trash it.

Step 38: Do not leave to crust for tomorrow what may be wiped up today

Here is something that I am so, so embarrassed that I had to be told not six months ago, as I somehow had never absorbed it in child-hood: When there are little spills or splatters, wipe them up right then.

For years, this was my mental process for spills:

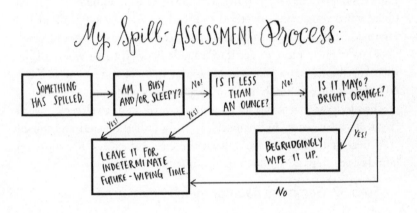

But here's how actual adults do it:

Seriously! It will never be easier to wipe up something than right when it is fresh. It is less likely to stain, dry, crust, et cetera, and you will have to wipe it up eventually. Just do it now.

Step 39: Be mindful about your garbage

This means getting decent trash cans, making sure you have liners and/or leftover plastic grocery bags for them (do *not* neglect this step or your garbage can will grow tiny, smelly civilizations in the bottom by this afternoon), and figuring out what the recycling process is in your neighborhood.

It's nice to have a little garbage bin for each room; I'll store extra plastic grocery bags in the bottom under whatever bag is currently in use. I also have a small, cute box by the front door so that when I bring in the mail, I can quickly recycle almost all of it.

If you live in a place with curbside recycling, learn the rules. It'll be run through either the city or the county, so just Google "[my city name] recycling." If you don't have a bin, call and ask for one.

Remember that leftover, crusty food is not made into anything except compost. (And if you want to do that, *congratulations*, because you are super functional and caring.) You will never buy a sketchbook made of Post-Consumer Dried Pizza Cheese. So generally speaking, items that are contaminated by food in a way that can't be washed (think porous things, like cardboard) should just be thrown away, and items that can be washed (glass, plastic, waxed cardboard) should be washed, then recycled.

If your curbside recycling doesn't take glass, then figure out where to take it to recycle. Or just accept that you're going to throw it away. Whatever you do, do not allow an army of white wine bottles to amass under your kitchen sink, like those terra-cotta soldiers, except made of shame.

A bucket list

So this is not a bucket list as popularized by the 2007 Morgan Freeman–Jack Nicholson movie of the same name, but rather a list that contains a bucket, which I did not own for my first three years of solo living.

Some basic cleaning supplies that everyone should own:

- Dawn dish soap. It is truly astounding what some dish soap in warm water will clean, but more on that later.
- A broom and dustpan.
- A mop.
- A bucket.
- Paper towels.
- Rags. **Note:** It's best to have old towels and some (unused, obviously) cloth diapers. The towels are great because they attract dirt, while the cloth diapers won't scratch your mirror or windows. You really don't need to buy rags; if there is a beloved piece of clothing (particularly a robe) that is too worn out, stained, or hole-having to give to Goodwill, go ahead and cut it up; then it may continue to live with you and serve you. Editor Morgan suggests old socks, which she puts on her hands for a prehensile Swiffer-esque cleaning experience.
- A scrubber.
- A toothbrush, for little crevices (think between the faucet and back of the sink).
- Bleach. (More on this later, but in the meantime, remember that anytime you're working with bleach, you should have gloves on.)
- Cheap white vinegar; a solution of one part vinegar to two parts hot water is a wonderful glass cleaner.
- Spray bleach solution. This can be used on many things, including mold, floors, painted surfaces, and so on.
- Knee pads, which make scrubbing a billion times less painful and Cinderella-like.
- Latex cleaning gloves.
- Pledge for wood.
- Goo Gone, which does wonders on weird sticky messes.
- A duster.

Cleaning supplies that I really like:

I've found a few things over the years that are either inherently great *or* are such a pleasure to use that they make me forget, for a moment, my deep aversion to cleaning. Here we go!

• Mrs. Meyer's Clean Day Multi-Surface Everyday Cleaner Spray in Honeysuckle: This smells very nice, and if I spray it on things, my house will smell nice, and, as long as I'm spraying it, I may as well go ahead and wipe down the surface in question.

• Melamine foam (aka Magic Eraser): It really does remove all sorts of weird stains, even Sharpie on painted surfaces! Magic Eraser is the brand name, but you can get generic melamine foam for waaaaaay less on Amazon, which is probably a good idea, as they can be single-use. I suggest cutting them up into tiny two-inch bricks for precision and adorableness.

• Swiffer 360° Dusters: I do not know what kind of black magic goes into these, but I don't care. You will think a surface is clean and then you run one of these little guys over it and then it is *actually* clean. I'm also very down with the Swiffer WetJet mops, which is perfect for people, like me, who are too lazy to actually mop.[3]

• A non-frustrating vacuum: Vacuums are strangely expensive, especially if you want one that isn't constantly falling over and clattering or is easy to empty. Do your homework, then buy the nicest one you can afford—a base model of a well-reviewed, trusted brand is better than the fanciest version from a cheaper company. I'd suggest looking around for a used one, ideally refurbished and with a warranty from a local vacuum store (bonus: Every vacuum sales clerk I've ever met is a weird garden of delights!). If there are no stores around, follow the same principle for buying any used expensive thing—buy from the most neurotically tidy, fastidious person you can find.

• A Dustbuster or small handheld vac: *Hot tip* for pet owners! Sometimes, you can just use the Dustbuster around the perimeter of the room, stopping to snag any dust bunnies along the way. Also, if you're feeling really lazy, sometimes after I sweep I'll just suck up the little pile instead of futzing with the dustpan. They're also very good

---

3. Full disclosure: One time, I was asked to host an eighteenth birthday party for Swiffer and then I freaked out because *of course I will celebrate with you, Swiffer!* Point being, they sent me a big box of Swiffer products and that is how I first bonded with the duster and Wet Jet. But I fell in love and regularly buy them now.

for when glass breaks, but do be sure to use two wet paper towels together and wipe up the area afterward to catch any little glass shards.

• A Roomba: So I got Carl the Roomba off Craigslist, and I'll be honest: He didn't do the best job, but man oh man was I emotionally bonded to that lil guy! I would actually talk about him with my boyfriend as though he were our child, as in, "Yeah, poor Carl got stuck under the coffee table *twice!* And I told him—Carl, do *not* go over there!—but he wouldn't listen." Carl was great when it was just Marigny the Cat, though he was no match for a giant longhaired dog, *and* Eleanor lived in very loud terror of him, so eventually I put him back up on Craigslist and the circle of life continued. It was really nice, though, to have the floors just passively much cleaner. I miss you, Carl.

• Fancy latex gloves: Mine are elbow-length dominatrixy black with a ruffle and I enjoy snapping them on with a flourish. But any cleaning gloves will do, and the magic here is that *you can touch almost anything with it and not get squicked out.* Cat vomit? Dog poop? Soggy sink bits of food, which, in reality, are way less gross than those first two but somehow seem just as bad? These are powerless against latex gloves.

Step 40: Get a toilet plunger

Toilets are actually pretty easy to fix, but not without a plunger. First, if it's overflowing, turn off the water using the little knob shaped like a football that is probably somewhere around the base. It is almost certainly a righty-tighty, lefty-loosy situation. A quick how-to: Plunger goes in the bowl over the drainage opening. Make sure there is a nice seal (visually, obviously), then plunge four or five times. Remove plunger, try to flush the toilet, and if that doesn't work, give it another go. Wash off the plunger using household cleaners and a good spray of Lysol. If possible, it's nice to keep it out of sight *but* in an obvious place so someone who didn't live there would be able to find it pretty quickly. Have you ever been at someone else's house and the toilet clogs? Like me, did you instinctively glance to the window and try to gauge whether you could make it through and survive the fall, get in your car and drive until you ran out of gas, walk until your feet were bloody, then start a new life?

Step 41: And a toilet brush

If, once per week, you spray some bleach solution (perhaps even *stored under your sink?*) in there and let it sit, then swish this guy around, well, you will never have a truly disgusting toilet. Also, every day or so I just use a couple sheets of toilet paper to swipe at the base where the seat attaches. This area truly disturbs me; is it *growing* hair and dust? Like, organically, from pores? Is my toilet alive? Best to turn away from these emotionally destabilizing questions by keeping it clean.

Step 42: Master other basic toilet repairs

Happily, toilets are fairly simple creatures, and most things that ail them are easily fixed. Nearly all home-improvement stores sell toilet repair kits that have blessedly simple instructions. If it's anything that you can't immediately diagnose when you take the top off the tank (for example: That little chain is broken! It should be replaced with a *non*-broken chain), then go ahead and ask your landlord.

Weekly cleaning

It's best to pick a two-hour window in which, every week, you do your weekly cleaning. Saturday mornings are perfect if you are not liable to be hungover; then you have a pretty clean house to enjoy all weekend. Per Karen's suggestions, here are the weekly chores:

- Clean your bathroom—that means the shower, tub, toilet, and sink.
- Do your laundry, including your bed linens.
- Sweep and then mop any non-carpeted surfaces.
- Check corners for cobwebs.
- Wipe down surfaces that wouldn't be cleaned regularly, like the coffee table, desk, chairs, and so on.

Again, doable.

The miracle of soapy water

A bucket of dish-soapy water feels very Cinderella-ish, which it most certainly is. But it's also an extremely useful go-to solution for cleaning most surfaces in your home. You can effectively use it to mop, clean counters, gently clean hardwood floors, clean sinks, wipe off many non-wood furniture items, and more.

One really effective strategy is to have two rags, a wet one and a dry one. Use the wet rag to wipe down (really use that elbow grease), and then use the dry one to clean up and wipe away any remaining flecks and dust.

Whenever either rag is getting dingy, wash it, wring it out, hang it up to dry, and grab another rag. Also, this sounds obvious, but rags can be laundered, albeit not with your other laundry. It's gotta be a rag-only load, unless you are cool with your clothes being washed in all that detritus you removed from your countertops.

Step 43: When cleaning, first do a garbage and recycling sweep

I'll usually grab a garbage bag and a paper bag, then move through each room getting any little scraps of paper or errant bits of plastic thrown away. Then, as I'm tidying the room, I keep the bags near so I can easily get rid of things I don't need, *particularly* unneeded papers.

Step 44: Tackle glass, mirrors, and windows

Of course, you'll want a glass cleaner for this. Karen said she found the most effective cleaning implement to be a cloth diaper, which doesn't leave behind lint or streaks. Spray down the surface thoroughly, then use one rag to wipe and a dry one to polish. Windows should be cleaned every six months.

Step 45: Sweep slowly, and think about vacuuming if you have a pet

One mistake lots of people make when they sweep, Karen said, is that they try to do it fast, which just ends up kicking the dirt and dust into the air. Use slow, deliberate strokes. Sweep three-by-three-foot areas, only moving on to the next one after you are sure the current one is totally clear. Also, because I have a cat, I vacuum my hardwood floors, which seems to get them much, much cleaner than sweeping.

Step 46: Master bathroom cleaning

A clean bathroom, more than anyplace else, demands that bleach spray I mentioned earlier. A toilet gets wiped down pretty much all over—everywhere from the top of the tank to the grimy base part that seems like a disgusting magnet for hair and unspeakable filth. You'll want to clean the inside of the bowl using a toilet bowl cleaner and toilet bowl scrubbing brush, which gets washed afterward.

Step 47: Find a tub cleaner that works for you

Karen strongly recommends Soft Scrub with Bleach. Of course, you're welcome to branch out, but be sure to read the directions—lots of bathroom cleaners want to be left on for several minutes before you scrub with a scrubber.

Step 48: Every so often, bleach your sink, tub, and toilet

This assumes you have the usual surfaces (the white porcelain kind of sink and tub) and not some exotic expensive material. Fill them with hot water, add perhaps half a cup of bleach to a tub or between an eighth and a quarter cup to a sink, then let it sit for twenty minutes. After you've drained and rinsed, any remaining grime is super easy to get off—and the sink or tub will be so, so white.

Step 49: Do at least a little spring cleaning

Wipe down all the surfaces in your home (doors, baseboards, windows) and tackle at least one big organization project; I always end up tackling what I refer to as Chernobyl Closet, which is wild and unknowable and always reverting to chaos. Get rid of stuff. You should also do this in the fall and winter. Why not?

Step 50: Master advanced cleaning

Here are some chores that I never, ever think of and so need to write down and check off a list every now and again, perhaps quarterly:

- Dust baseboards.
- Use a broom to brush cobwebs off ceilings and ceiling fans; clean out any vents (read: the bathroom one) that have gathered dust. Take out and wash any window-unit AC air filters.[4]
- Clean inside of windows and outside, if possible.
- Remove every item from the pantry or kitchen cupboards, then vacuum and wipe down the insides. Do this for any particularly debris-ish drawers in your house.
- Clean your doors and walls using a sponge and an all-purpose cleaner or Dawn solution; use a Magic Eraser–type sponge on any lingering stains.
- Vacuum any upholstered items using an upholstery attachment on your vacuum.

Step 51: Do not keep things in your house that make you feel sad or bad

The world is full of things that make us feel sad and bad. There is no need to allow any of them in the one small corner of the world you can control.

If, every time you see an item in your home, it makes you cringe, then *throw that shit out*. If for whatever reason it's something that pains you to part with (like old love letters), ask a friend to store it at their house for the time being. Give the smaller clothing to a smaller friend.

If the item in question belongs to a roommate, and you really hate it as opposed to just finding it unattractive, ask in your sweetest, most non-confrontational voice if they'd consider moving it out of the common area.

---

4. If you live somewhere that gets above 90 degrees for more than a week per year and you don't have AC, a small window unit for your bedroom is some of the best money you can spend. Try to think of it before you need it; it will be way cheaper to purchase in late September than during the first heat wave of the summer.

Step 52: Go a step further, and don't allow things in your house that you do not love

Yes, you *could* own this (fast-fashion dress, almost perfectly cute candleholder, thing at Goodwill that is so strange that it feels irresponsible not to buy it because c'mon, it's a larger-than-lifesize clown-face candle that you *can* and *should* leave on your significant other's pillow while they sleep, and that is *more than worth* three ding-dang dollars!) . . . but should you? We live in a materialistic, capitalist society, angelbugs, and it's so easy to acquire things. But if you only allow things in your house that you love—and yes, this is a truism—then you will love everything in your house.

Step 53: Think about strategies other than keeping every single item that may have a scrap of sentiment attached to it

This is hard for me, as I am the sort of person who keeps receipts from memorable manicures. I always have to remind myself that the vast majority of this emotional detritus never gets looked at. Some questions to think about when you consider saving something:

- Could you take a picture of it, or scan it/otherwise make it a file?
- Will you ever look at this again? Why?
- Do you have other, more significant items that speak to this memory/person?

Step 54: Replace things when they become disgusting

Here I am thinking of bath mats. Bath mats are like hamsters in that they have a very defined and short life span, although unlike hamsters they are sometimes kept around for years after their natural passing.

Shower curtains, hand towels, the little metal dish that goes around the heating element on an electric stove, kitchen sponges—these things, too, have a beginning and an end. If you ask yourself, "Hmm, should I replace this [unsalvagably funky-smelling item]?" the answer is almost always yes.

MOVING

If you've ever moved anywhere, which obviously you have, you know that moving is the second worst process in the world (ethnic cleansing is the first). After I moved my stuff across the country, I swore that I would never move again, that I would die in that little apartment by the railroad tracks.

But sometimes it's necessary. And you can do it.

Step 55: Get a big five-subject notebook, one with pockets to hold pieces of paper, one large enough to hold back the tide of moving insanity

Moving involves about 137 interconnecting processes, every single one of which is a huge pain in the ass. There's getting out of your old lease, getting the old apartment clean, finding a new apartment, forwarding your mail, squaring away pet stuff (one of the most amazing moments of my life was when a customer service lady for a major airline who didn't speak the best English asked what a "cat" is), getting rid of stuff, saying good-bye to people, and of course the question of how your things will get from one place to another.

Your patron saint of this process is a big notebook. Saint Notebook of Office Depot. It will have at least four sections: OLD APARTMENT, NEW APARTMENT, PACKING/MOVING, and MISC. In it, you will obsessively make and cross off lists. You will write down phone numbers and estimates of U-Haul trucks versus U-Pack. You will doodle a palm tree and dream of the carefree days before you foolishly decided to move. Any scrap of paper, no matter how inconsequential it seems, will be embraced by Saint Notebook's loving pockets.

Step 56: Give a bunch of stuff away

Moving provides the ultimate opportunity to decide how you *really* feel about each of the ten thousand items you own. Particularly if you are paying a huge amount to go cross-country. Ask yourself: *If I left this somewhere while on vacation, would I pay the hotel to ship it back to me? Or is it easily replaced? Would I even care it was gone?* Because when you pack something, you commit to it. You commit to carefully wrap it, carry it downstairs, put it in a truck with expensive and limited space, go days or weeks without it, carry it up the stairs, tenderly unwrap it, and find a place for it in your new home. If all this sounds reasonable, take it. If not, leave it.

Step 57: Get some decent boxes

Free grocery and liquor store boxes are good for two things:

1. Moves of less than ten miles, where they will travel exclusively via car.
2. Books and other ultra-heavy things that should not go in big boxes because they would quickly get way, way too heavy.

They just cannot be your everything, box-wise. You need to get some real, larger, sturdy ones, and chances are you'll have to pay for them. Yes. This sucks. They should be free. Trusty boxes should be like rain. But they're not.

The money you spend here is emotional pain you save when all of them make it intact, rather than sharing their contents with the gutter at 2 AM when all you want to do is go to bed. While you're acquiring the boxes, get two rolls of packing tape, a sharp pair of scissors, and a couple of Sharpies. Fashion yourself a moving necklace by putting the tape and scissors onto a long ribbon that you can wear around your neck.

Step 58: Things that live in the same room can and should go in boxes together

The box, of course, will be labeled with that Sharpie you just bought—LIVING ROOM! BATHROOM! OPIUM DEN!

Now. Obviously the caveat here is that big, sturdy things cannot travel with little breakable things, because they will unintentionally kill them. They don't mean to. But it's the inanimate version of Lennie and the puppy from *Of Mice and Men*.

Another good way to organize is by how quickly you need this item to reenter your life. Toiletries, hair dryers, underwear, anything that you'll need immediately should be labeled as such: OPEN ME NOW!!!, then put them on the truck last. Add smiley faces on your boxes. It reminds you that you actually like your possessions, that they are not just hundreds of pounds of dog poop that you have to transport across state lines.

Step 59: Wrap fragile items thoroughly

Your first move is to acquire a giant pile of newspapers. More than you think you could ever, ever use. Then, every fragile item gets a lot of newsprint wrapped around it—again, more than seems reasonable—sealed with a little bit of tape.

After your items have been properly cushioned, find a sturdy vessel they can fit snugly within. Pots are especially serious about their work as protectors of the fragile; just make sure they're stuffed with newspaper so nothing can move around.

Step 60: If an item holds something in your apartment, it should hold something during the move

The idea here is to minimize empty space, so this is especially crucial for non-collapsible things. Baskets can hold pillowcases or towels. Tote bags can hold other tote bags. Pots hold other pots, plus bundles of silverware held together with strips of packing tape. Oh, packing tape. You're my only friend. You and Saint Notebook.

Step 61: If a larger item needs a smaller item to function, tape them to each other

TV remotes get taped on to the TV. (Not the screen. You know.) Once you have disassembled your IKEA furniture, the screws should get taped to the underside. Really, these items are going through enough stress already. No need to separate them from each other and add to it.

Step 62: Soft things go in big garbage bags

This includes non-delicate clothing, bedding, towels, cushions, and curtains if you have them. These things get casually tossed into a giant Glad bag, which you then kneel on to compress all the air out of. You're left with a dense yet soft nugget that can be placed between furniture items in the truck to keep them from knocking into one another. Or thrown at people in an affectionate but still semi-destructive way. We all need to blow off steam when moving.

Step 63: Precious things that could be ruined by water get wrapped in plastic and put in big plastic bins

You can't waterproof all non-waterproof possessions prior to a move. But some things are not merely things. Photo albums, love letters, your grandmother's sketchbook, and so on, should be wrapped in plastic, then put in sealable waterproof containers. And really, unless you want them out on display, it's nice to leave them there once you're in your new place. You can still take them out and love them; just put them back when you're done.

Step 64: If your friends help you move, you owe them pizza and beer

You don't *have* to give them pizza and beer, but any decent person would. No one wants to help you move, but they will, because they love you. Nourish them, body and soul, with pizza and nice beer.

On the flip side, when your friend is moving, offer to help without their asking. This is great, great karma, and lets them off the hook for asking you something that they know you want to say no to. And hey, free pizza.

Step 65: If you can, hire movers

Yes, this is a luxury, and if you're moving, you're probably also super tight on cash. But if you can swing it, it is some of the best money you'll ever spend, I guarantee. There are some moving companies out there where you rent and drive the U-Haul and they just send over some giant men who will swiftly wrap all your furniture in protective blankets and pick up all the heaviest boxes like it's not even a thing. You will definitely want to do your research ahead of time—go to Yelp, search for movers, and limit your results to one $ sign. Make sure that they are licensed and bonded.

Step 66: Breathe, because it will eventually be over

Moving can make you crazy like a breakup makes you sad, which is to say, more than you ever thought possible. But be that as it may, eventually, it will be over. Slowly, the pain of moving will recede into a vague memory of hard times, as happens to women with childbirth. You can start your new life, decorate your new apartment, and swear to never, ever, ever move again. Thus, the cycle of domesticity begins anew.

DISCUSSION QUESTIONS
& Activities

1. Name one thing that you overlooked before you signed a lease for an apartment that you really, really wish you hadn't.
2. What is the very, very worst chore that exists in the whole world?
3. Make a diorama of your house when it was its very messiest, then share with the group. How did revisiting this scene make you feel?

Chapter 3
COOKING

Unless you aspire to a lifetime of going broke on takeout, followed by Lunchables and Top Ramen, you need to figure out how to make tasty and sustaining things for yourself.

Yes, yes: Technically, sometimes it's cheaper for people who live alone to purchase premade food, but if you do this, you are cheating yourself out of something very human. For tens of thousands of years, we've prepared food and eaten together—it's sort of our species's thing. Even if you're just doing it for yourself (for now), there is something to be said for taking the time and care to make something delicious. Plus, nearly everything that you create in your kitchen will be healthier, less chemical-y, and tastier than things that go directly from your freezer to your microwave.

To achieve these lofty goals, you'll need to stock a kitchen, figure out what you like and what ingredients it requires, learn a little about basic cooking techniques, and so on. You will get about 10 percent of that in these coming pages, since there are entire television channels and sections of bookstores dedicated to explaining the advanced ways of the kitchen. But if the word *sauté* makes you feel nervous, then angry at yourself for feeling nervous, then too apathetic to Google what sautéing actually entails, read on.

Here, I have the immense pleasure of introducing my two cooking northern lights. First up, we have Young Brooke. Brooke is precisely ten years younger than me and writes about food and wine and beer, but otherwise we are oddly indistinguishable. She is my darling roommate, and I cherish her for many, many reasons. One of those reasons is that Brooke cooks amazingly delicious food multiple times per day and always asks me if I want any.

Then we have Sarah. Sarah is the friend who, when the rest of us were subsisting on ramen in college, had everyone over to roast a chicken. This, at the time, seemed impossibly adult. From there, she quickly moved on to impressive dinner parties, cooking breakfast every morning, and, on occasion, making her own damn cheese. She is the best home cook I know.

Brooke acknowledged what many of us who are *not* food writers know to be true: "Trying to cook for yourself when you have no history with spatulas or flame is scary," she said. "Recipes seem like a truly horrid amount of effort and work, and hummus and carrots cost like, what, five dollars?

"You *should* really cook for yourself, however. I am a firm, loyal believer in the religious text by Tracie McMillan titled 'Cooking Isn't Fun.' In it, McMillan basically admits to something every young adult I know could admit with varying degrees of comfort: We just don't cook for ourselves, definitely not with any sort of regularity. 'Even while espousing the ideals of the communal table and cross-cultural exploration, I rarely cooked dinner for myself in my 20s. Where was the fun in *that*?' she writes. 'When you have no *choice* but to cook for yourself every single day, no matter what, it is not a fun, gratifying adventure. It is a chore. On many days, it kind of sucks.'"

I will echo Brooke echoing McMillan here and say yes. It does kind of suck, sometimes. But it's worth it, because this is a skill you will always need, and it is a way to save money, eat healthier, and take ownership over what your own body is made of. Off we go, to the proverbial cooking races!

Step 67: Find an apartment you can cook in, at least a little

Per always, New York and San Francisco residents are excused, but everyone else: Do your best to find a spot with at least a decent kitchen. It won't be anything magnificent, but a few extra feet of counter space go a long, long way. Ditto a full-size stove and, if you can pull it off, a dishwasher.

Step 68: Start to put together your kitchen

First stop on the Putting Together Your Kitchen Train: pans!

Sarah had the following advice for poor would-be home cooks:

"Get a medium-size saucepan, a large saucepan, a large frying pan, and a griddle," she said. "If you're on a budget, check out thrift stores or garage sales. Look for signs of quality, like copper bottoms, cast iron, or stainless steel. Someone with limited money would do far better buying used than buying cheap stuff from Walmart. If you are determined to buy new, check out places like T.J.Maxx, the HomeGoods store, Ross—anywhere that's likely to have top-quality items for low prices."

Brooke said that she also recommends a stock pot, which can be used for everything: making a big pot of soup; cooking pasta in a space that won't cause it to stick together; mashed potatoes!

As for knives, you really should spend some cash, although on the upside, you only really need one right at first. Get a chef's knife, and a sharpener, which you should acquaint yourself with. A chef's knife can do almost anything, if it's of good quality. Once, I dated a chef, and he had exactly three knives at home, two of which were chef's knives. You will also eventually need a paring knife and a bread knife and so on, but in a pinch, Sarah said, the chef's knife can do most of those things.

Step 69: Get you some plates, bowls, and so on

It doesn't have to be a ton—six place settings is good; eight is better. If you're just starting out and are quite poor, go with this: six big plates, six little plates, six bowls, six glasses, six forks, six butter knives, six spoons, six pint glasses, and six of something you can drink booze out of—perhaps stemless wineglasses.

These things can be had very, very cheaply at IKEA or Walmart, and unlike pots and knives, quality does not really count. Or be quirky and get a bunch of charmingly mismatched ones at Goodwill.

Step 70: Get the most basic implements

Price-wise, you can scrimp on these things without serious consequence, but you should certainly have at your disposal:

- A can opener
- A spatula
- A ladle
- A couple of wooden spoons
- Salt and pepper shakers (or, better yet, grinders)
- A whisk
- Measuring cups and spoons
- A colander
- A corkscrew (unless you never drink)
- A vegetable peeler
- A box grater

Step 71: If you have the cash, these things make kitchen life easier

- A handheld juicer, to get every drop out of that lemon
- A rolling pin, which works better than a heavy round jar
- A little handheld grater or microplane—Brooke notes that if you have one of these, you never ever have to go through the improbably frustrating, Kafkaesque process of chopping garlic again. *Just grate it!*
- An immersion blender: Honestly, I use mine less for its intended purpose (pureeing things) and more for the attachments that came with. In one lil' helpful guy, I've got a hand mixer and a teeny food processor.
- A mandoline: This makes slicing things, mostly veggies, much, much easier *and* the pieces will be uniform in size, and therefore will cook at precisely the same pace.
- A spiralizer: Is this trendy and weird? Perhaps. But zucchini noodles are truly great, and cook in three minutes, and this makes them very, very easy. It could be used for other vegetables, too, theoretically, though I never have.

Step 72: Get some baking supplies

First thing: a baking dish. You don't need a big one; nine inches by nine inches should be fine. If you're going to have only one, go ahead and get glass, because it's hard to ruin glass.

You'll need two cookie sheets—nonstick ones are great. I find cookie sheets with a lip on them way easier than their flat counterparts, because then if you're, say, heating tater tots up in the oven, you can just open the oven and give it a good shake so they'll turn over and brown evenly, rather than rolling right off the edge and down to the charred oven floor.

Get a covered Pyrex casserole dish, in which you can bake everything from homemade mac and cheese to a deep-dish cobbler to...a casserole.

Advanced purchase: An enameled cast-iron Dutch oven is a remarkably versatile thing. Use it on the stovetop for soups; use it in the oven for braising. You cannot make a delicious pot roast without first having a good pot at your disposal.

Step 73: Get the basic appliances

A toaster oven does an amazing variety of things (and works great if you only have something little to bake). Some sort of small food processor will make most recipes a lot easier; spring for a big model if you plan on cooking regularly. Finally, and yes, I know this is cliché, but get an Instant Pot (more on this in step 94).

Step 74: Know where things are in your kitchen, and label when necessary

Make sure your kitchen has some sort of organizational system that makes sense, at least to you. If things do not come with labels, masking tape and Sharpie go a long way.

PROCURING FOOD SO YOU DON'T DIE

Cooking is wonderful; eating is great. But you know what most do not find pleasurable? That crucial first step of grocery shopping. Here is an adult person's grocery list:

- Eggs
- Milk
- Bread
- Chicken breast

...and so on. Here is my shopping list:

- 14 ingredients for whatever weird dish I am hungry for *at that moment*, like lamb-and-raisin empanadas
- ½ pound of sour strawberry belts, all of which will be eaten in the car

But so far as I can tell, there are in fact people who have the things for a delicious and sustaining weeknight meal right there in their homes. I asked Sarah what staples she likes to have on hand. Here is an abbreviated list (none of y'all are on the hook for, say, more than one kind of flour). But it's a great list, and you'll find on it most of the things you need for basic recipes.

Grains, legumes, and pasta:
- Black and pinto beans (these can be canned)
- Brown and white rice
- Lentils
- Oatmeal
- A couple types of pasta—maybe spaghetti and penne
- Cereal of choice (I like to have one responsible choice and one "I'm a seven-year-old" choice: say, Grape-Nuts and Cinnamon Toast Crunch)
- A good loaf of whole wheat bread

Fats:

- Olive oil
- Butter
- Bacon fat (seriously, pour this in a little jar after you cook bacon, then stick that jar in your fridge; it doesn't have that many more calories than butter, and it makes every vegetable in the world delicious when you sauté them in it)
- An oil that has a very high smoke point so you can stir-fry things without setting off your smoke detector. I recommend peanut oil![1]
- Sesame oil, which can radically change your ramen experience

Baking:

- Flour
- Sugar, brown and white
- Honey
- Vanilla extract
- Baking powder
- Baking soda
- Dried cranberries (these are also key for salads)

Spices and condiments:

- Salt
- Pepper
- Garlic salt
- Spice blend of choice—I have three decades of faith in Tony Chachere's and would feel unfaithful if I purchased Old Bay, but follow your heart (and family/geographical tradition) on this one; za'atar, tōgarashi, and herbes de Provence are other strong contenders
- Cayenne

---

1. If you are always setting off the fire alarm in your kitchen, you may want to invest in a photoelectric smoke detector, which is less likely to get all hot and bothered when you pan-fry something. You could also get one with a dedicated "hush" button. Either way, put it more than ten feet away from your stove and *for heaven's sake, please check and replace the batteries as necessary.*

- Crushed red pepper flakes
- Balsamic vinegar
- White vinegar (which you can also use for cleaning and laundry!)
- Parsley
- Onions
- Garlic
- Ketchup
- Mustard
- Mayo
- Hot sauce
- Soy sauce
- Mirin
- Chili oil
- Thyme
- Rosemary
- Tarragon
- Bay leaf
- Dill
- Oregano
- Basil
- Curry powder
- Cumin
- Paprika

Hot Adulting Tip, Part 1: I know, I know: Spices are *very* expensive and if you were to try to collect everything on this list in one go, it would cost an absurd amount of money. I recommend looking in natural and health food stores for bulk spices, which can be a lot cheaper, particularly if you only get a tablespoon or so until you figure out whether this is something you need to have on hand. Also, feel free to get one spice every time you go to the grocery store so as to spread out the financial pain.

Hot Adulting Tip, Part 2: Brooke recommended sorting your spices into flavors that work well together, and get used to easy combos that are consistently delicious—lemon, garlic, and olive oil; soy sauce, mirin, and sesame oil; et cetera.

Weekly shopping items:

- Milk (always reach behind the cartons in front and find one with the latest possible expiration date)
- Eggs
- Potatoes
- Onions
- Garlic
- Apples, grapes, oranges, grapefruit—whatever your snacking fruit of choice is!
- Cauliflower, zucchini, or whatever veggie you regularly enjoy
- Baby carrots, for snackin'
- Chicken thighs (chicken breasts are for chumps! So dry! The meat equivalent of a PowerPoint presentation that no one asked for!)
- Salad greens
- Fruits and veggies of choice for snacking
- Smoothie ingredients (see step 86)

There's no reason not to have a lot of your protein of choice frozen in individual portions—this could be chicken breast, or ground beef, or fish fillets. When you get it at the counter, ask the butcher to cut it into smaller portions and wrap them individually.

Step 75: If your produce or meat is constantly going bad, freeze it or even buy it prefrozen

This alone could save you, forever, from foul vegetal slurry!

MONTHLY SHOPPING LIST:

Brooke listed some items that you may not get all the way through in a week but are still nice to have on hand. Brooke?

- Kimchi: Brooke asserts, and I agree, that kimchi is delicious on all kinds of things. Plus, fermented stuff does magic for your digestive system, and this is so much better than pickled herring!

- Cheese: Frankly, I'd have put this on my weekly list, but here we are. It's nice to always have a good Parmesan or Asiago on hand, for the gratin', plus string cheese and a good melty cheese.
- Butter.
- Citrus: Lemon and lime are key, but you can and should also cook with sweeter citrus fruits, like oranges and tangerines.
- Better Than Bouillon: When we were going over these items, I literally hissed "Yesssssss, BETTER THAN BOUILLION!" because I loooooove this product. Like, my mom gives me a little jar in my Christmas stocking every year type of love. Even if, unlike me, you do not enjoy recreationally drinking mugs of stock,[2] this is a fantastic way to add flavor to all sorts of dishes; it tastes way better than most store stocks and, if you should find your homemade stock (see Step 87) lacking, you can always stir a bit of this in.

Step 76: Get in the zone while grocery shopping

This tip came courtesy of my friend April. She always gets bottled water and a PowerBar before she shops, then puts in her headphones and listens to music while she goes down the list. The PowerBar helps her avoid my sour strawberry belts mistake.

I suggest you use whatever songs inspire you to get on your grind and get it, as Young Jeezy would say. It's hard to go wrong with Florence + the Machine's "Drumming Song," or Kanye West's "Stronger." If it is an especially grueling trip, you may need to up the ante with Reba McEntire's "Fancy."

Step 77: Have a slated grocery shopping time that includes prep time built in afterward

After you've made a list that includes replenishing any staples that are running low, includes any special items from recipes you'd like to try, and does not include more than two items that obviously have no redeeming value (I favor Hot Pockets)—and after you've successfully navigated the rocky aisles of Safeway—your job is still not quite done.

Christina, a truly gifted grocery shopper, weighed in with some tips.

---

2. Weird.

"It helps if you set aside a few hours each week to prep. While this sounds hard, it just means that you make assembling meals as easy as possible for yourself later in the week, when you are tired and your feet hurt and every part of your body is screaming to order Chinese takeout," she said.

She recommends you go ahead and wash the greens and herbs, then makes the adorable observation that storing a glass of herbs in water is like "a bouquet of flowers for your fridge."

You could also take this time to mince onions and such, then perhaps go ahead and make a big batch of food that ages well for later in the week if you're tired and don't feel like cooking—think a bunch of roasted veggies, or grilled pork loin, or a pot of soup. There are approximately 8 billion blogs[3] dedicated to how to #mealprep for the week, and you can and should avail yourself of them.

Step 78: Do put produce in the crisper drawer

It really does make a difference. But do not forget about it once it's out of sight and allow it to rot into a foul-smelling vegetal slurry that will coat the bottom of your fridge. That is something real and true and horrible.

IF YOU ARE VERY, VERY POOR AND CANNOT AFFORD FOOD:

First, I've been there and I'm so sorry. It's really, really hard. If you've got some money, eggs, beans, lentils, rice, frozen veggies, and ground beef are all great choices; also, look into bakery and grocery outlets in your area. But if you really and truly do not have money, you can and should go to a food pantry in your area. It doesn't have to be a big deal. You probably don't need to apply or fill out a bunch of forms. You can just quietly stop by, get some good nutritious things, and,

---

3. And a subreddit called /r/MealPrepSunday with almost 400,000 like-minded individuals.

FOUL VEGETAL SLURRY

I once was celery...

CRISPER

when the time is right, donate to the organization or pay it forward.

Step 79: Store and freeze things properly

Always remember: Air is the enemy when it comes to storing or freezing leftovers. Get all possible air out before it goes in the freezer.

Yes, you can go the rinsed-out-yogurt-container route, but it's probably worth investing in some Tupperware or, even better, glass containers with Tupperware-style tops. Freezer bags and Mason jars also work well.

Meat should be put in the freezer within two days, except for bacon, which seems to keep longer. Also remember that once things are frozen, it's really difficult to separate out individual portions, which is why you asked your butcher to separate things out and also why, if you're freezing soup or something, you should dole it out into the amount you want for any given meal. Ziplocs are great for this. Things in the freezer should be eaten within six months, and that is a maximum. Shoot for three.

COOKING

So what will you do with all these ingredients? Cook them, obviously. But how? As stated earlier, about a million books and two television channels are dedicated to answering that question, so I'll skip the in-depth recipes (except for a few that everyone should know) and instead talk about basic techniques and how not to hurt yourself in the kitchen.

Ways to cook things

Cooking things, of course, involves heat, which can be either moist heat involving water (think boiling) or dry heat (think baking). Here are the basics:

• **Baking:** This happens, obviously, in an oven, or even a toaster oven for your smaller jobs. Warm, dry heat rises from the bottom. Used on everything from cakes to roast chicken. Generally dry heat.

• **Boiling:** Submerging an item in water—or, really, it should almost always be stock—that is boiling. The gentler forms of this are poaching (which happens in hot but not super-hot water; bubbles shouldn't be showing) and simmering (tiny bubbles are forming continuously on the bottom). **Quick note:** A rolling boil is different from a boil. A rolling boil involves the whole surface of the water moving as one—it's pretty violent-looking, and throws off splashes with big bubbles. A boil is calmer, and involves constant bubbles perhaps the size of the tip of your pinkie.

• **Braising:** Some of the most delicious meat you will ever have is braised—think pot roasts, say, or lamb shanks. Essentially, braising involves partially covering the item with liquid (in the case of pot roast, maybe beef stock and red wine), then putting a lid on the pot so it is sort of both poached and steamed. This usually happens in an oven and takes several hours, but seriously, it's worth it.

• **Broiling:** The top element in an oven gets very, very hot. This is a wonderful way to melt cheese or finish off meat for a delicious crust, but you *must* stay in the kitchen while this is happening, because it rarely takes more than two or three minutes. Use the minutes it takes to tidy up something in your kitchen, which is also a good plan when microwaving anything. Also, when you're broiling, be sure to move the oven rack so it is close to the top—you want the food only inches away from the broiler.

• **Frying:** Enough fat is put in a pan to cover the bottom, then the item is placed in the hot fat. This will nearly always take the form of pan-frying, assuming you don't have a deep fryer at home. This is a great way to start meat that will be baked, as it gives it that crispy delicious exterior. But don't put too much of anything in at once when you're frying. When things are fried, they're generally giving off moisture. And if there are too many other things close by that are also giving off moisture, you'll end up with mushy steamed food instead of delicious fried food.

• **Sautéing:** This happens in a pan on the stove over medium-high heat. Turn the element on, then add some fat (oil, butter, whatever) and let it spread out. Then add your ingredient and use a wooden spoon to stir frequently. As with frying, be careful not to put too much in the pan at once.

• **Steaming:** You use a little steamer basket to raise food above water boiling down below. The rising steam cooks the food. So, like boiling, it adds no calories, but unlike boiling, it's much gentler on the food.

Step 80: Until you are a good cook, follow recipes

Recipes nearly always work, but you must follow them. Especially baking. No one is allowed to go out on a limb while baking unless they are a professional baker, because there is a huge difference between a quarter tablespoon and quarter teaspoon of baking powder, and things will be ruined.

With non-baking, there is a little more flexibility, but until you learn your way around the spice rack, it's a good idea to go with what recipes suggest, then if necessary add more salt or whatever when everything is done. It's obvious but bears saying: You can never add less salt (although you can water down soups, if need be), so it's worth going slowly and tasting frequently.

But if the recipe says a sauce should be thick enough to coat the back of a spoon, then cook it until the sauce coats the back of a spoon.

Step 81: Buy The Joy of Cooking

It has recipes for everything and, more important, tells you how to do things like sift flour and store mushrooms.

Step 82: Plus How to Cook Everything by Mark Bittman

Mark Bittman is an angel who has come down to earth to teach us all how to ~~love~~ cook simple and delicious recipes that will make you feel so in control of your culinary fate.

Step 83: And maybe some other cookbooks, too

Personally, I have yet to prepare an Ina Garten (aka the Barefoot Contessa) recipe that isn't simple and ridiculously delicious. When

I want New Orleans food, I turn to the aptly named *New Orleans Cookbook*, which—fun trivia!—was the only physical possession my parents bickered about when they were getting divorced. It was out of print then, but can now be easily found on Amazon. Brooke also had some excellent suggestions for those of us who want to take it a step further and actually get really good at cooking:

• *Salt, Fat, Acid, Heat*—Here, Samin Nosrat explains the very, very basics of how flavor works, and how to cook on the fly with a certain level of mastery. The gist, from her website: "Master the use of just four elements—Salt, which enhances flavor; Fat, which delivers flavor and generates texture; Acid, which balances flavor; and Heat, which ultimately determines the texture of food—and anything you cook will be delicious." She's not wrong.

• *The Food Lab*—For all my cooking nerds out there who want to know the best way to do things, J. Kenji López-Alt wrote the ding-dang bible. He tests out a ton of theories surrounding how you should properly cook a steak, an egg, a chicken thigh. Then, he gives you the basics on how to do it well (with a ton of pictures, so you can follow along), plus a few recipes so you can get started. Everyone should have *The Food Lab*, but it's wicked expensive. If you're just starting out, check out his page, Serious Eats, and look up some of the Food Lab posts. It'll get you started.

• *Dinner: Changing the Game*—Oh, Melissa Clark. What a goddess. Clark writes recipes for the *New York Times*, and she's a wildly prolific cookbook author. Her most recent is my favorite, because it's organized by main ingredient *and* method. You figure out how to do a sheet pan chicken dish, a grain bowl, whatever, and then you can just continue to swap out ingredients without learning a new technique. It's genius. And whether you like it or not, you start to actually develop a wheelhouse of go-to cooking techniques. Without telling you, "You're going to learn how to cook now," she teaches you how to cook.

• *The Fannie Farmer Cookbook*—My best editor and all-around East Coast mom gave me this book as a gift, and I will never be able to express what it meant to me. Fannie Farmer was New England's Paul Prudhomme. Her cookbook is not only a pocket-sized wonder of pastoral cooking, but she also teaches you how to be a domestic goddess, from your breakfast table and its butter dish to how best to throw a dinner party. Fannie Farmer is a step up from these basics, but it'll transform you into a cool, collected culinary queen. She's what Martha Stewart wanted to be, but *will never be*. Martha Stewart has cemented herself in the role of Snoop Dogg's cooking bud, probably because she couldn't handle the stress of not being Fannie Farmer. That's what I tell myself, anyway.

Step 84: Figure out how to make the breakfasts you like

This means mastering at least one style of egg cooking (Scrambled? Fried? Over easy? *The choice is yours!*) and perhaps frying bacon. Happily, both these things are pretty easy. The eggs I'll leave up to you, but here's how to make bacon:

Put some bacon in a pan and fry over medium heat until crispy but not browned, turning when necessary to avoid burning. If you are frying a lot at one time, pour off the fat halfway through. Set the bacon strips on a paper towel to drain.

If you want brown sugar bacon, which is great for salads and desserts, dip both sides of the bacon strips in brown sugar, then put a baking rack in a cookie sheet and lay the bacon on it. Put it in the oven and bake at 400 degrees for 17 to 20 minutes.

Step 85: Master oatmeal

It is hard to convince people of this, but oatmeal truly is miraculous. It gives you an amazing amount of energy, like cocaine, if cocaine were really good for your digestion and didn't ruin lives. Get some rolled oats, follow the very easy directions, and then add any of the following:

- Brown sugar and a little butter
- Raisins and almond butter
- Dried fruit of any kind

- Peanut butter and dried cranberries
- Honey and fruit
- Yogurt and walnuts

And...I can't attest to this last one but Sarah swears it is amazing and she never lies about these kinds of things:

"Make it, put it in square Tupperware, let it set, slice it, salt it, fry it, eat it with fried eggs," she said, then anticipated every single one of your reactions. "Yes, do it. Do it now."

Step 86: Maybe have some smoothie stuff on hand?

A few years ago, a well-meaning uncle gave my little sister one of those single-serving blenders, which she promptly on purpose left at my house. *Her loss was my gain!* For though I would have never purchased a tiny smoothie blender for myself, I quickly realized that if I have frozen berries, yogurt, and a banana, I could have a smoothie any damn time I wanted.

That little blender-that-could gave up the ghost last year (and it smelled/sounded very troubling as it passed), so I got a top-o'-the-line blender-for-one online for $19. SMOOTHIES ALL DAY EVERY DAY.

Step 87: Learn to make soup

Soup is so easy and satisfying, and it really does get better with age. A couple of quick soup pointers: It's not hard to make stock (just boil savory veggies, like onion and celery and garlic, and, optionally, animal bones, over low heat for several hours) but I've gotten great results by simmering store-bought chicken broth with garlic and onions and some herbs as a base, then adding my ingredients. In general, you'll want to sauté veggies in fat before you add them, or they will become sad and limp. It's also a good idea to sear your meat. (That means cooking it, not all the way through, in a little bit of oil or butter in a very hot pan until a tasty brown crust forms. Be sure to leave it in place until the crust is really formed. No stirring.) Potatoes, rice, and pasta are all great to add bulk. Use two good herbs; rosemary and thyme will do you nicely until you figure out which ones you like best.

Remember that some veggies—potatoes, carrots, and other hard ones—take a lot longer to cook than, say, spinach. If something is delicate or quickly cooked, add it toward the end. Finally, be seasoning and tasting as you go—you want the flavors to meld.

HOMEMADE CHICKEN NOODLE SOUP THAT WILL MAKE YOU FEEL MUCH BETTER WHEN YOU ARE SICK

Chop up half of an onion, one carrot, and a stalk of celery into roughly equal-size pieces. Melt a tablespoon of butter in a pot, then sauté the veggies until they're soft, probably about 7 minutes. Add 4 cups of chicken broth (or 4 cups of water and enough condensed bouillon until it tastes right), 1 chopped cooked chicken breast, and a giant handful of noodles (egg noodles are traditional but I actually like Israeli couscous, which is these teeny little balls that do a great job of spreading themselves out and being spoon-able). Add some salt, pepper, thyme, basil, and oregano (adding the spices slowly, then tasting the broth), bring the whole thing to a boil, then reduce the heat and simmer for 20 minutes.

Hot Tip: If you are feeling too sick (or, alternately, too lazy—that's fair!) to cook chicken, go grab a rotisserie chicken. It will be delicious in your soup. Add it when your noodles are almost done—give it, say, three or four minutes to heat through.

Step 88: Make good sandwiches

There is a reason that every culture has its version of the sandwich: You pick any of the four things you love most in the world, then get to eat them all at once and can even walk around while you do it, through the magic of carbohydrates.

Sandwiches are not rocket science. Generally speaking, one meat, one cheese, and an assortment of veggies will do you proud. Bread counts, though, so skip the Wonder Bread and get something decent. Toast it so it doesn't get soggy. Mayo, to me, is non-negotiable, but smushed avocado, mustard, or a thin spread of soft cheese can easily play the same role. The classic combinations are BLTA (bacon, lettuce, tomato, and avocado); salami and provolone; roast beef and cheddar; turkey and Swiss; and ham plus pretty much any cheese.

Remember that your vegetables are providing two key roles here: flavor and crunch. The latter should *not* be otherwise present in your sandwich. Brooke recommends tomato and cucumber, or pickles and romaine lettuce. Personally, I feel offended that lettuce is so omnipresent on sandwiches; if I notice it, it's not for good reasons. Nevertheless, the world at large seems to disagree with me on this point, so lettuce on, I guess?

When making grilled cheese: Remember to butter the outside of your bread and that a lot of cheese will soak into the bread. Put in more cheese than you think you need—maybe a layer that is half the width of a slice of bread—then a small sprinkle of salt over. Grill on a griddle over medium heat. Put a lid on the top for the first half, but leave it off after you flip the sandwich.

Step 89: Master the art of the meal salad

This is actually a great way to dip your toe into the waters of entertaining, because lunchtime is a great way to have people over and give them food without having to go full-dinner-party on them.

Sarah makes glorious salads, and here are her guidelines.

"What you need for a really good salad is greens, a fruit or vegetable, a nut or meat, and cheese," she told me, then suggested choosing at least one each from the following categories:

• **Greens:** Mixed greens, spinach, thinly sliced chard, mustard greens, watercress, and lettuce.
• **Fruit or vegetable:** Apple, pear, asparagus, cucumber, steamed broccoli, avocado, tomato, carrot—go for two or three of these.
• **Nut or meat:** Bacon, chicken breast, most nuts (as long as they are toasted).
• **Cheese:** Anything. There's almost no cheese in the whole world[4] that won't be nice on your salad.

---

4. Except American cheese, which is *strictly* for grilled cheese and Tex-Mex queso.

HOW TO MAKE DRESSING:

Most of the time, it's easier just to buy nice salad dressing, but every now and again a person gets a wild hair and wants to tackle the process head-on. Here's one of Sarah's easiest salad dressing recipes:

MUSTARD VINAIGRETTE

1 part vinegar—apple cider is great, but white or red wine also works
3 parts olive oil
A few spoonfuls of mustard
Pinch of salt
Smaller pinch of pepper

Combine all the ingredients in a bowl and whisk, or put them all in a jar and shake it right before dressing the salad. Generally, you want a three parts fat to one part tart ratio, whether that's vinegar or citrus juice or whatever. Remember that it's easy to overdress salads, so a good strategy is dressing your leaves: When your leaves are in the bowl, begin slowly pouring the dressing and mixing, then taste a leaf and decide whether you need more. Add the rest of the salad ingredients later.

Step 90: Make non-bullshit potatoes

Here, I am thinking of instant mashed potatoes, which are just awful, especially since real mashed potatoes are among the easiest and most wonderful things on the planet. Eating delicious, non-gruel food is one of the prime advantages of being a human being in the twenty-first century, you know.

Here is how you make the real thing:

1. Cut some russet potatoes into quarters or eighths. Peel them first if you feel it necessary, which I do not.

2. Put some water on to boil, and add salt until it is less salty than seawater, but still noticeably salty to the taste. Put the potatoes in the water while it's cold.

3. Boil until the potatoes are done, maybe 16 minutes or so. You'll know because you can poke them with a fork and encounter no resistance.

4. Drain the potatoes, then put the pot back on the burner for 30 seconds to evaporate excess water. Mash them to the right consistency or, better yet, use a hand mixer or the beater attachment on an immersion blender. Add a couple splashes of milk or cream, then salt and black pepper to taste. Then, as a waitress at the Movie Star Restaurant in Purvis, Mississippi, once told me, "Yew jehst keep adding butter until it tastes *raight*."

5. MASHED POTATOES.

Some optional but delicious things to add are dill, grated cheese of any stripe, sour cream, crumbled bacon and some of the grease that came with it, a little bit of ranch dressing powder, and roasted garlic.

BONUS ROASTED GARLIC RECIPE

Cut the top off a whole head of garlic, then set it on a sheet of aluminum foil. Drizzle olive oil on it, wrap it up in the aluminum foil, then set it in a muffin tin. Bake at 400 degrees for 35 minutes; when the garlic squishes easily, you are done. When adding this to the mashed potatoes, I just squish out the individual cloves and use most of the head, because more roasted garlic is better than less roasted garlic. You can also smear this on bread, or add it to pastas, or anything. It's roasted garlic, and we humans are lucky to have it.

BAKED POTATOES

Get a russet potato. You will know it by its dry, brown skin and the fact that it looks like every other baked potato you've ever eaten. Turn your oven on to 375 degrees. Wash the potato and get all the dirt off, then rub the outside lightly with vegetable oil. Any oil, really.

You now have two options: You can either poke it all over with a fork *or* you can get a long, clean nail and insert it lengthwise through the middle, then skip the poking. Wrap it in aluminum foil, then bake for about an hour. You'll know it's done when you can (gently and carefully while wearing an oven mitt) squeeze it.

Cut it down the middle, then top with whatever your heart desires.

Step 91: Marinate your meat

Full disclosure: If you're buying amazing $24.99 per pound Kobe beef or lobster or Kobe lobster, then you don't need anything other than salt and pepper. But if that's your life, why are you reading this book and, more specifically, this chapter?

Marinades are a fantastic way to tenderize and flavor your meats and veggies. Live them, learn them, love them! The very simplest one is just soy sauce, which can really do a lot for chicken or beef.

Here are a few of Young Brooke's go-tos:

- Sesame oil + mirin + soy sauce + garlic (bonus if you have ginger to add)
- Olive oil + chicken stock + lemon juice + garlic + herbes de Provence
- Orange juice + chipotle peppers + chicken stock + garlic + oregano/cumin/chili flake/cayenne/bay

Finally, it should be said that both the internet and your favorite grocery store have a lot to contribute in terms of marinade ideas and/ or mixes. Just throw whatever it is in a big shallow bowl; pour marinade over. Let it sit in the fridge, the longer the better (long as in an hour or two, not a week). Take out. Cook. Savor the flavor *of life*.

Step 92: Cook your chicken thoroughly

Here is how to make some delicious, simple, salmonella-free chicken for yourself.

1. Go to the store and get some chicken thighs. They are the best part of the chicken, anyway. If you're a boring person, go ahead and get boneless breasts instead, although if you can't handle bones you don't deserve to eat meat.

2. Turn your oven on to 400 degrees.

3. Put the chicken on a cutting board and rub olive oil all over, then salt and pepper it generously (as in, way more than you'd think), and add lemon or rosemary if you want. *Or* pour some soy sauce, chopped ginger, and garlic into a dish and turn the chicken over in it a few times so it's completely coated.

4. Put the chicken in a *baking dish*. If you don't have one, go to Target and get one. If you are really poor, they have them at Goodwill, too.

5. Remember that it doesn't matter how raw-chicken-y your hands get during this process, but don't touch anything until you wash them, which you should do now. Any part of the counter that may have been contaminated with chicken should have a bleach-based cleaner sprayed on it.

6. Put the chicken in the oven, and watch a 30-minute sitcom or drama of your choice. Then turn the oven down to 350 degrees, and check on the chicken. It might be done! But you also might have 10 to 30 minutes of cooking time left. Probably closer to the 10-minute side of things.

7. But here is how you'll know for sure that you've emerged from the salmonella valley: Poke the chicken with something sharp. The juice will always, cooked or not, be translucent, but if it's undercooked it'll have a red or pink tinge to it. If so, back in the oven! But if it's clear and colorless, your chicken is ready.

8. Enjoy not having salmonella.

If you want more chicken, or to impress someone, this is my strategy, which is adapted from Ina Garten's amazing and aptly named Perfect Roast. Also, go buy one of her cookbooks because every single one of her recipes turns out perfect.

CHICKEN

1 (5–6 pound) roasting chicken
Kosher salt
1 large bunch fresh thyme, plus 20 sprigs
1 lemon, halved
1 head garlic, cut in half crosswise
2 tablespoons (¼ stick) butter, melted
Freshly ground black pepper
1 large yellow onion, thickly sliced
4 carrots, cut into 2-inch chunks
8 small red potatoes, cut in half

Olive oil

The night before, do a dry-brining, which sounds complicated but is not and will ensure juicy, perfectly seasoned chicken. For every pound of chicken, use 3/4 teaspoon of kosher salt. Put your chicken in a pan, then reach inside the cavity and get out the giblets. (You are so brave and so strong! You are not afraid of a tiny chicken liver, even if you have to touch it with your fingers! Throw it away, and never think of it again!) Rub the salt evenly all over the bird. Cover loosely with Saran Wrap and put in the fridge overnight. At first, the chicken will give off a lot of water, but then it will all be reabsorbed and the skin will be taut and dry.

Turn your oven on to 425 degrees. Stuff the cavity with the bunch of thyme, both halves of lemon, and all the garlic. Brush the outside of the chicken with the butter and sprinkle with pepper. Place the onion, carrots, and potatoes in the baking dish. Toss with salt, pepper, 20 sprigs of thyme, and olive oil. Spread around the bottom of the pan and be sure the chicken is breast-side up.

Roast the chicken for 1½ hours, or until the juices run clear when you cut between a leg and a thigh. Remove the chicken and vegetables to a platter and cover with aluminum foil for about 20 minutes.

This is perfect for a dinner party, because it's impressive-looking and delicious and you'll have at least ninety minutes of downtime after you put the chicken in. Remember that one 5-pound chicken serves about four people.

Step 93: Make a decent steak

This can be done beautifully in a cast-iron pan, or semi-beautifully in any heavy-bottomed skillet. I suggest a rib eye, which tends to hit the sweet spot between flavor and tenderness. In general, the less tender cuts (skirt, flank) have more delicious beef flavor, while the more tender steaks (filet mignon) have less.

I love using Allegro Marinade, which I was first introduced to in Mississippi, where people understand how meat should taste. If you're a purist, you can certainly also just use salt and pepper. Take your steak out of the fridge about 30 minutes before you cook it, then either marinate it or generously salt and pepper it.

Get a pan very hot, then add just a little bit of oil (butter, ideally).

If you're using cast iron, you can put the steak right in. Sear it for at least 3 minutes on each side, more if it's thicker.

Here's how to tell if your steak is ready, using nothing but your own hand and the magic of human touch. It involves the fleshy ball of your palm directly under the thumb, which you will touch while holding the rest of your hand in various positions. The result is how the steak will feel at various cooking points. The way it feels when your hand is relaxed is raw. If you touch your thumb to your pointer finger, then that little space feels rare. Your middle finger is medium-rare; ring finger is medium-well, and pinkie finger is well-done.

Once you take your steak off, it needs to rest. Let it sit on a cutting board, loosely covered in aluminum foil, for maybe 10 minutes.

Step 94: Get an Instant Pot that also works as a slow cooker

Listen close, young ones: Pressure and/or slow cooking is The Way, The Truth, and The Life when it comes to delicious winter meals.

My Instant Pot entered my life a few months ago, and it is *astonishing*. It is the speedy cousin of the Crock-Pot, an equally wonderful gadget. Most Instant Pots also work as slow cookers; both of these functions are very important. Toss a bunch of raw meat and sauce in your Crock-Pot in the morning, set it on low, and return 10 hours later to fork-tender pulled pork. Crock-Pots make your whole house smell like delicious meat, and then you come home and feel all domestic and satisfied and have a big pile of slow-cooked meat. Seriously. Crock-Pots.

However! If you, like me, are the sort of person who treasures an extra fifteen minutes of sleep over pretty much everything else, you'll want an appliance that can pressure-cook, too.

"If you want the simplicity of 'throw everything in pot, make it taste good,' but don't have time to 'throw everything in pot, make it taste good,' get an Instant Pot!" said Young Brooke, and I concur.

Step 95: Throw a dinner party

...or an after-dinner party. Or a lunch party. If you're freaked out by the concept, it can be nice to ease yourself into it by a trial run where you're not on the hook for a full meal. Having people over for desserts, coffee, and drinks at eight is a wonderful way to do this, as is having people over for a big delicious lunch salad (see step 89). If you add bread and cheese to the mix, it's an inarguably complete meal.

Then, when you're ready, you can make the leap. First, let people know well ahead of time that you're having a dinner party and want them to come, and get a firm guest list. Four people is a fine number; eight is somewhat ambitious but doable. Six is a sweet spot, especially since you have your six place settings.

Cook things you know how to cook, because it's a bad time to experiment. Also, consider what your afternoon beforehand will look like. One reason it's great to cook something that will take a long time in the oven is that you have plenty of downtime for preparing the other components.

Serve an appetizer of some kind that people can snack on while you put the finishing touches on dinner. Plan on forty-five minutes between the time people walk in the door and the moment dinner is served; it's great to invite close friends from whom you can get help if necessary.

Go ahead and set your table ahead of time, so you don't have to worry about it. If you want to be really fancy, here's how the multiple-fork-and-knife thing works. You'll have one implement per course (so if you serve a salad ahead of the entrée, that's a separate course). The implement you use first goes on the outside, and you work your way toward the inside.

Usually, people anticipate a meat, a starch, and a vegetable with dinner; something like roast chicken and potatoes with a salad is perfect. You don't need bread if you're serving potatoes, pasta, or rice with the meal. A dessert is nice but strictly optional, and when people ask what they can bring, you can and should say dessert or alcohol.

Step 96: Make a dope cheese plate

If you don't want to go the puff pastry route (see below), then a cheese plate is an easy alternative. Here are the components:

- One soft cheese (Brie, Camembert, Roquefort, Muenster)
- One hard cheese (pecorino, Manchego, Emmentaler)
- One orange cheese (cheddar, Cotswold, Gouda)

- Bread or crackers (one for two cheeses, two for three cheeses)
- One accent (strawberries, olives, pickled asparagus, sautéed mushrooms, artichoke hearts, et cetera)

Set the chunks of cheese on a board along with cheese spreaders (or butter knives, which work just fine). It's nice to cut the bread into elongated rounds; make diagonal cuts down the length of the bread.

Step 97: Do not fear the puff pastry

Mediocre cooks everywhere have a tremendous ace up their sleeve that they do not even realize. Puff pastry can transform almost anything dull and lame into something that looks intimidatingly hard and tastes delicious, thanks to all that butter. Every person in the world feels a little bit happier when they are eating a puff-pastry-based appetizer, and as such it's perfect for a dinner party.

Here's Sarah's take on the subject:

"The best way to thaw puff pastry is to put it in the fridge the night before you want to use it," she said. "If this isn't possible, put the puff pastry in its package on the counter and leave it for about an hour. *No longer*, because then it will get too warm and stick to itself and you should just go ahead and throw it out because otherwise you are in for a whole bunch of frustration.

"After the hour, remove it from the box, take off the plastic, and lay one sheet on a cutting board, covered with a piece of plastic wrap or towel, then lay down the other piece and cover with another piece of plastic wrap or towel. Wait a little longer (about 20 minutes), then use as directed. Make sure that you use lots of flour with puff pastry, but not too much. It should not make the puff pastry white."

It usually comes in a square, so a good way to handle it is to cut it into nine little squares for small turnovers.

So now that your puff pastry is ready and willing, what to do with it? You could put any number of things in it, then bake according to directions! Like sautéed sausage and diced apples, or minced sautéed mushrooms with salt, pepper, and thyme, or even berries mixed with a little sugar. You can also bake it on its own with sugar on top, then put fresh fruit and whipped cream on. The world is yours!

BONUS WHIPPED CREAM RECIPE

Homemade whipped cream is...I wish I could come up with the right metaphor, but I can't, because it's beyond description, especially when set next to its fake, sad counterpart. When He feels so happy He could burst, God probably cries real whipped cream.

Here's how you make it: Put your mixer blades in the fridge for at least 20 minutes, or until they are cold. Put some heavy whipping cream in a bowl, then beat with an electric mixer until soft peaks form (when you pull your mixer out, the cream will sort of rise up in anticipation of getting eaten, then collapse back down on itself in disappointment). Add about a tablespoon of sugar per cup of cream, then beat a little more until it holds its shape. You can absolutely add dashes of things like vanilla extract, spices like cinnamon or nutmeg, and even essential oils, like lavender, or even a *liqueur*! Amaretto and Grand Marnier are aces for this. Try hard not to take a spoon to it.

Step 98: Have some snacks and non-alcoholic beverages on hand for when company comes

One time, someone will unexpectedly drop by, and innocently ask if they could have a snack, or a glass of water. When you are forced to offer them leftover Chinese food and tap water, you will decide to always have around some crackers and cheese, or grapes. It's also a nice idea to have some chilled water, either in a pitcher or from a Brita filter, depending on how tasty your local municipal supply may be.

Step 99: Hand-wash dishes properly

Even if you have a dishwasher, there will still be times when it's necessary to hand-wash things, especially anything wood (think cutting boards and steak knives), anything cast iron, anything especially delicate like those terrifying giant wineglasses, and anything really nice (china or silver).

Here's how to wash things besides cast iron and wood: Fill a clean kitchen sink with nice, hot water and add some squirts of Dawn, then a splash of bleach. Let your dirty dishes sit in this for twenty minutes, then put on your latex gloves. One by one, take the items out of the water, scrub with a Dobie sponge, then rinse thoroughly in hot water. Put them in a drying rack, remembering that anything that can hold liquid (cups, bowls, plates with a lip) should be placed in a way that drains all the water out—either upside down or tilted that way.

Wood shouldn't soak in water because it gets warped easily, so just clean it thoroughly using your soapy, bleachy water.

Cast iron should never, ever soak in water because it rusts so, so easily. To clean it, rinse with hot water and use a scrubber, but not steel wool, to get all the food off. Put it on the stove over low heat to evaporate all the water, then put a small amount of vegetable oil on a paper towel and carefully spread a very, very thin layer around the inside of the pan.

DISCUSSION QUESTIONS

1. Why does cast iron feel fine about being so impossibly high-maintenance, and *who are those people* who are like, "Oh, cast iron is sooooo easy!"?
2. Does it weird you out that your hand is made of meat, just like steak?
3. What could make a sandwich unacceptable? Give examples, and show your work.

Chapter 4
FAKE IT TILL YOU MAKE IT

Now that interior elements of your life are in order, it is time to work on your fake adult veneer.

"But wait," you say in a concerned, alert voice. "Wait. Isn't faking wrong?"

No. Faking—or, to reframe, setting aside one's immediate impulses and reactions because we as humans are social animals, fancy ants that all need to get along to do pretty much anything—is *terrifically underrated*. Remember that thing about intentions versus actions back in chapter 1? If you spend your time now faking pleasantness and tidiness, during that process you actually *are* pleasant and tidy.

Besides, a little bit of faking is necessary to keep us all sane. If we were all our most real and raw selves every moment of the day, things would be just awful. Think about the person you know who prides themselves on "always being real"; do you want a world full of them? Do you even want to be in a *room* full of them for five minutes? What people describe as "authenticity" is an excuse to treat others poorly at least 70 percent of the time.

But how does one go about developing a smart, clever, socially adept, and charming veneer? By actually behaving in a smart, clever, socially adept, and charming fashion. And it's easier than it seems.

Step 100: Remember that the outside world only sees your outermost layer

This is easy to forget, since we spend all day sloshing around in our own inner monologues, but it's true. No one hears your thoughts except you. No one sees what you were like in high school, or how red your face looks after you've been crying, or even where you were this morning or ten minutes ago. They can only see whatever is on your outside *at this very moment*. Thus, it is easier than it might initially seem to fake it until you make it, which, not so coincidentally, is the title of this chapter. See what I did there?

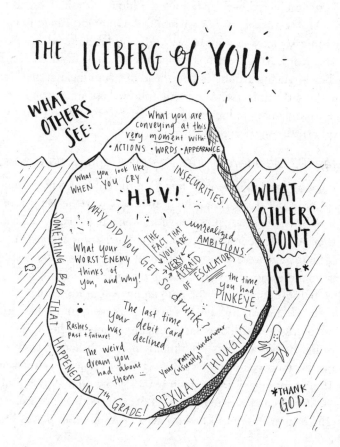

THE ICEBERG of YOU:

WHAT OTHERS SEE:

What you are conveying at this very moment with:
• ACTIONS • WORDS • APPEARANCE

What you look like WHEN YOU CRY

INSECURITIES!

H.P.V.!

WHY DID YOU GET SO drunk?

SOMETHING BAD THAT HAPPENED IN 7TH GRADE!

What your WORST ENEMY thinks of you, and why!

THE FACT THAT YOU ARE VERY AFRAID OF ESCALATORS!

unrealized AMBITIONS!

WHAT OTHERS DON'T SEE*

the time you had PINKEYE.

The last time your debit card was declined

Rashes, past + future!

The weird dream you had about them ☺

Your ratty underwear (usually!)

SEXUAL THOUGHTS

*THANK GOD.

Step 101: Watch ya mouth

You know that terrible feeling where you have put your foot all the way in your mouth, and saying sorry will not smooth things over? It's awful, right? And it gives you archival mental footage for when you're reviewing your own personal worst moments, to be sand-wiched between that terrible day in eighth-grade gym class and the time you begged that guy to take you back. I do it all the damn time—mouthing off, at least. I am always, always, always saying something I shouldn't, but as I've gotten older I've learned it doesn't have to be this way.

There's an incredible Tupac song that does not mince words in its hook: "Motherfucker, watch ya mouth." Granted, Tupac is issuing threats to associates of a mid-1990s hip-hop label, but these are still powerful words to take with you wherever you go. Just because there is an idea bouncing around in your head does *not* mean it needs to be sent out into the universe. And if you follow these steps, you'll greatly reduce your chances of having to explore your toes with your tongue (metaphorically speaking).

Step 102: Be aware of local, national, and world events

You don't need to have your finger on the pulse of, say, parliamen-tary elections in Estonia, but grown-ups know who the prime minister of Germany is, what NATO stands for, how a bill becomes a law, and why they vote Democrat or Republican. They know who their presi-dent, senators, representatives, and local officials are, and the broad gist of what they do. They are registered to vote.

Just because something isn't happening in your direct orbit doesn't mean it's not important. I'm a frivolous person, and I like to dis-cuss frivolous things, like what political parties various animal spe-cies would belong to (cats are monarchists; Labrador retrievers are Democrats; raccoons are anarchists). I don't cram every interaction with Important Heavy Facts about what's going on in Africa. But just because it isn't my favorite topic of conversation does not excuse me from the responsibility of knowing what's going on in places besides my head.

Surely everyone wants to stay informed for information's sake and needs no additional motivation. But just in case...staying abreast of current events will help you be interesting (see step 136) and minimize your chances of saying dumb things. Like the time I asked someone from Puerto Rico how they were enjoying their visit to the United States. (Puerto Rico, as everyone involved in the conversation immediately pointed out, is *in* the United States; in this moment, I fantasized that the student union floor beneath me would open up and I would fall down, down, down to a place where I had not just said this, a place where I could make a new life among the subterranean Crab People.)

Learn your national and local leadership and, um, geography. Try to stay aware of world events.

REGISTER TO VOTE, EVEN—ESPECIALLY!— IF IT'S HARD

Unfortunately, many of us live in places where elected officials are trying to make it *harder* to vote. This is terrible, and undemocratic, but here we are. Let their icky-kabong actions fuel your desire to vote, hopefully for people who aren't making it harder to participate in democracy. Don't wait until Election Day; at least three months ahead of time, look into what you need to do to vote, then double-check that your registration is correct and up-to-date. If you do live in a place where voting is hard and you need extra help, I guarantee you that there are local organizations dedicated to helping with just this situation, so do reach out. Google "voter registration [your county]," then call the number listed under the "contact" tab and tell them you'd like some help.

Step 103: Spend ten minutes a day gathering news, at least

One lovely habit to get into is putting on either NPR or C-SPAN while you get ready. Why just straighten your hair when you can straighten your hair *and* quietly absorb the fact that there is unrest in Liberia? I'm a big fan of those daily podcasts from the *New York Times* and NPR that come out early each morning and will tell you much of what you need to know in twenty minutes.

Step 104: Develop your own opinions

There is a group of people who dedicate themselves full-time to telling you what you should think about news, politics, and other information. They are called pundits, or commentators, or analysts, or columnists. Make sure that you don't confuse them with journalists, because they aren't the same thing. Developing your own opinion is great, but it can only be properly done when you've taken in all the facts, digested them, and then weighed them according to your values in your own mind.

This should be your method:

take in facts → process/analyze according to your own personal
value set and belief system → form opinion

This should *not* be your method:

take in opinion from media, parent, or significant other →
regurgitate opinion from media, parent, or significant other to
anyone who will listen, then sloppily defend it to the bitter end

When you watch a news channel, you should be able to discern what is actually news versus what is an opinion-yelling party. The latter make you stupider every time you watch them. So don't.

Step 105: Read opinions from people who disagree with you

As you may have guessed, I'm a pretty liberal gal. But it's important to me to understand viewpoints from people who are not. Yes, it's soothing to only read things you agree with, but you need to be able to approach and listen to differing viewpoints, as the world is *full of them*.

You do not need, as you are reading or listening to said opinions, to work as hard as you can to refute each and every point mentally in real time. You can sit with this idea, even if it upsets you. You can tumble it around in your mind; you can assess its strengths and weaknesses. You can decide that it's incorrect, or you can decide that perhaps it's a little closer to correct than you thought before. It won't kill you.

Step 106: Get to know people with different political opinions, and do not make "convincing them" the center of the relationship

Our country is so polarized right now, and it's not good for anyone. No matter what you believe, it's important to know that people can hold opposing views—perhaps even ones you vehemently disagree with—and still be good people. Conservative does not equal racist. Liberal does not equal Satanic Commie. When you think this way, you're doing black-and-white thinking that, frankly, helps *no one.*

It's easy to decide on your tribe and then root for the other side to fail. This is yet another example where "easy" is not synonymous with "healthy for you as an individual or our country as a whole."

The best way to convince anyone of something is to have their respect and affection, and that will not happen if the basis of your relationship is your desire to change who they are. The worst way to convince anyone of anything is to call them an asshole publicly.

Don't join a Facebook group dedicated to "respectful" political conversations between left and right folks, as the internet is No Good at making things civil. A much better approach is to actually get out in the world, meet and get to know people from all walks of life, and, when you have a friendship with them, listen to and don't demean their beliefs. When you ask questions, listen to the answers. When you share your beliefs, talk about how you came to them and use language that can reframe the issue. Whatever you do, don't imply that people who think differently are, by definition, willfully ignorant or hurtful, and remember that the more defensive someone feels, the more likely they are to dig in to their position. Give people the benefit of the doubt.

A personal example: When someone is talking to me about how political correctness is ruining the country, I'll ask what they mean, and then really listen to the answer. It often just sounds like there was a time when this person felt really embarrassed or called out for something they hadn't intended. I'll put myself in their position: It hurts when I make a faux pas or do something wrong and then someone calls me on it even (especially?) when I deserve it. That is a feeling I can relate to, so I might say that sounds really hard. Then, the pivot:

I say that to me, I don't think of it as political correctness so much as politeness. I'll say that we've all done things that are unintentionally hurtful, and while it's not pleasant to hear that we're wrong, it seems like if we know something we do hurts people, it's worthwhile to try not to do it.

Step 107: Do work to make the world as you think it should be

For many of us,[1] protesting is relatively easy and relatively fun. I like to chant as much as the next gal,[2] and it *does* motivate those who may be quieter in their beliefs to signal support to causes and people who need it, and it sends a message to elected officials.

But sometimes—not always, but sometimes—people confuse earnest displays of emotion with actual work. The former is mostly impotent without the latter.

If you care enough about something to take time out of your day, think up a good sign, and then march around and yell about it, that is awesome, and a great first step. But know that you can and should go beyond that.

Here, I will introduce Lelia Gowland, who is not only a lovely friend but *also* teaches women to negotiate, and for a time taught sex ed to New Orleans middle schoolers. This is a terrifying prospect in any venue but New Orleans especially. Also, she had some wise words for all of us.

Step 108: Look around at the current framework, and see who it is that's doing the work you'd like to do

"One of the biggest challenges, when people leave college, is that there's no longer a clear pipeline for action," Lelia said. "It's very hard to find the access point, but a good first step is knowing the issues that you're most passionate about, and then find out who is doing that work. In New Orleans, there is this one woman who is very, VERY

---

1. Who are white.

2. Favorite chant ever was from my friend Justin: "We WON'T be LED to CHANTING!" *But we were, and there is the brilliance.*

involved with the state legislature, and will tell you who you need to call and what you need to say—she even has a MailChimp."

So when Lelia got the chance, she reached out and asked what she could do.

"Ask those people for access points or recommendations—there are people who are plugged in and doing that work," she said.

Step 109: Feel free to call your elected officials—but be polite (even if you don't feel polite)

Lelia is quite familiar with the legislative process, and said that calling your state and federal representatives is absolutely a good use of your time—she even has an app that helps her track the issues that are important to her and provides the phone numbers.

"Other than an in-person visit, the next best way to be heard is to call—with one issue," she said. "Start off by giving your name and address and ZIP code, and saying you're a constituent—'My name is Lelia Gowland, I'm a constituent calling from 70119, and I'm happy to spell that or give a street address.'

"'As a small business owner who relies on the Affordable Care Act for my health coverage, I'm very concerned that my preexisting condition won't be covered.'"

Don't call with multiple issues, and whatever you do, be kind to the person on the other end because all they're doing is fielding these calls and a lot of people aren't kind at all.

"'I know you're busy and you're working very hard to serve us, and I really appreciate it,'" she said. "These are young people, fresh out of college, working insane hours for very little money, and even if I detest, with every fiber of my being, what their boss stands for on this issue, I don't need to take it out on them. It makes a better experience for them and a better experience for me."

And if you agree with what your elected official is doing, all the better! Call and say that.

"'I saw the senator's position on X, and I wanted to thank them for that vote,'" she said. "Calling people to thank them for their position shows support and it gives them a little bit of political capital—'I know my constituents want this.'"

Step 110: Perhaps even think about running for office

Here is a doozy: Someday, everyone in charge of the country will be our age! Except for the ones who are younger.

But in order for us to hopefully do a better job than the baby boomers,[3] we need to get elected for things. It can and should start small: Could you be on a local school board? A neighborhood council? Not only will you get the chance to see, firsthand, the pleasure of municipal meetings, but you'll also get a chance to advocate in a very concrete way for the changes you want to see.

Particularly if you're a woman, or a person of color, or LGBTQ, or any group, really, other than white dudes in their thirties who went to law school, there are a lot of incredible organizations out there dedicated to helping get people like you elected. So holler at them.

Step 111: Revise your perception of partying

Partying as a college student and partying as an adult are two very different things. Yes, there are house parties hosted by non-professional friends, which are a blast. But there will also be more and more parties where getting drunk and hooking up are not the goal.

Bonnie is a family friend who has unfair amounts of graciousness to her name—she is a pro champion at entertaining and at making others feel at ease; best of all, she has that intangible quality that makes you feel like an equally elegant person when you're in her company. She was willing to weigh in on conversation, dos and don'ts in social gatherings, how to get in to the best parties, and what to wear once you are invited.

Step 112: Do not RSVP "maybe"

When someone asks you to do something, you have three options:

---

3. YES I SAID IT. How does it feeeeeeeel, baby boomers? Also, as long as I'm on the intergenerational haranguing train, I have a bone to pick with you. In your many, many, maaaaaaany think-piece takedowns of the millennials, you always mention our dumb participation trophies. *Who do you think gave us those trophies?* Linda? Gary? Brenda?!? We were seven. *We were not the ones ordering or handing out those ding-dang trophies.*

- **Option A:** Say yes.
- **Option B:** Say no.
- **Option C:** Say "Gosh, that sounds wonderful, but please let me check my schedule," then get back to them within twenty-four hours with Option A or Option B.

You'll notice there was no Option D: Say maybe. Because *maybe* says many things, none of them flattering:

- "Perhaps I'll go if nothing better comes up between now and then."
- "Your invitation isn't important enough for me to decide one way or another, until the day of."
- "I am a flake who can't even commit to an afternoon of something."

I am really terrible about RSVP'ing, because I feel guilty saying no to invitations; then I tell myself that not replying at all is better than saying no. It isn't. If you say no, maybe it's slightly disappointing (because honestly, your presence isn't going to make or break anyone's afternoon). If you don't say anything, you are compounding the slight disappointment of your non-presence with rudeness and flakiness.

As Bonnie notes, the trouble your host or hostess is going to is very large compared with the smallness of just saying yes or no. It's inexcusable not to choose.

Obviously, there's a much higher expectation level with, say, a wedding than a house party. Here are some considerations:

- Is this person going to spend money and/or plan ahead based on my presence? (Think weddings and dinner parties or really anyone who is providing tasty, expensive things like steak or alcohol.)
- How did the invitation arrive? Facebook invitations are, by nature, lower stakes than an Evite or actual invitation that arrives in the mail. You should RSVP to all of these, but the second two show the host is taking things seriously.
- Are more than fifteen people invited? Your non-presence will be felt in a gathering of less than fifteen, and should be noted accordingly.

• Is this your last chance to see someone for a while? Going-away parties, even if they are large, should be RSVP'd to and, if you can't make it, do reach out to the guest of honor—knowing that they may be really, really busy in the run-up to the move, hence their desire to see and hug everyone at once.

• If you wonder, *Should I RSVP to this?* the answer is yes. Remember, if everyone assumes it's not that important to RSVP, then the host really has no idea how many people will come and therefore no clue of how much meat, goat cheese, baby spinach, whiskey, et cetera, to buy. And that is the worst. So do unto others and RSVP.

Step 113: Err on the side of attending events even if maybe you don't totally feel like it

Do you know how hard it is to organize a party? Especially an elaborate, grown-up one? It's a huge pain in the ass. But this person is making that effort, and they want you to be there with them. It's only a few hours of your time. If you are being really, really good and doing something you hate, then do what my friend Sarah does and make a deal with yourself: *If I go to this baby shower, I will get myself a pedicure afterward.* Or, *I only have to stay long enough to talk to three people, and then I can leave.* And on that note...

Step 114: Learn how to make an appearance then bounce

So you've sucked it up and are going to something you don't totally want to. Yay! Pat yourself on the back for the consideration you are showing others...and console yourself with the fact that you don't have to stay forever, assuming it's not a formal sit-down dinner or what have you.

This is what you do: Show up right on time, which gives the host a feeling of relief that someone has shown up to their party and gives you social karma points. Hang out for a while—thirty minutes, minimum—and chat with at least three different groups of people. Then kind of casually drop the chestnut that you Cannot Stay. This should come in a voice of deep regret, one that conveys you wish you could stay right here, with them, forever and ever. Don't qualify your Not Being Able To Stay-ness with elaborate reasons why. Just, "I can't stay, but this has been *such* a great party."

Hot adulting tip: In general, the more you labor over explanations, the flimsier they seem. Don't explain why you have to leave and what you're going to do and that you wish you didn't have to do that and could stay here but [super-pained, elaborate explanation redacted]. Just say you're so sorry you have to go. Period.

If they ask why—which would be strange—just say that you have a prior commitment. They don't need to know that your prior commitment is a promise to yourself that you wouldn't stay somewhere you didn't want to be for too long.

Step 115: Do not be intimidated by glamorous people

Every now and again, you will find yourself somewhere that is way above your normal schmancy-ness paygrade. Maybe you got an unexpected free ticket to a ball, or maybe a friend of a friend is dating a quasi-celebrity. Get excited, because you are going to have a *blast*.

And you're not going to feel intimidated by your fellow guests. Glamorous people, in real life, are not all that glamorous, generally speaking. And it likely makes them uncomfortable being stared at or treated as such. The idea, here, is to just treat them with the same politeness you would any person: introduce yourself, say it's nice to meet them, and make normal small talk.

By the same token, don't underestimate yourself, or assume you shouldn't be there, even if it's not your normal crowd. As Bonnie put it, "You all arrived on the same guest list."

Step 116: Act like you've been there before

These are Bonnie's words verbatim, and I've found the advice valuable across many arenas in life. Whatever the event or situation, act as though you've been there before, not like a small and excitable country mouse. If you act like you belong, people will think you most certainly do.

Step 117: If you show up at a party and don't know anyone, don't flip out

I'm not sure why it's so hard for us to be alone for even three minutes at a bar or party, but...it is. You assume everyone is looking at you, feeling many things: pity that you clearly have no friends, vicarious loneliness from your lack of companionship, and disgust about whatever personality qualities you possess that leave you void of human company.

In actuality, people are probably not noticing that you're by yourself, or really noticing you at all (see step 11). But to alleviate your feelings of anxiety, just head to a place in the party where you stand in line with others—the bathroom, buffet, or bar, for instance—then give a neutral, amusing opening comment to someone. You already have lots in common: You are at the same party, waiting for the same thing. Go from there. If your target is not the chatty type, then get whatever you came for and head to another line.

You can—and should!—follow this wonderful bit of advice, courtesy of Young Brooke's mentor, Sheryl Julian, who recommends always talking to the most miserable-looking person at the party. One, it's good karma, and two, you really have no idea who you might meet.

Step 118: If you forget someone's name, try to trick them into saying it

Some people (me) are wretchedly bad with names. Every time I hear someone say their name, it's like a wispy cloud that wafts quickly through my head before evaporating in the morning sun. This is really, really awful of me, because there is nothing worse than when people can't remember your name. And you never hear people mention with admiration someone's ability to never remember a soul.

This is fairly transparent, but if you absolutely cannot remember someone's name and there's no sign of them saying it, wait until someone new whose name you do know joins the conversation, then say to Nameless Person, "Oh! Do you know So-and-So?" Now let So-and-So do the heavy lifting for you.

You could also ask for their number and, when you get your phone out, ask how to spell it. Finally, if all else fails, starting a conversation about names in general ("I've always wondered if life would be different if I were an Esmerelda instead of a Kelly") will usually prompt Nameless to tell you theirs.

Step 119: Listen more than you talk

People will love you for it. Everyone is really dying to answer questions about themselves. If you treat every person like the most interesting person you've ever met, they will be. Every single person on this planet has fascinating things to say; they have a moment where they were happiest, or saddest; they know things you do not but would like to. Think of them as crabs, and your job is to extract all their delicious (if sometimes hard-to-reach) information meat.

Step 120: Ask good questions that take the speaker's answers into account

The secret to interviewing is not being so in love with your own questions that you don't listen to the answers given. Each question (so long as it's not a yes-or-no question) will open itself to an array of follow-ups. Even if the initial answer is short, you can draw shy or quiet people out on the second go-round.

Q: So where are you from?
A: Houston.

Possible follow-ups: Are they an Astros fan? Have they been to (Texas city you've been to)? Do they have any secrets to tolerating the humidity? How long have they lived there? What's Houston like? Is it anything like (city that you are in right now)?

Step 121: Do not talk about your deep, passionately held beliefs

This goes for Jesus, the Green Party, Judaism, numerology, the importance of never dating Scorpios, whatever. If you believe in it passionately but know the rest of the world doesn't, keep it to yourself unless other people ask you specifically. Even then, keep your answers brief unless this person really, really wants to hear about it.

Either they agree with you, which is sort of nice and makes for a superficial bonding moment, or they will be bored and/or offended. Since *boring* and *offensive* are among the worst adjectives that can be applied to a conversation (others being *spittle-flecked* and *grope-y*), better not to roll the dice and just steer clear.

"You shouldn't discuss something you feel intensely about, because your side of the conversation will probably sound like a lecture," Bonnie said. "Interests are great to share; passions, people need to be careful about."

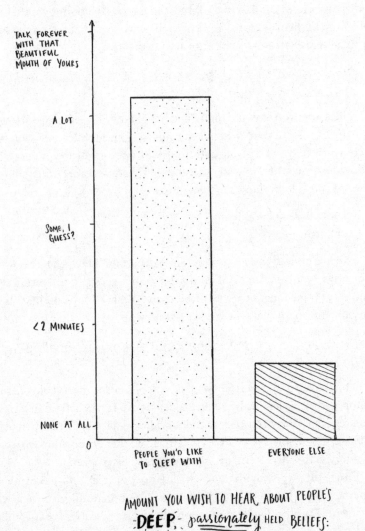

AMOUNT YOU WISH TO HEAR ABOUT PEOPLE'S
DEEP, *passionately* HELD BELIEFS:

Step 122: Curb your instinct to comment on other people's bodies aloud

This should be obvious, but it's not. People's bodies are not good conversational grist. Do not verbalize any details you may think you observe—that they are pregnant, or sunburned, or look really tired—unless they say it first. Because there is always that chance that they are actually just large and round, or have reddish skin, or feel at the peak of their vim and vigor but are naturally quite haggard-looking. Women you encounter are not pregnant *unless they say so or are actively in labor.* Pregnant women usually refer to their pregnancies every ten seconds anyway, so it shouldn't remain a mystery for long.

Even if this person has a really, really obvious affliction, like a cast on their arm, you still don't need to mention it or ask what happened. Chances are that this cast on their arm, being their one distinguishing characteristic, is all that anyone has talked to them about for weeks. They are probably tired of relaying that they were walking through a Safeway parking lot (or, as I call it now, "UnSafeway"), tripped over their own feet, broke their elbow, and were totally not drunk even though everyone assumed they were. For eight weeks, this is all I said to anyone, and it got very, very old.

If your conversation is with the kind of person who loves discussing their injuries (even though they shouldn't; see step 129), then they will find a way to weave these into the conversation.

One important exception: If someone has something in their teeth, or a smudge of BBQ sauce on their face, or something *very temporary* that can be *easily remedied*, it's nice to make sure no one else is in earshot and quietly murmur, "I think you might have something in your teeth. Would you like to borrow my compact?"

Step 123: Don't comment on things people are; comment on things people do

The simplest example of this is not telling a tall person that they're tall.

So much in our lives is shaped by weird rolls of the genetic dice, or fate, or God, or however you choose to interpret that particular mystery. Whether someone is short or tall or originally from Canada or gay or Asian or born to rich parents or redheaded or whatever—that's not something they chose or cultivated in themselves, and it's not something they work for.

What makes someone good and valuable is not these traits. It's the choices they make and the things they do. I'd always rather someone tell me I'm a good writer than that my red hair is pretty, because one of those things is something I work my ass off at, and another is some protein encoding. Both are sweet things to say; one means a lot more to me.

It's not that you can't be proud of/pleased by these intrinsic things, but don't forget that the things you (and others) deserve credit for are the things you have control over.

FRIENDSHIP ACROSS DIFFERENCES

I hope so sincerely, dear reader, that you have lots of friends who are different than you, because that makes us kinder and more compassionate and *real* in the *Velveteen Rabbit* sense, although sidebar, *why is that a beloved children's book?* It's messed up, right? All the toys we got to know being burned in a fire?

Anyway. There are two options out there, which are:

(1) **Have friends of different ages, genders, races, cultural backgrounds, sexual orientations, and so on, or**
(2) **Not.**

I would certainly vouch for (1). The key here is that you must not frequently make those differences a topic of discussion,[4] particularly if

_____

4. This is not to say you should pretend those differences don't exist. They do, and they impact things a whole bunch. But please do not make your friend tell you how. This is what the internet is for. Even more importantly, do not ask them to make you feel okay about racism or sexism or whatever, or reassure you that you're none of the above.

you are a part of a group that is larger and/or more powerful than that of your friend. Centering a conversation around How We Are Different (And What It Says About You... And *Me!*) is not a winning strategy.

Think about the last time you were made to feel bad about your Otherness, even if that was a super trivial thing like you not being able to laugh uproariously at all the hilaaaaaaaarious things that happened in that storied Kickball Season of '15. Was that nice?

If you're curious about the experiences of people who are not like you (a good way to be!), you do not have to make your friend the authority on, say, what black people think about zoos. Unless they are an academic in the field, chances are they have zero idea.

But you know who *does* have an idea, and won't be even slightly irritated when you ask? The internet, or any of the thousands of books by authors who are not at that very moment feeling flustered by your question while they're just trying to enjoy some tater tots.

This isn't to say those conversations can never happen between friends. But tread lightly, be respectful, and let them take the lead.

Also, spoiler alert: You will say and do some things incorrectly. That's a fact! None of us has a 100 percent winning streak on being respectful with these Big Things, unless we never ever mention or even notice them, which has its own set of problems.

When and if someone corrects you on something, be open and don't take it personally. Remember that this was probably the 874th time someone did this, and also remember that even though you feel (understandably) embarrassed and bad, you'll be okay and this means that you'll never do it again. Hurrah!

Here is the proper response: "Oh my goodness, I'm really sorry. I didn't mean that at all, and I appreciate you taking the time to explain that to me," and here, you may add some clarifying follow-up questions *as long as they are actual questions and not sneaky verbal missiles aimed at poking holes in this person's experience.*

It's okay—and even great!—to be wrong and have someone else let you know. It does not get better by refusing to admit it or getting angry. Trust me, there is the most beautiful freedom in saying, "Whoa! Man, *was I wrong!* I thought X but clearly it's Y. Hoo boy! *What a THING!*"

Step 124: Be polite to trans people

Here, I have the pleasure of introducing Davey Shlasko! Davey is the founder of Think Again Training, which has been teaching people to be ethical and kind since the early 2000s. Davey is also the Sotomayor Fellow at Smith College and the author of the *Trans Allyship Workbook*.

The first rule of being polite to trans people is: Do not treat them as your personal AskJeeves.com on What It Means To Be Trans, or What Trans People Think, or Really Anything That You Could Go To The Internet And Learn About Without Putting Someone On The Spot.

"Let's say you have a trans classmate for the first time, and you're getting to be friends and you see a *New York Times* article about trans people," Davey said. "You don't need to immediately send it to them. They have other interests. Someone who is trans doesn't want every conversation to be about their trans-ness; they're still someone with a life and a job and everything else."

There is no need to show off how very accepting you are based on your ability to click on articles about transgender issues and then pass them along. Just read them for yourself, okay?

Step 125: Pronouns are important

Pronouns, Davey said, can be a tricky thing.

"Asking is almost always better than guessing or assuming wrong," for the same reasons that cisgender people feel uncomfortable when someone guesses their gender incorrectly, Davey said. "It's really useful to say why you're asking—'I'm going to be introducing you to some of my friends and I want to respect your identity.'"

Purposefully using the wrong pronoun is vulgar and cruel—"People don't change their pronouns casually; there's a lot of internal and external process and it's a lot of work," Davey said. "[Being misgendered] is like being called the wrong name—not only the wrong name, but the name you *least* want to be called in the world."

Your friend may not be out to everyone, so especially if they're newly transitioning, be careful and sensible.

"If you know you have a friend that people often guess [their pronoun] wrong, ask what the friend would prefer," Davey said, and then use the pronouns in conversation without making it the *point* of the conversation.

"You can ask who they've told and who they haven't," Davey said. "Some students I work with use 'they' at school, but when it's commencement and their grandma is walking down the street with them, I may not use 'they' in that situation."

Step 126: Do not ask people about their genitals unless you are on a face-to-face basis with them (the genitals, not the person)

It's troubling that people do this, but Davey assures me that it is a Thing—asking people whether they've had or are going to have surgery.

"That stuff is almost never your business unless you're their doctor," Davey said, adding that even seemingly innocent comments can actually be fairly creepy.

"Someone complimented me on how well I was hiding my boobs that day, and I was like, 'I don't really want to know you were looking closely enough to notice how my boobs look today,'" Davey said.

If you're not their doctor or not having sex with them, you do not need these details. When's the last time you inquired after a friend's labia shape or testicular sagginess? Same deal.

Step 127: No need to mentally fill in tragic backstory details

Here are two things that are true: It's generally harder and more dangerous to be a trans person than someone whose gender identity lines up with their biological sex at birth, and there is no Universal Trans Experience.

"There's this story out there that the only way someone would ever transition would be if they were in so much deep distress," Davey said. "I know I had a little bit of distress, but it was much more that I found so much joy doing my gender in a different way—there was more pull than push for me. People can have quite a lot of distress and pain, and that's real, but that's not the only reason someone would transition."

In short: Identity does not equal trauma, and it's rude to assume otherwise.

Step 128: Don't emotionally rubberneck

If someone reveals a detail about themselves to you that suggests they went through something heavy, do not ask them about it. If they say their mother died, don't ask how. Don't ask people who say they are from New Orleans about Hurricane Katrina; don't ask people from New York City about where they were on 9/11. Revealing a biographical detail during small talk is not an invitation for you to ask anyone to rehash something that could be terribly painful. If they want to offer this information to you, they will.

If you're on the flip side of this and someone asks about something similar, you can absolutely say, "You know, it was very difficult and I don't generally talk about it in light situations." Yes, this is a tiny reprimand, but probably a good reminder for this nosy person.

Step 129: Quit talking about your own body

Remember that time someone told you in loving detail every single medical thing they've been experiencing lately (even the poop-related problems) and it was incredibly fascinating and not at all disgusting? No? That's probably because someone talking about their own body almost never makes people feel anything but uncomfortable. So apply this principle to yourself, even though it's hard, and realize that although the fact that you are valiantly soldiering through strep throat is very interesting to you, others don't care, and discussion should be limited to a need-to-know basis. What could they even add to that? They have no idea what your throat feels like.

Now. If someone who is dear to you is in bad health, of course they're welcome to talk to you about what they're going through—and if you're in that situation, you are welcome to do the same. There are mild and temporary inconveniences and then there are life-changing illnesses that warrant emotional support. But before telling your tale of tendinitis woe to co-workers, passersby, the checkout lady at UnSafeway, whomever, just realize that your body isn't good small talk.

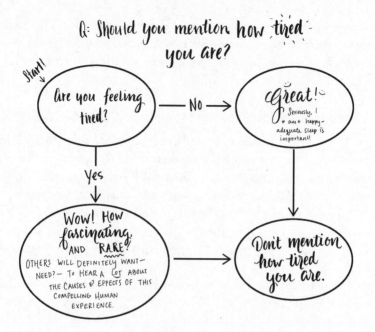

Q: Should you mention how *tired* you are?

Start!

Are you feeling tired? — No →

Great! Seriously, I *am* happy— adequate sleep is important!!

Yes ↓

Wow! How fascinating. AND RARE! OTHERS WILL DEFINITELY WANT— NEED?— To HEAR A LOT ABOUT THE CAUSES & EFFECTS OF THIS COMPELLING HUMAN EXPERIENCE. →

Don't mention how tired you are.

Step 130: Don't tell people you've just met about your problems

There is one exception here, and that is the random stranger who, for some reason, you find yourself opening up to and then they tell you something brilliant that gives you an entirely new perspective on life. This usually happens on cross-country train trips.

The rest of the time, best to keep things positive.

Step 131: If a stranger tells you something inappropriately intimate, be sympathetic and graceful

"If they're opening up like that, it could be poor training or it could be a call for help," Bonnie said. "In your mind, you must distinguish whether they simply don't know they shouldn't be talking about this, or if they're in actual need of assistance."

Is this person just talking to you because you're present and willing to listen to them? Or do they legitimately feel like you're a safe person that they can confide in because they don't feel safe? If it's the former, you can politely excuse yourself whenever you please. If it's the latter, please remember that you can't fix everyone and boundaries are so, so important. You can, however, point them toward resources that may be helpful.

Step 132: Rescue a conversation from the brink of disaster

This is a great, characteristically brilliant Miss Manners trick for situations when someone has said something so egregious that the conversation has come to a halt. And there you all are, stuck in the agonizing awkward place this person just created with their words.

Pause, and take a beat to kind of reinforce the utter wrongheadedness of what they just said, thereby distancing yourself from that particular thought or sentiment. Then, say this in a slightly sympathetic voice:

"I'm sure you didn't mean that the way it sounded." And then change the topic *stat*.

For example:

"I'm sure you didn't mean that the way it came out. Anyway, oh! You guys! I forgot to tell you, [good news about your life]."

Take everyone in the conversation to a faraway, safe verbal space that is *light-years away from what was just said*. Yes, it's awkward, and yes, everyone at the table will know exactly what you are doing. Still, this is the best possible course of action in the face of such verbal ruin. Pause, pivot, *go*.

Step 133: If you have said something really offensive, apologize

That is all you can do. Say sincerely, "I'm so sorry—I *really* did not mean that the way it came out." Wait for them to respond, add a quick follow-up sorry if necessary, and then change the subject.

Whatever you do, don't try to justify or explain away what you just said, because then you are holding everyone hostage in the offensive place you've created. Again, you need to move away from there.

Step 134: Use the sandwich method when saying things people may be upset or hurt by

THE SANDWICH METHOD
OF DELIVERING FRANKNESS

COMPLIMENTARY BREAD:
"It is so sweet of you to ask about me."

REAL-TALK MEAT:
"I'm actually really private about these things, and tend to process quietly, so I don't need to talk about it now."

SECOND SLICE OF KINDNESS:
"You're a great friend, and it means so much that you checked up on me."

Step 135: Other people's sex lives are none of your business

...unless you are having sex with them, in which case it isn't other people's sex lives, it's your joint sex life.

Here, again via Miss Manners (seriously, she is the best and everyone should put this book down and go read her now), is an ideal takedown of homophobia and prudery. Someone wrote in asking her what they could possibly be expected to say when introduced to a gay couple. After one of her perfectly curt answers ("How do you do? How do you do?"), she had a great line, which I will paraphrase: "I've come to believe there are only two kinds of people in this world—those who believe other people's sex lives are their business, and those who know they are not."

A non-comprehensive list of stuff that is none of your business:

- Who is fucking whom.
- Who likes what in bed.

• How many people someone's slept with.

• What other people's orientations are, particularly if they've not felt like coming out and telling you. If they have, keep that to yourself unless you are really 100 percent sure that they are completely open and out. Don't assume they are.

• Who might be trying to have kids, or, if they are currently pregnant, the circumstances in which they got that way (planned? unplanned? fertility treatments? et cetera).

Have you ever had someone discuss your sex life? Did you like it? There you go. What other people do with their penises and vaginas doesn't need your analysis or attention. Some things can and should be private except with close friends.

Step 136: Be interesting!

Figure out what your own talking points are—quirky and unique things about yourself that might amuse others and/or help segue into a topic where everyone is comfortable. Also, know these facts about your friends who might be at the party with you—for example, one of my friends is winningly Minnesota-modest and would never tell people that she was an ice-skating cheerleader in high school. (Which is a thing in Minnesota! Since hockey is the big sport, they need cheerleaders... *on ice skates!*) But you know who *can* tell people that she was an ice-skating cheerleader? Me. And I did, all the time. Because let's face it, ice-skating cheerleaders are the most incredible thing ever, and I'm pretty sure people will want to know when they are in the presence of one.

Step 137: Know how to wrap things up

Every conversation you begin must at some point come to an end, because you do not want to spend the rest of your life talking talking talking in the host's living room, passing the years and growing old together on this one conversation. And, nothing against you, but the person you're conversing with doesn't want that, either. Leave them wanting more, not less, of you. So start to mosey the conversation back to the light, early topics (how fun the party is) and then you can end the conversation on a positive note.

Bonnie broke it down thusly: "It's simple—just say, 'It's been so nice to meet you! Kelly's told me lots about you,' or 'It's been so nice to meet a fellow Oregon State Beaver'—whatever it is—or 'I've really enjoyed our conversation'…ending it that way should put everyone on the same page."

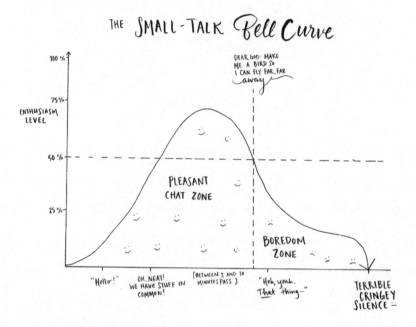

THE SMALL-TALK Bell Curve

Step 138: Send a thank-you note

Yay! You made it through this party—almost. You are not quite off the hook because you still need to send a thank-you note to the host.

Now, the same thing as with the RSVP applies here—if your host cooked you a delicious dinner, or let you stay at their house, or took you boating, or just generally showed a higher level of care and hospitality and attention than they would for a house party, go ahead and send a note.

The truth is that there is nothing bad and everything good about thank-you notes, so you should send them all the time. In fact, this book's spirit animal is a thank-you note.

Someone takes you out to dinner? Thank-you note. Takes the time to interview you for a job? Thank-you note. Present? You *know* that's a thank-you note, and in the words of an etiquette expert I interviewed once, the note should be written before you open, eat, play with, look at, listen to, or in any way enjoy the gift.

I saw the apex of thank-you notes several years ago in the Gamma Phi Beta sorority house on SMU's campus. The chapter had a bulletin board full of thank-you notes from other chapters, because of course Texas sorority girls love nothing more than thanking one another on official sorority stationery.

These notes...they were just so *perfect*. I'd been writing thank-you notes for years—good ones, that others always commented on—and I had nothing on these bitches. NOTHING. Comparing their thank-you notes with mine was like watching Michael Jordan play one-on-one against a seven-year-old with a broken elbow. They had, essentially, shut the thank-you-note game down.

I copied their format and have used it ever since. I will give you an example of me thanking my best friend for inviting me to her wedding, then parse below.

> Dear Anne,
>
> You were such an unfairly gorgeous bride. Seriously, you single-handedly stole the show from that delicious salmon, charming decor, wonderful company, and excellent/ridiculous dance party there at the end. I had such a great time; it's the best wedding I've been to in years. Thank you so, so much for inviting me.
>
> *Love,*
> *Kelly*

A breakdown:

- Start with the word *you* if possible, because everyone loves reading about themselves more than anyone else, and this sends a loud and clear signal that you'll be doing just that.
- A couple examples of what you were appreciative of. Be specific!
- How you felt or benefited (so they get the warm fuzzy of knowing they made you feel happy).
- Don't thank them until the very last line, and do it simply. "Thank you so much for this wonderful gift." Et cetera.

Step 139: Determine what you care about, then dedicate some of your time to it

Maybe it's disabled children, or animals, or the environment. Maybe it's the incarcerated, or their kids. Maybe it's the homeless. No matter how black your heart may be, somewhere there is something that you care about the fate of. It is a good, grown-up thing to exert a little bit of energy trying to make things better. It's also a great way to meet new people, bulk up your résumé, and get out of your comfort zone.

"Figure out how much time you've got and then call up a non-profit and say, 'This is who I am, and this is what I'm capable of doing,'" said my friend Jacob, who is an astonishingly talented volunteer.

OPPOSITION

Step 140: Imagine rude people as jellyfish

Someone once told me she imagines crazy mean people as jellyfish, mindlessly floating in your direction, ruining your day with tentacles of unpleasantness, and then float-

Is that a grilled cheese sandwich? ...Ew.

Mean Person Jellyfish

ing away. On the upside, when she encounters these awful human beings, she thinks of a jellyfish noise, sort of like *bloop...bloop* in her head. I have started doing this as well and find it very satisfying.

Jellyfish do not respond to reason, they usually don't respond to kindness, and they will always show up to ruin a fun party if possible. Therefore, your strategy is threefold: avoid, neutralize, and, in rare circumstances, poke with a stick.

Step 141: Develop your own Teflon qualities

Oh, this is so much easier said than done. But in the long run, this is the best and most universally effective way to deal with the unpleasantness of others.

From here on out, always, you are a smooth, unblemished surface to which even the most crusty meanness, bitterness, anger, and craziness cannot affix themselves. The gross social output of others slides off you. The bad moods, the dark looks, the curt replies: All of this you process, yes, but only in passing, and not in a way that changes anything in the long run. To move on, you need nothing more than a gentle swipe with a paper towel, not the emotional equivalent of soaking in dish soap overnight.

You're a grown-up, and you get to decide what behaviors affect you for five minutes versus what behaviors change you as a person.

Step 142: Accept that some people are just jerks

Some people have blond hair. Some people are really good at baseball. Some people find nothing more pleasurable than organizing a drawer full of buttons. Some people are assholes. This is the human spectrum.

Step 143: Try to pity them a little, for your serenity

Being a bad, mean person is punishment in and of itself. Think of the most difficult person you know. Do you think they're happy? Do you think it's fun living inside such a taut, prickly shell? Chances are good that they're prickly to themselves, too.

A slightly modified version of the Serenity Prayer:

Lord, grant me the serenity to ignore the assholes I cannot avoid;
The luck to avoid the ones I can;
And the self-awareness not to be one myself

Step 144: It's probably not about you

Let's say you're checking out at the grocery store, and the clerk is dismissive and short with you. Here are the possibilities:

- They hate their low-paying job and the attendant bullshit.
- They had an ugly fight with their significant other this morning and are stewing about that.
- They're developing strep throat.
- They are a sour person generally.
- They dislike you personally and are out to get you, even though they just set eyes on you and you've said nothing to them yet.

Now. Of those possibilities, which is the likeliest? But which one does your mind jump to?

Usually, when people are being dicks, it's not about you; it's about them. Think about the last time you were rude or dismissive to a stranger. It's probably because something else bad was happening and you were in a foul mood. And such is the case with others, too. It's more than likely that either something shitty is going on in their life, or they're just bad, mean people.

Step 145: Just accept that some people won't like you, and never will

...and it's not because they're jealous, either. They can just not like you. Do you like every person you meet? Every song you hear? Every food you taste? Extrapolate that. All around this world, there are people of all stripes—men and women, young and old, of every color and station—who, for whatever their reasons, *do not or would not like you*. Just move on.

As my friend Kate put it, if you don't like someone and they don't like you, that's not a problem; that's mutual agreement.

Next time you find yourself fretting about this, think of someone really, really neat—Albert Einstein, maybe. Then remember that there was at *least* one person who thought Einstein was a colossal dick. I guarantee it.

Step 146: Do not engage with unhinged people

Here, I am not talking about the mentally ill, but rather people whose perception of the world is so odd and skewed that it is difficult for them to interact with the rest of us. Think people who scream at waitresses. Those types of people.

Engaging with them will never, ever provide the desired effect for you. You cannot make unreasonable people reasonable; you cannot explain to them why it is not okay to, say, get drunk and have a breakdown at a toddler's birthday party or threaten nuclear war with North Korea via Twitter. There is one direction sanity will flow, and it is away from you as the madness spreads. Soon your thoughts and words won't be even slightly reasonable. Drunk counts here, in both the short term ("Oh, she's drunk") and the long term ("Oh, he's *a* drunk").

The next time you find yourself interacting with someone who is just completely out there, don't tell them they're being unreasonable, because that won't do anything.

Remind yourself that you do not engage with cuckoo-bananas people (silently, of course; saying this aloud will probably make things much worse). Treat them kindly, and gingerly, and then get away.

WARNING SIGNS

Here is a collection of things that should sort of set off some Unsettling Person Alarm Bells. They can also be said or done by benign weirdos, but just make sure your little ears perk up when you notice these things:

- "Those guys are all out to get me." Possibly, yes. Possibly they are all out to get him because he is a crazy jerk.
- Any sort of slur against a group of people.
- Discussion of conspiracies of any sort in casual conversation.
- Intense, prolonged eye contact.
- Walking any animal that is not a dog.
- Immediate revelation of an overly personal detail, like the fact that they don't talk to their mother anymore.
- Returning to a topic that you are not returning to, more than twice.
- An unnecessarily cutting comment, particularly if it's disguised as a compliment.
- Discussion of bodily functions, or (true story) telling you that they didn't get any sleep last night because their husband is passing a kidney stone, then doing what must have been a very accurate imitation of the noises he was making. While standing in my cubicle.
- Asking questions that even a socially ungifted twelve-year-old would know are not appropriate things to ask.
- An insistence that they *know exactly what is wrong with you*, and—great news!—there is a *wonderful* organization—some people say it's a religion, but it's not, it's just an *organization*—that brought

them great peace and relief and will no doubt bring you the same. Would you like, some time or even right now, to go there with them and begin your new life?

Step 147: Accept, in the deepest part of your heart, that just because you are right or have the upper moral hand does not mean you'll win

You know why movies are so satisfying? Because they reflect back a reality that we all wish were true, that being good is its own reward and that being right means we will win.

This is often the *opposite* of the case in real life. People who have lots of power, people who care less about others, people who are more interested in what they want than what is just—sadly enough, these people tend to do pretty well for themselves, because they are more concerned with what works than what's right.

So if you find yourself the David to whoever's Goliath, fight valiantly. But also...

Step 148: Know when to drop the banana

When my sisters and I were little, we maintained a pretty steady argument for about seven years. I don't know if she got this from a child psychologist or what, but my mother's ingenious strategy was called Drop the Banana.

When we were having a pointless back-and-forth, the first child to say, "Drop the banana" and leave behind the bickering was rewarded. So, if you're stuck in a perpetual pointless-argument orbit—one that, *even if you were to win*, would not tangibly help anything except your desire to hear them apologize and realize how very, very wrong they've been, well, drop the banana and move on with your life.

Step 149: Do not allow yourself to be abused

While preserving your sanity by heading off pointless arguments at the pass is a great skill to acquire, do not do this all the time because you are afraid to fight with someone who picks on you constantly.

Know deep in your heart that you are not someone who tolerates the shitty treatment of others. Or at least don't let it get to you. Again, easier said than done.

But a good way to gauge this accurately is to try to take yourself out of the situation. Imagine that a close, dear friend you love is relaying the circumstances to you. Is it abusive?

STRANGER DANGER, OR AT LEAST INCONVENIENCE

It is so easy to come to the conclusion that every single person in the world whom you don't know personally is out to ruin your day, what with the loud movie-talking and non-turn-signaling and mouth-breathing and every single other repugnant human behavior.

And yes, there is little you can do to permanently alter the behavior of others. But you can be a folk hero who shushes people in the movie theater and doesn't tolerate line-cutters.

Let's start by not being an asshole yourself.

Step 150: Give up your seat to pregnant people, elderly people, and others with obvious physical burdens

Come on. No one needs to tell you that. Just do it.

Step 151: Speak patiently and kindly to people

Even if you feel neither patient nor kind. Just do it. Know that in some way, you will be rewarded for upping the earth's pleasantness level.

Step 152: Remember that you catch more flies with honey than vinegar

Here's one reason to be kind and patient: It gives people more incentive to care about you enough to do what you want. Just because you're kind and good doesn't mean your motives have to be pure.

Step 153: Deal with line-cutters and their ilk as though they are sweet but dim people who need some gentle correction

This can work with people of all stripes who need to straighten up and fly right, although line-cutting is a perfect example. Assume your friendliest, most open expression that lets them know you are all on the same team. Your voice will express *sympathy* that they didn't get this right the first time, but *optimism* that with your guidance, they will manage.

"Actually"—pause—"the line starts back that way." Then put a bright happy smile on your face, one with just the slightest hint of steel. Ninety percent of this smile will say, *Glad we've cleared this up!* Ten percent of this smile will say, *I see you, you mouth-breathing son of a bitch. Get to the end of the line.*

This also works with drunk bros harassing women, someone who is talking loudly on the cell phone, and teenagers playing loud and terrible music on public transportation.

Step 154: In general, don't cause a ruckus in public

Unless people are paying to see you perform, it's nice to just go with the flow. Be quiet in movies. Don't cut in line, physically or metaphorically. Don't raise your voice to strangers as a means of signaling that they need to pay attention to you, even if they are the worst customer service agent ever. Look at what the people around you are doing, and do that. If you are in a space where people are all walking or moving in one direction, then walk or move in that direction with them. If everyone is being quiet, maybe you should be quiet, too. If you don't care to, then relocate yourself.

Don't be an unnecessary impeder.

Step 155: Do not call people out on the internet

It's just almost never helpful.

Here's what you wish would happen: Upon seeing your scathing Facebook reply, this person will be shaken to their very core. They will realize that yes, in fact, that *is* a shitty racist thing to say and, now that they're thinking about it, they say and do a *whole bunch* of terrible things. They will commit, right then and there, to the hard work on themselves that is required to overcome our default setting, which is, generally speaking, not as kind and compassionate as we could be. They will log off Facebook and head to a library; they will tirelessly read theory, listen to the lived experiences of others. They will only return after months (years?) of education, and when they do, they would *never* respond to that *Atlantic* piece on the importance of justice reform with "ALL LIVES MATTER—and also, when is WHITE PEOPLE history month?" That old version of themselves now fills them with remorse and shame. For lo, they have bathed in the cool, clean water of you telling them what an asshole they are; they have been washed clean.

What will actually happen: They will immediately dismiss what you said because (a) you hurt their feelings and (b) they have no particular desire to listen to what you—a Random Internet Person—have to say, and instead will be angry because (c) telling someone you don't know that they're wrong, in a public forum, is not a way to change hearts or minds.

If you don't know this person? *Just let it go.* You could spend literally every second of your life from now until when you are dead bickering with random people on the internet—*you still would not make a dent in that vast, exhausting mountain.*

Step 156: Instead—when appropriate—call in

If you do know them—let's say it's your aunt whom you don't see much but you know in her heart is good—it's probably worth sending a private message to them. Do not immediately tell them that they're a jerk (even if they are maybe acting that way at the moment). Instead, gently explain your position, pass along something that might convince them, then end by appealing to their better angels and common decency:

Hi Aunt So-and-So!

I hope you and Uncle What's-His-Name are doing great. I saw that you commented on the criminal justice reform article I posted, and I wanted to let you know I am going to take down your comment. I know you have strong feelings on this, but to a lot of people, including many of my friends, this issue hits very close to home.

The phrase "all lives matter" can be really offensive to some people because it turns their words against them and implies that what they are working for isn't valid. This is a silly comparison, but if you sincerely wished someone a Merry Christmas and they immediately shot back that All Holidays Matter, it would be frustrating, especially because you never said other holidays don't matter in the first place! ☺ But on a more serious note, you might be interested in this article I read a little while ago that really helped me understand what the Black Lives Matter movement is all about. I know you would never say something hurtful on purpose, but I know this does hurt people, including many who are also commenting on the post.

Love,
You

Step 157: Wish them well

This is for the long-term sorts of enemies. There is a good bit of truth in that cliché about how acid hurts the vessel that carries it more than any object it might be poured upon. When you carry around ugly negative feelings about someone, guess what? It's your brain that has those awful thoughts living in it, not theirs. Chances are that your hatred does little to nothing to thwart your actual enemy, but rather keeps *you* in a state of icky resentment.

So here is one of those things that is so difficult, but that you can feel proud of. Next time you think something awful about someone, just take a moment and do your best to wish them well. You can wish that their wellness occurs far away from you, but finding a little pebble of positivity to fling in their direction does wonders for one's serenity.

DISCUSSION QUESTIONS
& Activities

1. Which is worse to talk about in polite circles: poop or herpes?
2. Name some other things crazy people do, then write a one-act play that includes all of them.
3. What is the most spectacular conversational clusterfuck you've ever witnessed in person?

TEN EASY STEPS TO REDUCE EVERYDAY SHAMBLES

1. Important information does not live on small scraps of paper for more than the time it takes to hang up the phone and transport that information to its permanent home. Phone numbers go in your phone. Dates go on your calendar. And so on.
2. Keep your phone charged and on you. Have extra chargers, 'cause why not! One lives in your car, one at work, one at home. An external charger is great, *particularly* if it's the kind you can also jump your car from.
3. Apply a similarly generous strategy to deodorant placement: again, one at home, one at work, one in your car, and one in a strategic fourth location—the gym, perhaps, or a significant other's house.
4. Develop your mantra of Things That Must Not Be Lost. Anytime you leave a place to go elsewhere, run down the list. Mine is phone-keys-wallet. Pho-Kee-Wah, for short.
5. Get online banking, then check your account at least weekly for anything surprising or terrifying.
6. Be on time to things.
7. Call and email people back promptly. These last two steps do more than you can imagine to convey one's grown-up-ness.

8. Attach one of those little beeping tracker thingies to your keys. I have a Tile and I love it, because not only can I make it chime from my phone (or anyone else's who has the app!), but I can *also* make my phone ring by pressing the button on the Tile, and *that little guy is super busy almost every day.*

9. Keep a few protein bars in your car or in your purse. This way, when you're getting crabby and you go through the HALT (Hungry? Angry? Lonely? Tired?) checklist, at least you won't be that first one.

10. Drink a bunch of water, all the time, but *especially* when it's hot outside. It happens very, very regularly that I'm upset or having a hard time thinking and I don't know why until I realize that I've been drinking nothing but caffeinated drinks all day.

Chapter 5
GET A JOB

Getting a job isn't usually optional unless you are phenomenally wealthy, in which case enjoy hanging out in your own private baby animal menagerie. Mine will have a bouncy castle full of red pandas.

But as seminal Atlanta rapper Young Jeezy put it, if you aspire to stack paper and ball sufficiently outrageous to someday have an adorable private zoo of your very own, you need to get a job. And unlike Young Jeezy, your job will not consist of rapping about Atlanta's cocaine trade.

Jobs are crucial to being an adult. Frankly, jobs are crucial to being a human being. We're social creatures, and we each need to do something that is useful to the other human beings, even if it's in an artificial capacity, like helping other humans get their hot pizzas in a timely fashion.

Side note: I know it is really, really hard to find a grown-up job, and the process can be painfully demoralizing. I promise: I feel your pain. Everyone does, because everyone has to start at this place of not having a job. If you're reading this and don't have a job, know this: You *can* and *will* find a job eventually and someday this will be an icky but receding memory. But for now, there are a few ways to maximize your chances of finding the right thing for you.

Step 158: Keep your head down and cook

This piece of advice, more than any in the chapter, will work no matter where you are or what you do.

An old boyfriend of mine was a cook who was good enough to open up his own restaurant. When he talked about the employees he loved best—the ones who got raises, the ones he would take anywhere—there was one thing they all had in common.

"He keeps his head down and cooks."

If you are the employee who shows up on time without fuss, doesn't cause drama, and quietly but competently does the job you're paid for, then you will always be sought after. Go with the flow when it comes to workplace regulations. Show up in a clean uniform and do the small, stupid things that seem pointless but are part of company culture.

Step 159: Let go of your pride

In the vein of non-Singular-Seahorse-ness (see step 1), it is important to come right out and accept that your first job will not be glamorous, lucrative, or fun. It may be one of those things, but it certainly won't be all three.

I have a friend whose work ethic is just unparalleled. It's not even his work ethic so much as his pragmatism: He always understood that having a job is not optional. He worked hard through undergrad, then got into a top-tier law school with a generous scholarship. And then…he decided he hated it and dropped out. Not knowing what to do but knowing that he had to pay rent, he got the first job he was hired for, which happened to be delivering pizzas, which is decidedly not as glamorous as being a lawyer. But he knew that he needed to make things work, and so didn't spend a bunch of time complaining about how it was beneath him or a waste of his intelligence.

So while you may not, personally, be delivering pizzas now, put yourself in a humble place. Nothing is beneath you, right now, except doling out hand jobs by the watercooler. That *is* beneath you.

This will not always be the case, so (last time Young Jeezy will be quoted) get on your grind and get it. A *metaphorical* grind that involves no cocaine, okay?

Finally, this should be obvious, but if you don't have a job and get offered one, take it. As my friend Joce pointed out, there is no reason to think you're too good for a paying job if you are without one.

Step 160: Figure out what you don't want instead of what you do want

So I'm using this principle for jobs, but it actually applies to lots and lots of things. Often, we decide that it is this *one job* or *one industry* that will make us happy. The truth is that you could do really well and find satisfaction with lots of different types of jobs, including some that you may never, ever have considered. So instead of being very specific, think about what you *don't* want in a job (or a partner, or a city of residence, or...), which will leave you open to all sorts of things. "I don't want to sit in the same space all day; I don't want to have to work mostly alone; I don't want to work in a super rigid environment," leaves you with a lot more possibilities than "I want to work on foot in a forest, with a team of seven people, for a start-up."

Step 161: Keep your chin up when the inevitable setbacks come

You may have always imagined yourself as doing X, and then once you're actually hired to do X, you truly hate it. You may want a job in an industry that, no matter how hard you try, you can't seem to get any traction in. You may feel incredibly limited by what you don't have—that particular degree, access to an impressive parental Rolodex, whatever.

First, know that persistence and resiliency are so, so important. Do not think that you must fill each and every requirement on the job posting to go for it; the worst they can say is no. When you don't get the job you were really, truly hoping for (and believe me, this will happen unfortunately often), do not take that as a sign that you are a failure or that you will never work as a blah blah blah. *The only thing that means is that, this time, you did not get this particular job.* It could have been a truly impossible decision to make, or maybe the other applicant was literally Beyoncé. It doesn't matter. If it makes you feel better, please remember that there is probably at least one job that Beyoncé applied for and didn't get.

But! If you take that one rejection as a sign of failure and become so dejected that you don't apply for another job, then yes, you *won't* ever work as a blah blah blah.

Step 162: Know that there are a lot of paths to happiness

In the chapter ahead, there's a lot of talk about more traditional workplaces, particularly office-type jobs. But that might not be what's right for you, even if you always assumed it was. You might be more happy starting your own company; you may have gone to school for business only to find out that what you truly want to do is work outside. At the end of the day, the right job for you is one that allows you to pay for your own life and not feel like you're slowly being driven to despair and/or madness. There are lots of right jobs for you out there.

Step 163: Accept the idea of networking

Networking sounds terrible and suggests the image of carnivorous fish (in people bodies), circling one another hungrily, business cards burning in their pockets.

And sometimes, yes, that's what it is.

But mostly, it's not that at all, in the same way that not all parties are frat parties. Networking is building a community of people you know and care about, and it really is important. You don't have to be an asshole to do it well.

Grown-up jobs, more often than not, come from professional and personal connections you've made.

But also know that networking isn't a transactional thing. It is not step 1: Meet people. Step 2: Said people offer you a job.

"It's not just a bank account you draw from—it takes a lot of ongoing work and maintenance and being willing to offer whatever kind of help and favors you can," Jared, a dude who is one of the few people in the world who is great at networking but also an excellent human being, said. So, in words that he would never, ever use: You are building, twig by twig, a beautiful nest of shared opportunity, cemented by the spit of your helpfulness and enthusiasm. You are not sharking for a job. You're trying to offer your resources to people who can use them, and maybe someday they'll want to do the same for you.

POSSIBILITIES FOR NETWORKING

Lots of business organizations hold mixers. These events specifically designated for young professionals are a great bet in terms of a lower intimidation factor. Conferences are nothing but networking. Job and career fairs, of course, are also great chances to meet people who may want to hire you. You can and should ask your professors, family friends, and colleagues if they would ever be willing to let you tag along on networking opportunities, or if there is anyone they could perhaps introduce you to.

There are also a bunch of helpful Facebook groups; I'm in some great ones for lady journalists and writers. Many of these groups are not public, so ask around (then, when you're *in* the group, definitely extend invitations to any friends or colleagues that you think would be interested and good group members). It's also a great idea to ask anyone you're taking out for coffee (see step 166) if there are any online or in-person groups they'd recommend.

Quick note: All the things that shouldn't be discussed in light social situations from the Fake It Till You Make It chapter are verboten here, too. Heavy political discussions, tales of your health woes, and gossip about who is sleeping with whom should also not be a part of networking.

It's not super complicated: They are there to meet people, and so are you. An introduction can be really simple: "Hi, I'm Kelly," and then, after they've said their name and you've established that it is, in fact, nice to meet each other, and they ask you what you do, you can say something along the lines of, "Oh, I'm graduating from Loyola in a few months and am hoping to work in PR."

Step 164: Ask for a business card when the conversation is winding to a close

"It was so, so nice to meet you. Oh, hey, do you have a card on you? Thanks! Here's mine."

This feels terrifically uncomfortable/intimidating (proposed new emotional state: uncomfimidated), but it's not. People are there with business cards *to hand them out*, and they expect it. Since you've already established yourself as a smart, confident person who would never dream of calling their office every hour on the hour just to hear their voice, they should be happy to oblige.

You can also make business cards of your own via any number of online shops. These can and should be really simple: your name, telephone number, email address, and website, with social media links *only if* they are super key to your professional life. You can put the industry or job you're going for on there, but please don't be too cute. The world does not need anyone else who describes themselves, in print, as a "wordsmith."

Step 165: Follow up with people you meet

Send them an email—a brief, non-manifesto-length email—to say what a pleasure it was to meet them and that you hope your paths cross again. You will get the email address off the business card you ask for when the conversation is drawing to a close.

Step 166: Ask those people out for coffee

When you encounter smart people in your industry, realize that it is perfectly acceptable (and encouraged!) to ask them out to coffee, then pepper them with questions. They may say no, but you'd be surprised at how often they say yes. They may not want to give you a job, but people, generally speaking, are happy to answer questions and give advice. The happiness that comes from helping others in a low-stakes way is pretty universal.

Before you go, brush up on their work and what they (not just the industry, but that individual person) have done. Then ask about what they do and what advice they'd give to someone just starting out, and really listen to what they are saying. Buy their coffee and baked good of choice and send a thank-you note afterward (see step 138 in Fake It Till You Make It).

Finally, this step is not just for people new to the working world. There will always be people older/smarter/more talented/further along than you. Take them out for coffee and listen to what they say.

Step 167: Go on informational interviews near and far

Here is one of the most useful phrases in life: "I'm going to be in town for a few days, and I'd love to stop by and introduce myself."

Here is how you employ that phrase: Whenever you are going to visit somewhere you would not totally hate living, scout out the businesses in your industry that are there, and see if you can't stop by and say hi. Send an email—not to the top boss, but someone who has some power in the division you'd like to be a part of. The "in town for a few days" thing implies that you are a Business-Minded Gal-on-the-Go who zips efficiently through airports and car rental counters en route to global domination. Short skirts, long jackets, and such.

Hopefully, you make a good impression, send a thank-you note (are you sensing a trend with the thank-yous?), and then, when a job opens up, your résumé will float to the top of the pile because unlike the vast majority of applicants, they have a face to put with the name.

This can also work closer to home: Simply say that you know they don't have any openings right now, but you'd just like to stop by and say hi.

Step 168: Make sure your social media presence doesn't raise more questions than answers

You will be Googled. They will Google you, then move to your Facebook, Twitter, Instagram, LinkedIn, and even, if you are old enough, your MySpace, which will float around forever. I love that everyone of a certain age has their embarrassing 2007 self trapped in cyber amber. So beat any potential employers to the punch, and if there is anything questionable online, *take it down*.

By all means, be yourself—an interesting version of yourself, not the wasted-during-a-college-party version. There's nothing wrong with that second one—okay, maybe there are some things wrong, like its propensity to yell "Woooooooo!" way too much, and its insistence that it *needs* a burrito *right now*. But when you're looking for a job, that particular card does not need to be laid on the table.

If you wouldn't show or tell your mom, boss, and ex-boyfriend, then don't put it on the internet.

Step 169: Customize your résumé

Yes, it's a pain. But so is almost every aspect of being a grown-up. How much do you want this job, anyway? Enough to spend thirty minutes tweaking your résumé?

Dana is a recruiter for a schmancy West Coast digital staffing agency, and she recommends that you use the same wording they do in the job description.

Not all jobs have thoughtful people like Dana looking at résumés; instead they employ cold and calculating computer algorithms. And even if someone is looking at the résumé, they're not looking for long unless they see what they're skimming for.

"The average hiring manager takes about seven seconds to skim through a résumé," Dana told me, then added that lots of job postings use computer programs to scan the résumés, and only those that match move on.

"You might have ten different versions of your résumé," Dana said. "Maybe you would think of *managing* being a keyword, whereas the company job description doesn't use one word about managing a team but instead talks about leading a team. You need to change your wording to match theirs."

Step 170: Proofread your résumé

Seriously. Read it out loud, word by word. This is also a good time to mention that writing like you talk works very well. If you're stuck on how to phrase something, find someone you're comfortable with and then try to tell them as directly and simply as possible.

Then get at least two other people to proofread your résumé—the kind of people who will help and not hurt the situation.

Step 171: You can and should send a follow-up email after you send in your application (unless it's specifically forbidden)

Dear Ms. Williams,

I wanted to drop a quick note to make sure you've received my cover letter and application for the general assignment reporter position, and also reiterate my interest in the position. I know you have lots of applicants to sort through, but I hope you'll consider me.

All my best,
Kelly

Step 172: If you are called for an interview on the moon, figure out a way to get there

"Too many times do I see candidates who, when I call them and say, 'Hey, you've got an interview request at this time and this day,' aren't willing to reschedule whatever their something else is and don't get a second chance to interview," Dana said. "The likelihood of them working with your schedule is slim to none."

However, if you really, truly, absolutely cannot get there because you're having open-heart surgery or whatever, come back with several other, similar options. "Oh my gosh. This is heartbreaking, but actually my wedding is scheduled for that Wednesday afternoon and I think my wife-to-be would notice if I were missing. Is there any way we could do the following Wednesday?"

If the job is far away and they aren't willing to pay for your travel, then ask if you can do a Skype interview.

Step 173: Do not bring anyone—not your mom, dad, boyfriend, cat, step-cousin, frenemy, anyone—with you to a job interview

I am sort of shocked this is a thing, but recruiter Dana assures me it is. If you need a ride to the interview, that's fine, but this person must remain invisible to the employer. As far as the employer is concerned, you just emerged, Aphrodite-like, out of the seafoam and into the office park, the winds of your own competence wafting you safely to shore with five minutes to spare.

Step 174: Show up looking and sounding smart

If you've gotten that precious and rare job interview, congratulations! You are so, so close, and needless to say, you are going to blow the interviewer away. They will be left trembling after the presence of such awesome competence, and gnash their teeth when they think of the years that passed when they could've had you, then feel relieved that *at least they have you now.*

So to ensure this is the impression they're left with, think of it this way. This interview is simply asking, "Can you fill this space/gap, this need that we have?" and you replying, "Absolutely." All of your responses during the interview need to convey that "absolutely."

The first way you will demonstrate your absolutely-ness is in appearance. You will look extra sharp in your best suit, unless you are in an extremely casual and creative profession, in which case take cues from those around you (or, even better, ask someone what is customarily worn to an interview during one of those many coffee dates you had earlier).

Step 175: Don't talk about how great this job will be for you; talk about how great you are for the job

Remember, this company or person isn't interested in hiring you because they want you to be as self-actualized and joyful as possible—they're thinking about hiring you because they have a need, and think maybe you can fill it. Your entire job is to convey to them that yes, you can indeed fill that need. Your needs are not important in this step of the process.

It's understandable to forget this—especially if you're fresh out of college. Up until now, your life has been about others teaching and instructing you in the hope that it will help you meet your life goals. But have you noticed that you pay to go to college? Generally speaking in life, the person who gives money is the one whose needs are important, and the person getting money is paid to meet those needs.

Step 176: Don't bad-mouth any past employers. Don't bad-mouth any current employers. Don't bad-mouth anyone

This may seem like a fun, conspiratorial, "Oh, you wouldn't *believe*," sort of thing, but to a potential employer, all bad-mouthing does is establish that you are gossipy and potentially not a team player. It introduces doubt in their mind about you and your abilities—if you're so great, how come this person didn't like you? Remember how the only thing you are doing right now is conveying how capable and essential you are? This does not fit in with that.

No matter how terrible things were with a past job—and they may, indeed, have been really, really bad—it's not valid interview conversation fodder. If you can say good things about the boss or company, then do so. If you just can't bring yourself to say anything even slightly positive, just say, "You know, it wasn't the best fit for me. Anyway, [more statements that convey your professionalism]."

Step 177: Don't forget to ask questions

Frankly, you should have a million questions. This is a place that you will spend forty or more hours per week. This is a place that will assign you hundreds and thousands of tasks to be successfully completed. This is a place filled with people whom you will spend more time around than you do with your own family. Someone who isn't interested in what this means for them is a major red flag. Asking questions doesn't make you a pest; it reveals you as someone who is committed to making sure you are right for the job, and the job is right for you.

Here are some classic examples:

- What does an average day look like for someone in this job?
- What is the most challenging aspect of this job?
- In your opinion, what kind of person would be most successful in this position? (**Note:** Take the answer to this into account, then hopefully tailor your responses to demonstrate that you are that sort of person.)
- What makes your company's culture unique? What, in your opinion, distinguishes you from the others in your industry?
- Is there anything you'd like to share with me about the job that we haven't covered yet?

Obviously, after such a powerful interview performance, they will see there is absolutely no choice but to hire you and offer you exactly what you are worth. At which point you must...

Step 178: Negotiate for your salary

This feels really awkward. We're socially conditioned to not talk about money or how great we are, and all salary negotiations involve talking about how great we are *in the context of money*. If you're not used to it, it can be several layers of uncomfortable. Move past that.

The reason we have jobs is to make money. Yes, hopefully you love and are rewarded by what you're doing, but chances are you wouldn't volunteer there forty (or fifty, sixty, seventy, whatever) hours per week.

There may not be as much wiggle room in your first job as there will be in future ones. If it's clear that there is a particular, non-negotiable salary associated with this job, you will have to accept that.

But if the ad says DOE (depending on experience), then it's negotiation time.

Alan is the director of sales for his company and, in general, a very winning guy. This is probably why he's director of sales. He was willing to weigh in with a few tips on where to start the negotiation process:

• For your starting figure, request the **salary of someone with five years' experience in your particular job.** Ask the internet what that number is for your job of choice, but for the purposes of this book, let's pretend that figure is $40,000 per year.

• You will also want to have another figure in your head, and that is **how low you will go.** Decide, realistically, what this number is. Alan suggested perhaps 10 percent less than your initial offer, which in this case would be $36,000.

• **Pay attention to the person's reaction when you give your number.** See if they look startled, or blink, or take it in stride.

• **If they say your requested salary is too high, ask for what their budget is, then ask for the top end.** "If you go to work for a big company, there's a salary range," Alan said. "They won't go above it and they generally won't go below it."

• Negotiating only works, of course, if you can **demonstrate your value,** so be sure to figure this out ahead of time. It doesn't have to be a bar graph, but rather an anecdote that demonstrates what a bright young go-getting thing you are. "It could be a story," Alan said. "People love stories."

• Understand that no one will rescind an offer because you ask for a lot. You may not get it, but you won't be punished for asking.

Step 179: Some industries require an internship; if so, go get one

For a lot of glamour industries, this is the only way in. You don't necessarily need to wait for an internship posting; you can certainly take initiative and ask someone who is not at the very top, but a few rungs down, about the possibility of an internship.

Hopefully this is a paid internship but, unfortunately, many are not. Like so many, many, many things in life, this is not cool or fair and it's a huge advantage for people whose parents are well-connected and/or wealthy. But here we are.

If you don't, in fact, have parental benefactors, and most of us don't, try to figure out how to drastically cut your expenses. Could you find an internship in a more affordable city? Could you stay with relatives or friends' parents for a few months? If it is a truly incredible opportunity, it might be worth it to figure out what the bare minimum you need to live is for those months, then take out a small, extra student loan.

Step 180: Be prepared to do the worst, dullest assignments as an intern/new hire. Do them cheerfully

This is so unpleasant but so true: In almost every profession, you have to pay your dues. Unless your dad owns the company, there is no way around, over, or under it—just through it. And it's not always fun.

But what separates those who will, in time, get to hand off their own boring assignments to future interns is a willingness to do this shit *like it is the most exciting and important task of your life.* You are *unbelievably thrilled* to type up all the weekly senior center activities in town. God, you would *love* to go get this person some coffee. Et cetera. The key here is not to employ that sorority-style "YAAAAAAY!" enthusiasm, but rather the sort of serious enthusiasm with which you might set off on an epic quest in a big-budget fantasy trilogy. Summon all of your latent acting talent.

Step 181: Pick up on office etiquette and norms

There is a lot of leeway here if you're an intern or a young new hire. Everyone remembers what it was like to be twenty-one and feel really swamped and confused, expected to obey rules and concepts that are invisible to you but so obvious to everyone else.

But! You still need to be on your best behavior and follow others' lead. The charmed patience for your youthful foibles and indiscretions will end very quickly once you're paid to be there.

Every office has different social mores, customs, and etiquette, and when you walk in for the first time, you will naturally have no idea what they are. It is okay to be quiet and mouse-like for a few weeks. Just watch silently, with your beady but adorable eyes, and observe how and when people talk to one another. Is cursing allowed? Does anyone eat at their desk? Are said desks to be kept spotless, or are they piled with papers? Is lunch an hour long? Twenty minutes? If you leave the office for an errand, do you need to let someone know? These questions have all been answered long before you arrived. Don't go with your gut. Go with what everyone else is doing.

Whatever the standard-issue behavior is, make yours a notch or two more conservative until you are a fully integrated part of the group.

Step 182: The most important of all the above-type questions is "Who is actually in charge?"

This doesn't mean title-wise; it probably won't take that much time to figure out who is organizationally at the top. But there are other leaders, too. There's the one who knows every single thing that happens in the building. There's the person who may not have an intimidating title, but is the boss's favorite and always has their ear. There is the one who is the folk hero of the workers. There is the person you need to talk to when shit hits the fan.

You can't ask most of these things directly, at least not until you find a good friend at work (the kind who would be your friend even if you didn't have work in common). But again, keep your eyes and ears open. Notice who speaks in meetings; notice how others react to that person. Notice who always has really great ideas; notice who delights in shutting everyone down. Read the body language between coworkers.

Step 183: Treat casual Fridays as not-casual Fridays

Everyone says it because it's true: Casual Fridays are stupid. Actually, it's just me that says that, but prevailing wisdom does hold that you should dress for the job you want, not the one you have. Unless the job you want is dolphin trainer, and the job you have is funeral home director.

But if you show up looking spiffy (not formal, mind you...just spiffy) on casual Fridays, then everyone else looks kind of rumply by comparison.

Step 184: Don't be that intern

Internships tend to happen at a point in life when we get to drink lots and lots of alcohol pretty much consequence-free, a golden time that I will dub the Absolut Mandrin Years. And you, intern, have a great and wonderful gift in that unlike almost everyone else at the office, you can get near-blackout drunk at a Saturday-afternoon croquet game and not raise any eyebrows. Life is your schnapps-soaked oyster, so enjoy it.

But the people around you at your internship live in a very different world, one in which the above action would warrant, at minimum, some Serious Concern. You can tell it's serious, because the S and C are both capitalized.

To blend in seamlessly, you must drink as they drink, which is to say sparingly. Actually, no. Drink less than them. (See chart on next page.) Do not be that intern who (true story) got drunk and told all the men in the office that she had no gag reflex. No. Never. No.

Step 185: Do not tell the internet what you think of your job

Just don't. This is something that can, and likely will, get you fired. No matter how well you think you've veiled it on your anonymous blog, it will come back. It will live forever. The internet has a big mouth and a long, long memory, and it is so happy to remember and share whatever you've told it. Plus, people have an uncanny knack for *immediately* finding the unflattering things you've said about them.

Don't bitch about your boss on Facebook. Don't write emails detailing how much you hate everything on a work computer. Don't think that you can leak things without it coming back to bite you in the ass.

If you're over the job, and aren't worried about establishing yourself as the kind of person who (publicly) bites the hand that feeds you, then by all means. Otherwise, do what everyone else does and complain bitterly over happy-hour drinks with your coolest co-workers.

How Many Drinks Do You Get At This Work Function?

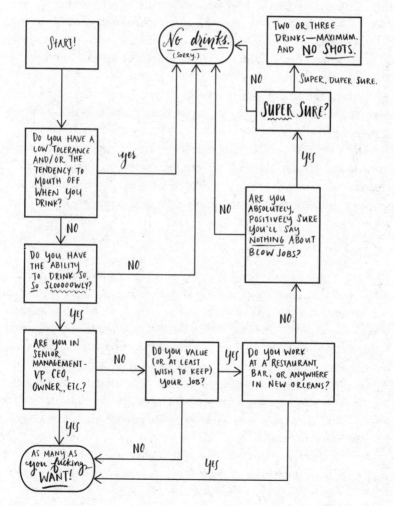

Step 186: Don't lose touch after an internship

Now that you've successfully made your way through your internship, congratulations! Even if it seems thankless now (and yes, it most likely is), the Universe sees your diligence and will smile upon you.

Internships can pay unexpected dividends and give you your first shot at networking. During your internship, there will probably be three or four people who have been especially helpful or that you feel close to. One of these will likely be your supervisor, but you'd be surprised how many people will reach out and teach you things about what they do. This is an awesome and self-selecting group of helpful, kind people who like you.

Toward the end of your internship, write them a thank-you note that tells them not only that you appreciate them, but also *why* you appreciate them.

And then stay in touch. Not every week or anything, but when something exciting happens in your life or theirs, send a friendly email. And then, when you're a few months out from looking for a job, let them know and ask if they would mind keeping their ears open for you.

Step 187: Ask for a raise

This can happen very naturally at an annual review, or right after you've finished kicking ass and taking names on a big project. For obvious reasons, you should ask at a time when you are doing demonstrably well. You are welcome to ask for as much as you want, though if you work at a big corporation, chances are good they have a set formula. Three percent is usually an acceptable figure to ask for. Again, you won't get in trouble for asking. Send an email asking for a meeting—perhaps during a time in which your boss will be in a jovial mood—and then compress your nervous gases into a steely core, because you deserve this.

Sample dialogue: "Thank you so much for meeting with me. I'm really proud of the work I've been doing here recently, and I was hoping you'd consider the possibility of a raise."

IS THIS OUTFIT OFFICE-appropriate?!?

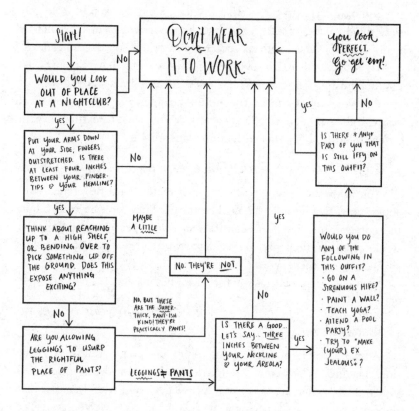

Step 188: Put together a work wardrobe

If you find yourself working in an office for the first time, chances are very good that

(a) you do not have a ton of clothing that is office-appropriate and

(b) you don't have enough cash on hand now to buy a whole new wardrobe.

On the upside, every career gal ever has faced this, and you can certainly come out on top. First, observe what people in your industry of choice wear. Then try to get a couple of non-cheap base items, and lots of cheaper supplementary options.

You may decide to get nice black slacks, a nice black skirt, nice gray slacks, and a nice gray skirt. Then find a blazer or two that matches all four items, and supplement with cheaper (but also mainly covered-up) blouses.

T.J.Maxx and other discount retailers often have steeply discounted business clothes. Also, chances are good that there is a thrift store in your town run by the Junior League or whatever the local equivalent benevolent rich lady society is. Find this store, then revel in seven-dollar BCBG pants with all the tags still on.

Step 189: Get some really nice, expensive black high heels

You know how people say you can really tell a difference with super-expensive high heels? Well, you can. They look beautiful, but, more important, they *feel* beautiful. Save your pennies, five dollars a week for a year, then go to a nice department store. Get sexy but classic heels. Wear them forever. You will not be sorry.

If you never wear black, go for nude ones instead.

Step 190: Don't hook up with anyone in your office, no matter how exciting the prospect

Actually, you're probably going to at some point. Almost everyone does. Having a poorly considered liaison with a co-worker is the chicken pox of the working life, so you may as well get it over with. But after that happens, you will look back and wish you hadn't. Have you ever once heard of someone saying, "You know, I'm glad I had that three-week fling with my cubicle-mate a few years back, because it's so great to sit across from him in meetings knowing what his dick looks like"?

After that one mistake, you will realize that it was a bad plan, at which point you will decide to . . .

Step 191: Live your life as though everyone in the office has plastic, featureless doll crotches

This includes you. Your sex life should never be a topic of conversation in the office, and neither should anyone else's. You may reclaim your genitalia once you are on non-company time.

Step 192: You did not come here to make friends

Like every reality show contestant ever, your focus must be *solely* on winning the heart of an aged rocker, except instead of fleeting glory and untold STIs, you are angling for the corner office. Or at least doing competently the thing you have come to do. You want to be warm and friendly with your co-workers, but this isn't subsidized socializing; you are being paid to do something and you need to do it.

Step 193: Find a mentor

There will be someone you click with, whom you feel close to. If this person doesn't work in the same office as you, all the better; they won't be tainted by any office politics and can always be impartial in their advice. Conferences are a great place to find mentors; after you've met them and sent your follow-up thank-you email (Follow-up email! Follow-up email! Follow-up emails, *forever!*), then it's time.

You really shouldn't ask them to be your mentor, the same way you don't ask someone you just met to be your best friend. Instead, invite them to coffee, pick their brain, establish a friendship. Then, at some point, mention that you consider them a mentor.

Their heart will likely melt in the face of this awkward yet touching message. Don't blow up this person's inbox, but do feel free to ask them "What would you do in this situation?"–type questions. I've gotten to a point where I have a protégé in the form of Young Brooke (see basically all of the cooking chapter) and I promise: If this person likes you, if they see something of themselves in you, it will make them very happy to feel like they can help you in the form of doling out advice. I love you, Tiny Bork!

Step 194: Develop a good meeting face

I've never yet met someone who likes meetings, but obviously they work in some way, because humanity keeps scheduling them and they are a Very Important Part of the office life. Bring a notepad, and don't let anyone see you doodling.

Meeting face is a curious, interested, yet neutral expression. Practice this in the mirror, especially if your default facial expression is bitchface. Subtle nods can be good, too, if you actually agree with what is being said. If you're all the way in the back and don't need to pay attention, I recommend trying to list all fifty states as a nice time-burner.

Step 195: Keep your desk tidy

Here, I will officially designate a time for you: At 3:17 PM each Wednesday afternoon, take the next thirteen minutes to tidy, straighten, recycle, and wipe down. Do that last one with the disinfecting wipes you keep in your desk drawer.

Things to keep in your desk at work:

- A deodorant stick
- Hem tape, which works shockingly well, or a sewing kit
- A lint roller
- A bottle of over-the-counter pain reliever
- Non-perishable, non-stinky, non-bug-attracting snacks—I recommend almonds and dried fruit
- Feminine hygiene products of your choice, if you are a lady or an over-the-top helpful dude
- Disinfecting wipes
- Hand sanitizer
- Quarters
- A travel toothbrush and toothpaste
- Tissues, particularly during the sniffly season
- Mint or gum
- Label maker (Nothing says *baddest bitch in the cubicle game* like matching tape dispenser, scissors, and stapler with color-coordinated labels with your last name. As a bonus, even when you move on and the scissors are handed down to someone else, either the label or its gummy afterglow will remain as a tiny testament.)

Step 196: Distinguish, in your mind, business etiquette from social etiquette

I have a pretty finely developed radar for when people are feeling uncomfortable, and my natural inclination is to make them feel at ease.

But as a reporter, sometimes I need to keep pushing. I ask questions that I would not ask if I met this person at a party, because it's my job and *grown-ups do their jobs*. So, while you are not given permission to be a total asshole, you have every right to be curt, businesslike, or cold with people when it's called for. Remember: Not here to make friends.

Step 197: Don't verbally undermine yourself

If you were the kind of really cool person who was on the speech and debate team in high school, you know never to start an argument with "I think" or "I feel." Obviously you think it or feel it, or you wouldn't say it.

This can slip away so, so easily, especially if you are new or feel like you don't fully have a handle on what's going on. And you will have this feeling for the first three years of nearly any job worth having.

"Well, I'm not the expert, but..."

"I don't know much, but..."

"I think that maybe..."

Knock that shit off. Seriously. If you're going to share your opinion, *say it as though it were a declarative statement.* Not a question? That you have? Floating around in your head? And you hope others will agree with? But if they don't, that's okay, too? Just say it. And if you really feel that unsure about it, then don't waste that other person's time with verbal waffling.

Step 198: Gchat if you must, but remember your bosses can legally read everything you're saying

Ditto for Facebook, email, Twitter, all of it. If you're doing it on a work computer, you legally have no right to privacy, and you shouldn't expect it. So just imagine these interactions being read aloud to the office.

Hopefully this goes without saying, but *never* look at anything that could even slightly be construed as porn at work. If, for some reason, you unwittingly click to something, go to your supervisor and say, "Hey, I just wanted to give you a heads-up that I clicked on a link in an email and it took me to CentaursDoingWeirdStuff.com, and I was *really* not expecting that. Should I say anything to IT?"

Step 199: You can only call in fake-sick one day a year

And no, being hungover is not being sick. So choose wisely, friend.

Step 200: You can, when it is truly warranted, take a mental health day

The key here is that whatever's going on with you does really have to go above and beyond general workplace (and life) ennui. If you're going through a wrenching breakup and have been crying for so long that your eyes feel sandy and your head hurts from dehydration and you can't get three words out without choking up, well, it is not inaccurate to say you don't feel well. When you do this, do try to actually make it a mental health day. Do some self-care, call a friend or your mom, take a bath, go on a nice walk, et cetera.

Step 201: Tell your boss the broad outlines when you're going through something really tough

This assumes that your boss is not a sociopathic monster or the robotic, never ever ever reveals even the teeniest detail about themselves type.

You shouldn't give them a blow-by-blow of your love life, or tell them the color of your snot, or detail every single difficult familial relationship you have. But if there is something big and ongoing, it's fair to tell them and, in turn, to give them a chance to be compassionate.

If a family member is very sick, they should know that. If your relationship of four years just came to an end, again, that is naturally going to affect your work, at least for a while. If your pet dies, tell them that. Chances are nearly 100 percent that they, too, are human, and will be able to cut you a little bit of slack...particularly if you don't go to them about the smaller stuff.

Step 202: If you're coughing, sneezing, or otherwise obviously infectious and cannot take over-the-counter meds to remedy the situation, stay home

Make your co-workers sick and they'll hold it against you forever. When I get someone's nasty ailment, it really makes me want to punch them. This is not an accepted form of workplace communication, no matter how much they may deserve it. So don't set these ugly thought wheels into motion. Stay home and get better.

Step 203: If you're sick, stay home and rest; don't try to do the work-from-home thing

A friend of mine has an awful boss; one of his many offenses is constantly telling her she looks too sick to work and then telling her to work from home.

If you really and truly *must* work from home, be very clear about what you can do: "I have a doctor's appointment at 9, and I should be back home by 10:15. I'm going to do as much as I can for two hours, then I won't be available after 12:30."

Step 204: Don't just be likable; be a good co-worker

If you are not a good co-worker—if you don't get things done when they're supposed to be done, if you drop the ball on group projects, if you don't speak up when someone else is being blamed for your mistake, if you don't reply to time-sensitive emails and calls promptly—people will figure that out. Being sweet and charming can cover for a while. But these things will come back to bite you eventually.

Step 205: Accept that there is no such thing as vacation

There's just working extra hard beforehand, spending your vacation feeling that something must be awry, then scrambling for weeks to catch up.

Step 206: Take yours anyway

If you get paid vacation, take it. Even if you're too poor to travel anywhere, you can at least spend your day off lolling around and watching TV and/or being hungover. It really is important to take breaks from your work, and remember that if you get two weeks' paid vacation that you don't take, that's like giving up 4 percent of your salary.

Step 207: Do not steal more than three dollars' worth of office supplies per quarter

Pens, I think, are reasonable. But not all the time. And no scissors.

Step 208: Shut down office creepers

First off, you do not need to feel uncomfortable at work. Everyone needs to be there, and no one should make it unpleasant for others to be there. But before you dash to HR, remember this: If someone is making you feel uncomfortable, it is okay to make them feel a little uncomfortable and it can be *such* a delight to discover, within yourself, the ability to call someone on their shit in a way that could never, ever be construed as you actually calling them on their shit. Natural consequencessssssss!

I've found that most offices have at least one middle-aged male employee who seems to delight in spending as much time as possible around the new twenty-two-year-olds. Remember, you can be cordial and icy at the same time. Forced, thin smiles that register for half a second then turn into a slightly squinty face, and curt answers without follow-up questions will do wonders.

If this person tends to invade your personal space while you're working at your desk, here is a brilliant strategy, courtesy of Miss Manners. The next time you turn your head and they are way, way too close, let out a little scream. Nothing overly dramatic; just enough that other people do the prairie dog thing of popping their heads up over the cubicle walls to see what is going on.

Then say, "Oh. Gosh. You startled me; *I didn't expect you to be that close to me.*" Period. Don't wave away the awkwardness this sentence will create. Let this painful silence roar, that the dude may remember this natural consequence of breathing in your ear.

If that doesn't work, go to HR with your documentation.

Step 209: If there is something shady going on, document everything

Not just on a work computer, either, because (not to be dire) if you were to get fired, you wouldn't have access to those files anymore. Send copies of your documentation to your personal email address.

Get time, date, location, specifics, a list of witnesses, and verbatim quotes if possible. These things must be quantifiable.

It's also a good idea to email these memos to a third party, whether that be a colleague or your mentor. That way, you have a paper trail that proves that you wrote about this *as it was happening* and not just, say, as revenge after you were let go.

It can also be useful to begin to leave traces showing that you tried to approach people within the organization about this; if you send an email to your boss via your work account, blind-copy your personal account.

Step 210: Remember that HR is not necessarily on your side

HR people can be really and truly wonderful—Gina, I am looking right at you. But—and this is particularly applicable if you work for a larger company—HR is not just there to be an arbiter of justice; they are also there to protect the company against liabilities and lawsuits. If your workplace issue is with someone who has a lot more political power than you (or is a lot more valuable to the company), know that things may not go the way you think they should in the court of HR.

Step 211: When possible, conflict via email

One, in the workplace it leaves a paper trail, and paper trails are *great* for proving a point, should it come to that.

But beyond that, letters are a great way to deliver a difficult message in a way that gives the recipient a chance to think about and digest what you've said without having to respond immediately. Often, people need a little bit of space when you've given them something difficult, and in the pressure of an immediate response things can come out wrong. If the person you're dealing with is even slightly reasonable, this can be a much calmer way of actually solving problems rather than just feeling angry and self-righteous.

This means that you cannot just write an email and put someone on blast. Email is not your chance to polish every mean thing you've ever wanted to say, lob a digital Molotov cocktail, and walk away without looking at the explosion.

Instead, email should be a place that you can be calm, reasoned, and open to a solution that works for all parties. And yes, if it gets into a back-and-forth, eventually you'll need to talk. But this is a good way to say the things you need to say in the way you wish to say them without being interrupted.

Step 212: Let that angry email you composed marinate for a minute

Every single time in my life that I've thought, *Hmmm, I wonder if this email is a little over the top? I should sleep on it*, I could just French-kiss my past-self for her measured control and foresight. Because each and every time, I revise the email.

Yes, it's not satisfying. But it's what grown-ups do.

Step 213: If someone dislikes you right off the bat, then do your best to either nip it in the bud or avoid them

This will be a function of power. If the person is beneath you, or clearly on your plane (not just position-wise, but power-wise), then you can adopt an attitude that says, *I'm confused why you're having this problem but it doesn't matter all that much and you need to move through it.* Come from a place of kind, patient confidence with it.

And you know what? If nothing else, you can let this person's dislike for you fuel your desire to do well, thus eventually putting yourself in a place where you *definitely* have the upper hand.

If they are above you, skip to step 216.

Step 214: Assess whether the work foe is actually an enemy, or just difficult

Yes, some people will genuinely have it out for you, and you may never know why. But when you're encountering someone new and difficult at work, it's best to leave the jury out for a few weeks on the off chance that they are just sort of confused and blunder-ish.

Step 215: Stand up for yourself when someone is constantly dumping stuff on you that is not your responsibility

It's great to go above and beyond at work, but when one person is consistently expecting you to do his or her job, it hinders you from doing yours.

My friend Shantrell once had a co-worker who turned to her for help when he was new...and then they got into a pattern where she did the work for him. Finally, when he dumped an enormous project on her lap two days before she was supposed to go on Christmas break, she asserted herself.

"I just kind of opted to say...I don't know what you've been told, and if I'm wrong please clear it up for me, but I'm not required to help out with these projects," she said.

It could even be as simple as "Martin, I've got so much on my plate at the moment; I'm afraid I can't help you out with *your work* right now." In real life, don't say the italics, but you are very, very welcome to think them.

Step 216: If the person giving you a headache is above you, then it's time to kiss a little ass

Yes, yes. It's horrible. Mean bosses are just wretched. Truly, they are the employment equivalent of the stomach flu, in that there is not even one good thing to say about them, and years later you'll still feel nauseous every time you, say, smell linguine Alfredo or hear someone say the name *Valerie*.

But they are what they are. Generally speaking, the boss will always, always be in a more powerful position than you. That's just how it is. And whether it's fair or not, whether they are good or bad, it is in your best interest to be in their good graces. Just do a really excellent job, keep your hatred cards close to your chest, and hopefully eventually you'll be in a position to fire their sorry ass.

Step 217: At a certain point, do your best to disengage

I worked in a toxic workplace in my early twenties, one where everyone new was looked upon with suspicion. The mean girl of the office, I was told, hated all new female employees. "It's just her way!" everyone said, as though this were a funny personality quirk instead of something that made it truly awful to work there.

Sure enough, the first time I was introduced to her, her lip curled and she said in the most acid voice imaginable, "I know who you are," and then left it there.

Things with her got worse. In retrospect, I assume that she felt like

I didn't deserve the position I had (which, truthfully, I did not) and resented the fact that the boss really liked me, which provided its own share of difficulties.

It came to a head at the office Christmas party about three months after I was hired. After a few drinks, I was feeling cheerful and felt like perhaps things could finally be put behind us.

"Melanie,"[1] I said, "I know things kind of got off on a bad foot between us, and I just wanted to let you know that I think you're a great reporter and I really hope we can work together."

(I'll pause here to allow you to start the horror-movie soundtrack strings in your mind, as she slowly turned a face contorted with rage I did not understand.)

"No one respects you. Everyone knows you're only here because [the boss] has a boner for you and we're just waiting for you to quit or get fired."

This was the opening salvo on what turned out to be a surprisingly extensive, flawlessly delivered invective. I stood there for maybe five minutes as she continued her awful monologue, paralyzed by shock.

I wish I could go back in time and save that very sad past-self o' mine. I wish I could whisper in my own ear, "It's not true; don't listen to her." I would not allow myself to be abused. I would not assume that some people can be reasoned with. I would not think that surely I had done something to warrant this.

Instead, I would have found my most crisp and dismissive voice. "Sorry you feel that way, [c-word],"[2] I'd say, then pivot on my high heels and walk. I was doing nothing useful for myself by staying in that conversation. I was just allowing her, once more, to assert cruel power over me.

Step 218: Discern between dues-paying and abuse in the workplace

Don't expect to be treated with deference or respect in any new office environment. People deserve decency, but you have to earn those other two. You will not instantly be the most respected and beloved

---

1. Not her real name, obviously.
2. Except I would have actually said the c-word, not said "c-word."

person when you walk into a workplace; those things come from months and years of doing your job well, pleasantly, and competently.

So a small amount of prickliness is to be expected while people sniff you out. But if it lasts and lasts even after you begin to prove yourself, then consider whether that's the right place for you.

Is your office a particularly cruel environment? Do certain people get singled out? Is humiliation, especially in front of others, an ongoing thing? Do people scream at each other, particularly if they're higher on the totem pole?

When you get criticism, is it about your actions and performance or about **you**?

Step 219: Realize that there is a difference between toxic co-workers and a toxic workplace

There will always be someone you don't like in the workplace, and someone who doesn't like you. This is just the law of averages. Also, a workplace nemesis is sort of fun, especially when you beat them for that promotion.

Step 220: If you work in a toxic environment, find a new job

When you work in a place where the culture is fundamentally flawed—where anger and abuse flow downstream from the boss, where there is a casual sexism or racism, where employees are controlled by fear and intimidation—then you need to go, for your own sanity.

Toxic workplace environments rarely get better. Instead of being hurt, allow that anger to fuel your drive to a new job.

Step 221: Wait at least a year to move on unless there is a really, really compelling reason

Some jobs are not a great fit...but generally, professional-type jobs should last a year, minimum.

If you just can't make it that long, then do your darnedest not to repeat that move within the next five years. You want to look grounded and competent, not flighty.

If after a year, you still dread going in, begin putting out feelers for your next move.

Step 222: Be quiet when you start looking for a new job

Transparency is not your best option here. While you can quietly approach people whom you trust that are not your direct supervisor to see if they'd be willing to serve as a reference, you should not say anything to your bosses until the new job is a fait accompli. As in, offer letter in hand, drug test passed, starting date established.

Step 223: Let people in your network know that you're looking

Remember all that wonderful networking that you did? Now is when it pays off. Hopefully you've been keeping up these ties in a friendly and selfless way, you like them, and they like you. Just send a quick email:

Dear Alan,

Hey! Hope everything's been great. Things here [personal details that are interesting but not lurid].

Anyway, I've really enjoyed my time here at [company] but am starting to think about what the next move will be. I'd so appreciate it if you'd keep an ear out for any openings in [industry].

Take care!
Kelly

Step 224: Write a resignation letter—a nice one

No matter how bad things have been, it's not a good idea to leave on an f-you note. So when it is a done deal that you are going elsewhere, you will write a formal, dated letter. No need to pour your heart and soul into it, because presumably you will be talking to your boss in person. But the note should convey a few things:

- You are resigning your position as [X].
- You so appreciate the challenges and growth that you've experienced in the past [X] years.
- Your last day will be [X] *or* you are willing to work until [X] date to help smooth the transition. Two weeks' notice, minimum.

Step 225: If you have an exit interview, don't burn the place to the ground—but you can be tactfully honest

This is especially applicable if you really, truly would never be willing to work for the company again. You should not name names, but it's fair to be honest about troubles you had, particularly if you can make concrete suggestions that would make things easier for whoever comes behind you.

Step 226: Help out someone in your professional network

The first time someone (a friend, or co-worker, or whomever) comes to you saying that they want to switch jobs, and you can say, "Oh, my friend works at such-and-such place, let me put you in touch," you will feel so, so satisfied and helpful. It is really a wonderful feeling. And in this moment, you will understand why all those people were willing to help you out.

You don't need to go crazy, but an email of introduction is always a wonderful start, and spares the person you are helping from having to cold-email someone. In this case, it's a good idea to make sure the person you are putting them in touch with is okay ahead of time. And once they say *yes, pass on my email*, then you can do something like this, adding the second person in the CC: line:

Dear Alan,

I wanted to electronically introduce Anne, my friend I was telling you about a few days ago. Anne's been working in marketing for a few years, but she's been very interested in public relations and I think is hoping to ask you a few questions. Anne, Alan is the head of communications for Bedwin-Fischer and an all-around excellent guy. Alan, meet Anne; Anne, meet Alan.

Cheers,
Kelly

In this way, it shall come full circle.

DISCUSSION QUESTIONS

1. If you were a carnivorous fish who was good at networking, what kind of carnivorous fish who was good at networking would you be?
2. Did you think I was talking about myself when I mentioned the intern that told everyone she had no gag reflex? Because, for the record, it wasn't me.
3. Do you know of any True Life Workplace Heroes who've called their co-workers on sniffling, fermented-fish eating, or flatulence? What lessons should we learn from such people?

Chapter 6
MONEY

Ugh, money. The worst. Being responsible about finances is terrifically grown-up—it requires impulse control, thinking about the future rather than the present, delaying gratification, and realizing that yes, you probably *can* survive without those vintage sunglasses. And it's really, really hard for some of us.

It's just so much fun to spend money! On delicious food, or ten-dollar drinks, or pretty hats, or airplane tickets, or any of the 16 billion things in this world that are a blast to purchase, own, and experience. And it's so soul-crushingly dull not to spend it, knowing that it's right there, calling to you. "Hey [your name]," it begins. It uses a whispery, conspiratorial voice like it's your senior prom date or something. "Hey. Wouldn't it be great to take me to that new boutique? And maybe stop for macarons? Didn't you need some stuff at Target? Oh my God, you know what? I am so hungry and I think the only thing that will make me *not* hungry is sushi. Like, a *lot* of it."

And then you spend it and it's gone because most of us aren't lucky enough to have lucrative jobs or independent wealth at twenty-three. The one advantage you have is that poverty in your twenties has a certain kind of glamour that cannot be said of, say, tuna fish casseroles in your seventies.

Do not underestimate the great pleasure that comes from outsmarting poverty, from looking nice even though you can't buy a forty-dollar pair of pants, from hosting a party on the cheap, from being able to actually handle a financial emergency without depending upon your parents.

The best reason to be good about money is that not being good about money is so, so painful. There is no moment that forces you to think about your poor choices more than when your debit card is declined when you are trying to purchase fried chicken at Popeyes. This is not something that I'm saying *has* happened to me, but I'm not saying it *hasn't* happened, either. At least the drive-through lady forgot she'd already handed over the Diet Coke so, hey! Free Diet Coke in exchange for any dignity I may ever have felt!

If you have never eaten at Popeyes Famous Chicken and Biscuits, you are missing out. Did you know that famous New Orleans chef Paul Prudhomme has helped develop some menu items? And that their biscuits taste like they are deep-fried? Run, don't walk.

Step 227: Set reasonable expectations for yourself, money-wise

Before we delve into the sexy, fast-paced world of financial responsibility, take a moment and decide to be gentle on yourself if you are not yet a financial Viking. Money is an arena where it's all about expectation setting.

Some people reading this are people with diverse investment portfolios—in which case, yay for you, go enjoy your yacht or whatever. And some people reading this live with their parents. And some people are one type now but have been another. We will all experience circumstances that are not entirely within our control, especially when it comes to money, so don't judge yourself too harshly.

Just decide, realistically, where you are and what you can do. But mainly decide that you *can* do something, that there are small pieces of this very important thing that you have control over. And do not get stuck in a shame spiral. *No matter what you've done, you can take steps to fix it.*

I don't know what the constellation of qualities that make someone good with money is, but I certainly don't have it.

I am never going to be, by nature, a frugal person, or someone who can honestly say she's never strategically bounced a check. If, God forbid, I were ever to be rich, I know I'd be a cautionary tale. The local TV news would play a clip of me crying when they repossessed the pair of hot-air balloons I commissioned in the shape of my and Rihanna's heads.

But I can be someone who doesn't ring up seven thirty-five dollar overdraft fees for transactions of less than five dollars apiece. I'm probably never going to be great with money. But I can be okay with money, and you can be, too.

Step 228: Ignoring money issues won't make them go away. In fact, the opposite will happen

It's so easy to allow money to flow away from you if you aren't paying attention. And the prospect of keeping a vigilant eye on each cent in your possession can feel like an unpleasant combination of shrewishness and drudgery. Shrewdgery. But it must be done. The only way you can have control over your financial destiny is to face it head-on. And the first, best, most important tool is . . .

YOUR BUDGET

Budgets are right up there with meetings and annual gynecological exams in both unpleasantness and unavoidability. But like any good Pap smear, you'll feel capable and in charge once all is said and done, even if the during was no fun.

Step 229: Know exactly how much money you have coming in

The first step to determining how much money you can spend is to figure out how much money you have coming in on a monthly basis. For most of us, our salary will make up the bulk of this figure, but certainly add in any side income, from freelance writing gigs or your business selling earrings made of tiny plants on Etsy.

Now. See that number? You may not spend more money than that. Period. No ifs, ands, or buts.

Step 230: Know what you are spending money on

Make a list of your non-negotiable monthly expenses—rent, bills, however much you spend on groceries, gas, any recurring expenses—and then add a 5 percent cushion for all the unexpected expenses, plus your ten dollars per paycheck to add to your rainy-day savings account (see step 242). This will be your monthly living expense. This number doesn't include long-term savings and discretionary income.

Step 231: Take a long, hard look at the things you don't need to be spending money on

Conrad, who is a mortgage broker and, generally speaking, a super-responsible dude, said that it's a good plan to get six months' worth of bank and credit card statements on the table.

"Tracking where you currently spend your money is absolutely the first step," he said. "You can go back and make a list: *Here are the places I spend money. I'm spending X on food, I'm spending X on gas, I'm spending X on entertainment, I'm spending X on shopping.*"

Man, is this humbling, but highlight every unnecessary expense on your monthly bank statement. Look at the sea of jabby neon decisions. Is *jabby* a word? The adjective form of the verb *to jab*? Because that's how $57.89 on coffee in a month feels. Very jabby indeed. Stop bleeding money.

Step 232: Stick to your budget not because it's the right thing to do, but because it gives you an out

This may seem counterintuitive, but one lovely thing about having a budget with built-in savings is that once you've been adequately responsible, you don't have to feel guilty about spending the extra, discretionary income on earrings made of tiny plants. They grow on *air*!

A wise blog reader put it thusly: "Like crash dieting or quitting something cold turkey, it's often harder to stick to something that feels like a punishment, when what a budget can actually give you is freedom...If I look at all my expected income, then subtract my necessary expenses and plan in some savings...then everything that's left over is mine to do with as I will! If I budget in a hundred dollars of 'me money' a month, then I can spend that dough guilt-free."

Step 233: Give yourself a per diem

Decide how much screwing-around/discretionary money you get per day—maybe five dollars, maybe fifteen—and then stick to that. Money can roll over, but you can't borrow against future per diems.

Step 234: Start writing down every time you spend money

If you want to lose weight, write down everything you eat. If you want to gain money, write down every time a penny leaves you. This is like that highlighting you did in step 231, but ongoing.

This small act of self-accountability means that you probably won't take a spoon to the frosting, metaphorically. You will have a much harder time unnecessarily parting with cash if you have to take a moment to think about what you're doing.

Step 235: Think of shopping like drinking

You know what's just real, real fun? Shopping because you can. Shopping because it feels good. Shopping because if you do it long, hard, and smart enough, then it is possible that you will someday own every single pretty thing in the world, and wouldn't that be *terrific*?

But shopping can be like drinking. You can do it in a normal way, you can do it maybe a little more than you should but not veer into self-destruction, or you can *straight-up ruin yourself*.

Are you shopping and buying things to make yourself happier, to quiet your sadness? Are you doing it despite consequences? Do you go through that icky mental progression where you think, *Oh, I shouldn't [shop/ drink]*, and then you think, *Okay, just a little bit*, and next thing you know you're down two hundred dollars and have a crushing fiscal hangover?

Step 236: Develop your anti-shopping mantra

You need to get your non-shopping game face on.

I have honed this skill until it glistens, particularly in IKEA. IKEA is a high-pressure crucible of young adulthood, and only the strong can hope to survive.

For four hours, my inner monologue sounds like this: *You don't need that. You don't need that. You don't need that, either.* And so on.

Step 237: If you don't have money to shop, do not window-shop as though that's a real thing

That's like advising people on a diet to watch other people eating steaks for a little pick-me-up.

I *love* thrift shopping, and seeing how cheaply I can find things is part of the thrill. But when I was twenty-two, making twenty-four thousand dollars a year, I *didn't* have that extra ten bucks. I learned, the hard way, that I will always, always fall in love with something at a thrift store, and there was no point in torturing myself by finding it and then having to leave it behind.

You are not going to want to shop less when you're in a store! Don't tempt yourself! Go somewhere that won't make you feel sad and poor, like a park, or your equally poor friend's house.

Step 238: Do not charge shopping sprees and other such foolishness on your credit cards

Just don't. I'm serious. Not for the work wardrobe that you are sure will get you the job you need. Not for the most perfect item in the world.

Debt is the Voldemort to financial responsibility's Harry Potter, which is to say, no good, very bad, all-powerful, doing awful things. You should do everything you can to vanquish it.

As my dad once said, being in a credit card situation where you can just barely make the minimum payment every month is as close as most come in our modern world to being in debt peonage. And, historically, being a peon is rough. Do not allow yourself to become one.

It's fine to buy a small something on your card every month or so—in fact, you should do that, then pay it off in full to build credit. But do not pay 30 percent interest forever on anything.

Let's say you're the kind of person who isn't great about paying off your credit card in full every month. It's okay if you're not, but accept that you're not that kind of person and that you are actually paying maybe three times the sticker price each time you put something on the card.

If you're *really good* at paying off your credit card every month, then by all means, use them—you get cash back, airline miles, rewards, and so on. *This only applies if you are an A+++ student when it comes to paying it off.* Airline miles are not a good reason to rack up insane debt.

Step 239: Freeze your credit cards

Thank you to blog reader Leah for this one: Literally encase them in ice. Put them in the bottom of a bowl full of water, then stick that in the freezer. If you want to use them, thaw it out. Once again, it seems unlikely that you will ball outrageous through Sephora if you have to spend hours and hours first considering your decision.

And even if you've got the money, and it's not a problem, you should still...

Step 240: Pause before you buy something

Lots of people say you should wait a week before you buy something, to determine if it's really necessary and gauge how badly you want it. This always seemed a little harsh to me, and I'm certainly not a saint about it.

But at least take a moment. Leave the store, maybe, and go somewhere else. By removing yourself from the immediacy of the situation and the item you want, it sort of sobers you up, takes you back to a time when you didn't desire or even know about this tiny tchotchke that has stolen your heart. Then and only then can you thoughtfully decide whether you actually need that item, or just want it.

Step 241: Get what you came for

If you are in the kind of place where you go needing one thing and leave with fourteen (I'm looking at you, IKEA, Target, Whole Foods, and H&M), then make a list and *do not allow the siren song of thirty-dollar coffee tables to lure you onto the rocky shores of eating ramen until your next paycheck.*

Step 242: Put away ten dollars per pay period in savings

I don't care how poor you are, you can handle ten dollars every two weeks. Of this I am certain. It really, really, really should be twenty dollars, but ten is the absolute minimum. So make it non-optional. From now on, your monthly expenses include twenty dollars for savings. Because you're not saving for retirement, though that is important, too. No, no. You are setting yourself up to have that teeny cushion.

Step 243: Be prepared for the three-hundred-dollar emergencies

Here is the beauty of putting away ten dollars per paycheck: At the end of the year, you'll have $260, which incidentally is how much minor emergencies always seem to cost.

These emergencies are and always will be part of your financial landscape, at least once per year until you are dead. Your car will need new tires, or you'll owe the government some money, or your roommate will flake out at the worst moment. Just this little tiny bit of money will be of assistance at some point. And the first time you handle one of these without busting out the credit card or, worse, calling your parents (see "A Short List of Things Your Parents Are Not," in the Families chapter), you will give yourself a well-deserved high-five. Which looks to the outsider like clapping, but you'll know the difference.

Step 244: Ideally, someday, you will have three months' worth of living expenses squirreled away. Or, if you're a superstar, six months' worth

I have never been one of these people, but that is what you're supposed to do. There are many names for this pool of money, ranging from the polite ("safety net") to the not-so-polite ("fuck-you money"). But no matter what it is, remember that money represents freedom to leave a terrible situation—an abusive job (see step 220) or your horrible boyfriend whom you live with or whatever it is.

Financial planner Ron Kelemen calls this the "opportunity-slash-emergency fund."

"Maybe a job opportunity presents itself in the next town, or maybe your car breaks down and this would help you avoid getting into more debt," he said. "Or maybe it's a shove-it fund, so you're not stuck in a job where you have to stay forever and can't leave."

Step 245: One month's expenses is better than none

Don't let great be the enemy of good when it comes to saving. Something is infinitely better than nothing.

MAINTAINING DECENT CREDIT

Yes, yes, everyone says this, because it's true. To do things that adults want to do (get loans, buy a house, get jobs), you need to have decent credit. There are several things that go into your credit score, but the basics are simple.

Step 246: Cut up credit cards, but don't close the account

The ratio of debt to credit you have makes a big impact on your credit score. You want to aim to have a very small debt balance and large limit. So aim for a $30 balance on a $1,000 credit limit, rather than a $450 balance on a $500 limit.

Step 247: Do not ignore a bill

Here are the ways that a bill will leave your life:

1. You pay it.
2. ...

Here is a way that a bill will *not* leave your life:

3. Leave it unopened on your hall table, then look at it anxiously every now and again.

Duh, bills are awful. No one likes receiving a bill, no one in this whole world. In this way, bills and tapeworms are not so very different. But they must be paid or, like an untreated tapeworm, they will get larger and more powerful. And with that, you can calmly enjoy what will, from here on out, be a tapeworm-free book.

Now. There is a certain group of people in the world, of whom I am one, that have the money to pay their bills, but don't, because bills are dreary and there is some weird anxiety dysfunction at play. If you are this sort of person...

Step 248: Pay your bills on time. Pay your bills on time. Pay your bills on time

That means signing up for online bill-pay and setting monthly calendar reminders that will alert you *several days before it's due*. If you pay it online, pay it the day before, latest.

I don't care what you have to do—set a monthly alert to go off on your cell phone, have the money automatically withdrawn, pay a friend to nag you, whatever—but make it a ritual. On the seventeenth (or whenever), you pay each and every bill.

Pick a day and a time to pay *all* your bills. That way, you won't have to do that thing where you get a call from an 800 number and don't answer it just in case it's T-Mobile wondering where their $45.27 is.

Step 249: Know which bills you can be late on

In a perfect world, none of us would ever pay a bill late. Collection agencies would disappear, because every grown-up would pay their bills, in full, three business days early.

MASLOW'S HIERARCHY OF BILLS!

YAY!

FUN. NETFLIX. SHOPPING

INTERNET. CABLE. PHONE

CAR INSURANCE/NOTE. STUDENT LOANS. DEBT

START PAYING HERE

POWER. WATER. HEALTH INSURANCE

RENT. GROCERIES. MEDS. CREDIT CARDS

Pay each layer before moving up to the next!

*NOT REALLY.

But. Suppose—just suppose!—that sometimes you are getting to the end of the month and cash is tight. This is pure, pure hypothetical territory we're moving into here, the quantum mechanics of grown-upness.

But if that were to happen, make sure you have your own internal order of who gets paid, first to last.

Rent and credit card companies should be right there at the base, rent because it's the biggest and most important expense and credit cards because they will slap you with a thirty-dollar late fine or a nastily high interest rate so fast your head will spin. Toward the top should be cable/internet/cell phone because if things became truly dire, your world could continue to turn without them.

In the middle will be utilities, insurance, and student loans. Again, utilities and insurance are really important, and student loan companies are nearly as quick to tattle to the credit agencies as credit card companies.

Step 250: If you find yourself in a serious bind, call and ask the people you owe money to for help

If something really bad has happened in your financial life, be proactive and *call companies ahead of time*. The truth of the matter is that even though they seem cold and impersonal—and many are—they are run by human beings, and these human beings understand that sometimes bad things happen.

A while ago, I had an enormous hospital bill—we're talking an amount that could buy a decent used car—out of nowhere. Rather than waiting until I got the horrible bills and freaking out, I called the hospital in advance and let them know that it was going to be really hard for me.

And in return, they helped work out payment plans and even forgave some of the debt, based on my income level.

But the key is that you need to be *proactive* here. Do not wait until your bill is ninety days past due to call your creditor or service provider. Call as *soon* as you know there's going to be a problem, and say that you want to figure out a solution, you want to be a good customer, and you want to get them their money.

"It's good for you, the borrower, but it's also good for the lender," said financial planner Ron. "What they ultimately want is their money back, and it's going to cost them money to try to get blood out of a turnip. It's in their best interest to find something accommodating."

Step 251: Get comfortable with the idea of refinancing

Refinancing is another one of those frightening-sounding words, but it can be something surprisingly simple. Refinancing is moving your debt from one place to another, resulting in lower interest. A while ago, I had about two thousand dollars of credit card debt with high, high interest rates. An extremely practical friend of mine suggested that I look into taking out a small consumer loan from my credit union, and sure enough, I took a 20 percent interest rate down to 4.75.

If you, too, are really struggling with credit card debt, please, please go into your financial institution and *talk to them about it.* That's what they're there for. They can help you figure out a solution.

Side note: Credit unions are awesome. They're not-for-profit, member-owned financial institutions, and they tend to have much friendlier, less predatory terms—think lower fees, higher savings rates, and so on. They can be less convenient, with fewer offices and ATMs, and some of them have closed membership, but it's at least worth looking into whether you qualify for one. You might qualify through your job, or your college, or even just your state of residency.

HOW TO BE POOR

Okay, so now you're not allowed to spend much money anymore.

"But wait!" I hear your tiny, shrill voice. "Wait! That sounds like no fun at all!" Rest that piercing voice, and realize that the poor can have plenty of fun; they just have to be smart about it. On with the fun, or at least bearable, poverty!

Step 252: Get good at shopping for clothes on the cheap

Given enough money, anyone can look stylish and amazing. Have you ever noticed that there aren't many frumpy rich people?

But you can also be cute and poor, I promise. Think about this in terms of spending time rather than money, because it's much easier to find the something that is just the perfect fit for $110 at Nordstrom than for $3.50 at Goodwill, but you can do it.

• Shop with a specific item in mind, then search single-mindedly for that one perfect thing. You shouldn't clothes-shop aimlessly, ever—that's a good way to buy a lot of stuff you don't need. So figure out what you do need, then go get that. You can rifle really quickly through racks if you know you're looking for a white lace blouse or a high-waisted gray wool skirt.

• When possible, buy vintage clothing. I can't afford new interesting clothing, but I can pay for old interesting clothing. When I'm in a thrift store, I rifle through looking for *old* stuff. Get familiar with what old material looks and feels like—what the stitching looks like, the buttons, the zippers, and then look for that.

Or find quality, designer duds for less. Again, look for good stitching, quality fabric, and so on. If you need to, creep around Saks Fifth Avenue surreptitiously checking out what nicely made clothes look like. Then leave, because no one besides Beyoncé should be shopping at Saks.

Step 253: Hold a clothing swap

These are so satisfying, you have no idea. All you need is an apartment, some similarly sized friends, and hopefully a bunch of wine. Everyone brings clothes, jewelry, and shoes they don't want and dumps them on tables or the floor; then you root around like pigs searching for truffles. Clothing swaps are the best. I can't tell you how satisfying it is to see that beloved dress or skirt that just isn't right for you anymore go to a happy home. And, obviously, it's a bunch of new (to you!) clothes, for free.

Step 254: Shop thoughtfully

A lot of this is just comparison shopping and common sense: Buy summer things at the end of summer when they're on clearance. If you love decorating for holidays, go to stores five days after said holiday, when everything is marked down 90 percent. Seriously—you can sometimes get hundreds of dollars' worth of Target Christmas décor for a cool twenty.

For furniture and home decor, look on Craigslist and at Goodwill because you'll be way better off getting quality used things than what you can afford new, right now. If you need a new (to you) laptop, then check online for refurbished ones sold by the original manufacturer. Figure out where the discount grocery store in your town is. Get to know the vintage/thrift shops in your town (the ones where dresses are $12, not the super schmancy ones) and make friends with the owner, in the hopes that they will set aside cheap things they know you'll like.

Before any big purchase, ask yourself: Do I need this new? Do I need exactly this model? What is a low, reasonable, and high price on it? How much is it selling for in stores locally? Can I find it on eBay or Amazon and, if so, does it come with a warranty?

Step 255: Get familiar with happy hours and, failing that, the sides menu

Yes, I understand that waitstaff doesn't like this, but it's a valid money-saving strategy. If you get an invite for a night out and you absolutely, positively cannot afford it, then turn it down. If you can afford about 50 percent of it, eat ahead of time! Eat an almost-but-not-quite meal at your house, then go and order something small.

You can get a salad, or a side, you know! Or an appetizer. Make sure that when the bill arrives you aren't a total jerk about it.

Note: You still must tip properly. Tipping properly is not contingent on how much money you have; it's contingent on whether or not you accepted service. If you don't have enough to tip—and in America, that's 15 percent at casual restaurants, 18 to 20 percent at fine dining, and a dollar per drink, minimum, at a bar—then you do not have enough money to go out. Period.

However, no matter what, you need to . . .

Step 256: Pay your fair share cheerfully at restaurants

Please, please, please bring cash. This is easiest for everyone; bring $60 in two $20s and change. Alternatively, be comfortable with Venmo.

If you absolutely must split the bill seven ways, ask the waitstaff if that's okay before you sit down. At the end of the meal, figure out how much you *think* you owe (don't forget tax, tip, and beverages!), then add two or three dollars and say you will pay that amount. For God's sake, don't spend half an hour quibbling to make sure you don't over-pay by thirty-seven cents. If you're out with a friend who got an entrée that was a dollar more or whatever, *just split it in half*. Friendship is long, and you'll recoup your losses eventually.

Also, if you must pay your check with several different cards, here is a convenient thing to do for your server: On the bill, write the initials and amount each will be paying. So it would look something like this:

KB: $23.50
RL: $16
SB: $21.25
Plus
$15 cash (no change, please)

Ultimate adulting move: Just pick up the check for the table, know-ing the favor will eventually be returned...and that doing so won't bankrupt you.

Step 257: If you are dying to go to a schmancy restaurant that you could never afford, go for lunch

I have no idea why more people don't do this. It can be so luxe and fun, and just as delicious as dinner for maybe 60 percent of the cost.

Step 258: Get good at having cheap fun

Get a French press and learn to make coffee for your friends. Buy cheap wine and three-dollar frozen appetizers from Trader Joe's. Host potlucks at your house in the winter, picnics in public parks in the summer.

Going out for drinks is going to cost you at least fifteen dollars, every single time. But you know what? You and your friends can totally split a decent bottle of wine for ten bucks and play a board game and have a delightful time for a third of the cost.

And if you have rich friends who are always suggesting that you go out bar-hopping or out to expensive restaurants, it's okay to—without laying a thick guilt trip—say something demure about trying to stick to a budget.

Step 259: Don't borrow money from your friends

Just don't. It will never, ever turn out well. Don't lend your friends money, either. If you want to help them out, just plan on making it a gift. Or do something cash-based, like spotting a friend dinner. It'll come back someday.

Step 260: Discern things that are worth spending money on

My brilliant friend Sarah once explained to me that paying to get her dog's toenails clipped is an absolute necessity. It's worth it in terms of not dealing with a terrified and potentially bloody dog. Paying for someone to change your oil, spending extra on a good-quality winter coat that actually keeps you warm, and not buying a janky old bicycle off Craigslist if it's your only mode of transportation all fall into this category.

Here are some things to consider:

- How reliant am I on this good or service?
- Is this something that I could *theoretically* do myself but in reality am more likely to mess up and cause possibly costly damage?
- Is this something that will last me four times as long if I spend twice as much?

Step 261: Think in terms of how much things cost over their lifetime

Going out to dinner is great, but that money is gone in one night. All forty dollars will be dedicated to that extremely short period of time. Even if you are an excruciatingly slow eater, it's over in two and a half hours, max.

Goods and services have varying degrees of durability, and it's reasonable to think about how much worth something provides over its lifetime. To pick the most frivolous example possible, when I can afford it, I buy nice foundation. Yes, it's thirty-five dollars at the department store rather than eleven for the drugstore brand, but that thirty-five-dollar bottle lasts me for at least seven months. Is it worth five dollars per month for me to have decent foundation? It's a pretty low cost for something I use every single day. The key here is that I can't apply this to everything, only things I'm willing to sacrifice other spending opportunities on.

Step 262: Remember the other side of the lifetime-cost rule

But here's the thing: You can use the lifetime-cost trick above to justify nearly any purchase (except maybe lingerie), but remember that if you don't have thirty-five dollars to spend, then it wouldn't matter if that incredibly luminous, acne-fighting, skin-perfecting shade lasted you for the rest of your life. Remember your budget? *If it's not in your budget, then it doesn't matter what a great buy it is.*

Okay, so there you have it. That is how to be poor. And it isn't so bad! But you know what's better than being poor? *Not* being poor. And you can do it. If you are straight out of school, know that, barring having a kid or drastic job loss, in five years things will not be nearly so painful.

ADVANCED ADULTING

So now you're sort of in control of your finances and are getting a handle on how to be poor. Now it's time to imagine a day when you're not poor. It will come. Now is a great, great time to talk to a financial planner. You don't have money, but you do have something that all the money in the world can't buy: time. It makes a big difference to start this process when you are twenty-two, versus thirty-two. A financial planner can also help you figure out how to get out of debt, which is not only the Voldemort to financial security's Harry Potter, but also the Ursula to financial stability's Little Mermaid and possibly even the Gaston to financial relaxation's Beast. Let's talk through terms!

A 401(k)? The 401(k) is, essentially, a big pile of untaxed money; really, it's an investment account that often encompasses a broad range of mutual funds (a mixture of stocks, bonds, and so on). Lots of employers will match your contributions up to a certain amount; if they do, what we're talking about is essentially free money, and it will compound faster than you'd think. This is also one of those things that benefits hugely from starting early, say starting a 401(k) at age twenty-three versus thirty. We're talking a massive difference in terms of savings, in the tens of thousands of dollars over the years.

Seriously. Contribute. Do not allow yourself to be frightened by that little (k) in parenthesis. Pretend it stands for "kumquat," or "koala," or another friendly k-word. It is your 401(koala), just idly munching upon eucalyptus of employer-matched income, and you *love* it and want it to be happy and fat.

In general, financial things stress me out and bore me. So my coping mechanism is to tie the concepts to things that relax and delight me, which is to say, animals. We've already met the 401(koala), but let's dip into the rest of the Financial Zoo.

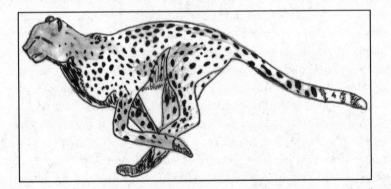

Compound-Interest Cheetah moves way, way faster than Simple Interest Snail when it comes to changing piles of money. If you are lucky enough that this benefits you—say, your savings interest is compounded—it's great. But if it's a debt situation with compound interest, then Compound-Interest Cheetah's swiftness can be as devastating to you as a regular cheetah is to a gazelle.

IRAguana is a retirement plan that, like real iguanas, is not required to pay taxes. So whatever money you give to him isn't counted as income for the year. Usually, IRAguanas are somewhat picky and you have to qualify to have one that counts as a tax deduction.

Savings Sloth: He grows very, very slowly, but Savings Sloth should have a place in each and every one of our lives. Do not let predators like Cute Art Print Cobra or Going Out To Bars Bobcat eat your Savings Sloth.

Pension Panda: Just like regular pandas, Pension Pandas are now sadly rare. A pension is an amount that a company pays a retiree regularly; they were much more common in our grandparents' generation. Social Security is a sort of pension.

TAXES

Step 263: Calm the F down; they're not that bad

Taxes are way, way less scary than they seem. Truthfully, if you just have one job, it should be pretty simple and you can probably do it on your own using an online filing program like TurboTax or H&R Block. Especially when you are young and poor, April 15 will probably result in the government giving money back to you. I *love* filing my taxes. I recommend listening to some sort of money-themed hip-hop while you do this. It's not required, obviously, but should get you feeling nice and rich and in control. Some good ones:

- "Money Ain't a Thang" by Jermaine Dupri featuring Jay-Z
- "Got Money" by Lil Wayne and T-Pain
- "Money to Blow" by Birdman, Lil Wayne, and Drake

- "Gin and Juice" by Snoop Dogg
- "C.R.E.A.M." by Wu-Tang Clan
- "Duffle Bag Boy" by Playaz Circle featuring Lil Wayne

Step 264: Pick an online tax-filing site of choice

Those programs are pretty straightforward; they simply ask you to fill out the numbers in the various tax documents you've been sent, then ask questions that should be easy to answer, like, "Did you buy a home in the last year?" Sometimes, it's free to file your federal tax return, but then you have to pay eighty dollars or so to file your state tax return, or vice versa. Either way, this is probably a simpler solution than having someone do your taxes for you.

Common tax documents include your W-2 form, which your employer should mail out toward the beginning of the year, plus the 1098-E form—a statement if you've paid a certain amount in student loan interest, or if you've donated money or goods to a non-profit.

If you have a more complicated tax situation—think lots of income from investments, self-employment, filing jointly if you just got married—then think about going in person to a tax preparation place. It really is affordable and worth skipping the headache.

Question: Do I need to save my receipts?

Saving receipts seems like the height of adulthood. Really, there are two good times to save your receipts:

1. Before the charges clear on your credit or debit card, so you have proof of the amount paid in case there is a dispute.
2. When you would like to write something off as a tax deduction.

There are about a billion and one things that can be written off—in addition to donations, there's moving expenses, business expenses including gas mileage, medical expenses, state income taxes, and so on. But it's a nice idea, if you're planning on writing something off, to keep the receipt around. Just get a shoe box, cut a hole in the top, write TAX RECEIPTS on it in big, friendly letters (or, better yet, glued-on rhinestones to add much-needed glamour to the tax preparation process), and pat yourself on the back.

Step 265: Wealth isn't that complicated

At the end of the day, it's a radically simple thing: There's just one way to save money, which is to spend less than you earn.

Discussion Questions

1. What is the most expensive item of clothing you've ever purchased? What was the pleasure-to-guilt ratio?
2. Have you ever had your credit card declined? Did you just slink off sheepishly, or offer a super-implausible explanation? Did you say, "Oh my God! I have to contact my bank! Something terrible has happened!" then rush off, as though the only possible explanation was that your bank account had been drained by an elite international ring of thieves? That's what I did.
3. Why can't we all just be rich already?

Chapter 7
MAINTENANCE

Everything is falling apart. Some things (like mountains) fall apart slowly, while others (like cars that never get their oil changed) fall apart quickly. At least compared with mountains.

It's frustrating that you can't do something once and have that be enough. It feels like once a problem has been solved, it should *stay solved*. But this is not how things work. Our universe constantly trends toward chaos, and adulthood often feels like nothing but solving the same recurring problems, over and over, again and again, forever.

On the upside, maintenance is not as big of a pain in the ass as you might initially think. Most items in your life need no more than two minutes of love per day, or perhaps an hour of affectionate attention every few months, to stay happy. These boring bits of time have immense payoffs.

So tattoo this on the inside of your eyelids: Spending a little time and money now protects you from experiencing great expense, inconvenience, and heartache later. Take the extra few minutes to hang up delicate clothes to air-dry so your shirt doesn't hang limply on you like a dead jellyfish. Change your car's oil on time not because you are a super-responsible person, but because you do not want it to break down on some backcountry road en route to a wedding.

If the mere thought of checking on something (your finances, your health, a friendship) stresses you out, take it as proof positive that you need to check up on it sooner rather than later.

This chapter is more about physical items than finances, relationships, and other intangibles, which are covered elsewhere. Just remember: You can have nice things…if you treat them like the nice things they are.

THE CONTINUUM OF MAINTENANCE!

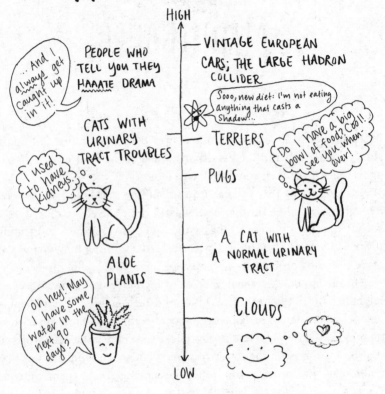

CARS

If your life requires a car, then that is likely your most important possession. No, it's not your beautiful vintage coat, your guitar, or your grandmother's wedding ring. The loss of the other things would hurt infinitely more in the long run. But the loss—even temporary—of your car will make almost all aspects of your day-to-day life super inconvenient, in a way those other losses do not.

While you can't prevent car troubles, you can take steps to lessen the possibility of it bursting into flames ten minutes before you're supposed to be in an important meeting across town.

Step 266: Name your car

With gas, insurance, maintenance, and whatever it cost you in the first place, you throw something like 15 percent of your income at the thing. So discover, in your heart, a deep love for this mass of metal, plastic, and gears. Name it, perhaps after yourself. Cherish it. Adopt a protective, benevolent attitude toward it. You and this car are on the same team.

Don't stomp down on the gas pedal two seconds after you turned it on, or pull out so fast that you squeal the tires. Drive it like you love it, because you do. It takes you from place to place, keeps you safe and warm, holds your Diet Coke, plays you the songs you want to hear, and all it asks in return is to be driven decently gently and given some new oil every now and again. Is that too much to ask?

Step 267: Find a mechanic you love or, more realistically, who will not rob you

Before you get that as-yet-nameless car, ask around for recommendations. Mechanics are like lawyers in that people will happily gush about a good one and spit venom about the bad ones. I lucked out massively in the form of Shane, who has all the crucial mechanic qualities: He's honest, never tries to upsell unnecessary repairs to my automotively ignorant self, and charges less than almost everyone else in town. He was also willing to sit down and explain how to take care of the damn things.

Step 268: Avoid used-car lots in favor of private sellers

Unless you own a Jet Ski or take trips to Vietnam for fun, you're probably in the market for a used car. So look for a good previous owner.

"Car lots tend to have the worst cars on them, because...no one will buy it, so [sellers] have to trade it," Shane said, adding that Craigslist, Nickel Ads, and newspaper classifieds are always a better plan.

You can certainly ask for maintenance records—not only to know the car's been serviced regularly (more on that later) but also to find that delightfully anal quality you should seek out in people from whom you wish to purchase an expensive, used, and hopefully well-cared-for thing.

Per Shane, do all the following when assessing a used car:

1. Start it, and make sure the engine turns over and starts right away.
2. Look for a big puff of smoke out of the tailpipe. If there's smoke, that's an indication of burning oil, which is a major problem.
3. Drive it, being sure to get up to at least forty-five miles per hour. If it's a standard transmission, make sure it shifts into all the gears smoothly. If it's an automatic, listen and make sure the car shifts itself at the correct time. Listen for any grinding, clunking, or banging, as these are all Bad Signs. "Go over some bumps, see if it feels solid; see if the steering wheel shakes," Shane said.
4. Park, then look under the car to see if anything's dripping. You should also look at wherever it was originally parked and make sure there are no suspicious stains.

My friend Sam has an interesting strategy for buying used cars: She always looks for leather seats in good condition. She doesn't particularly care about this, but the seats' higher price says that the car itself was likely to have been nicer when it was first purchased, and their preserved state shows her that the car's previous owner took pride in their possession.

Step 269: Do not buy a used European car

European cars are sexy and rare and a terrible plan unless you have piles of money for maintenance. Or are the type of person who likes to date people who unexpectedly and violently melt down.

Step 270: Do buy a used Japanese car, or American if you feel so moved

"Any Japanese car is a better-quality car than a European car—they're priced more reasonably, they're easier to work on, and easier to get parts for," Shane said, adding that domestic cars are second place to Japanese cars.

Step 271: Take it to a mechanic to look over

It doesn't cost that much—Shane said his shop charges $42.50 for half an hour of labor. This is a very, very small bill compared with the investment you're making. Whatever the mechanic says, listen to him or her. Do not allow your desire for this car to blind you to the dangers he or she may warn of. If it's something that can be solved fairly easily and he or she gives you a repair estimate, then go back to the seller and ask them to either fix it first or discount the amount from the purchase price.

Step 272: Do not skip oil changes

This is the very best thing you can do to ensure your car has a long, happy car life. Check your owner's manual, because lots of cars only require oil changes every five thousand miles. This counts as something that is Worth Spending Money On.

Do not remove that little sticker that says when you'll need another oil change, either. Leave that sticker be. If you look at it and feel guilty, go get the oil changed.

If you truly cannot afford an oil change, at least go get some oil and top it off. It costs maybe five bucks for a quart; you can do it.

Step 273: Know how to check your car's oil

Every car has a dipstick under the hood. Check your oil when it's cold, which is to say, after the car hasn't been running for a little while. Pull it out, wipe it off with a paper towel, then put it back in and pull it out. There's the full line, and then the add line. If the oil is below the latter, your car needs more oil.

Step 274: Keep a quart of oil, some coolant, and a rag in your car

If you're super low on oil (or, worse yet, losing it regularly), then go ahead and add half a quart, then check your oil again. If you need more, add the rest. Then, the next time you stop for gas, get another quart.

Step 275: Get scheduled maintenance every thirty thousand miles, or as indicated in the owner's manual

Spending $350 on car maintenance is the second most boring, sad use of $350 in the whole wide world. (First place: dental work. Third place: a visit to the vet to get the dog to stop vomiting, which at least has elements of danger and urgency.) But it has to happen.

"Every thirty thousand miles, there are usually some significant things that should be done. It depends on your budget, but you should change the coolant, you should change the transmission fluid, and you should have the car looked at"—especially brakes, belts, hoses, and tires, Shane said.

Step 276: Watch warning lights, especially the red ones

If a light comes on, pay attention to your car: Is it driving differently than it did before the light was on?

Car warning lights are amber if they require attention, and red if you are in imminent danger of causing irreparable (or, at minimum, incredibly expensive) damage to your car. The worst light to come on is the red oil light, which indicates that your car has lost oil pressure and is not lubricating itself. This is very, very bad. Imagine extremely vigorous, unlubricated sex, except everyone's genitals are made of steel and powered by exploding gasoline.

Your car tells you things via those little lights, but in ways you cannot fully understand unless you have a magic scanner. Which you don't. Mechanics and auto parts stores have them.

Many national auto parts stores don't charge to run the scan, whereas most mechanics do. Call ahead to make sure it's actually free.

CAR WARNING SIGNS

Here's a rundown of some ways that your car can be acting weird, and what it may be trying to tell you in its car way:

- If you're going slow and the wheel is shaking, or it feels like you're driving over speed bumps, that's probably a tire problem. It's usually pretty obvious when you have a flat—if it's in the front, Shane said, you'll have a really difficult time steering. If it's in the back, the whole thing will drive mushy. Pull over and change your damn tire. (Or better yet, call AAA [step 452]!)
- If it's driving normally except there's a thumping or jerking when you step on the brake, or a squealing sound, you may well need a new brake job. This is not as expensive as it sounds unless you

let it go on too long and start to wear down your brake disks, in which case it can get very expensive indeed.

- If you hear a *clunk, clunk, clunk* when turning but nothing when going straight, that probably means a front axle is going bad.
- "If you're accelerating and you hear a backfire or popping sound, a little *pop, pop, pop, pop*, that's usually a spark plug that's gone bad," Shane said. If there's no sound but there is jerking, that could also be a spark plug, but also potentially an injector or coil problem.
- If you let go of the steering wheel and the car immediately decides on a new course for itself, that's likely an alignment problem. You can also have problems with alignment that don't manifest during driving—check out your tires every now and again, and make sure that they are wearing evenly. The treads should be pretty even, but if the outer treads or inner treads are notably shorter, HEY. Go get it aligned.

Step 277: Get new tires when necessary

Remember when I said that car maintenance is the second most boring expenditure in the world, after dental work? Well, I lied. Tires are the clear winner of Things That Are Really Expensive But Not Even Slightly Fun To Purchase sweepstakes.

Once, when I was especially angry about how expensive and boring tires are, I called a spokesman for a major tire manufacturer named T.J. Now, T.J. is a true believer in tires—at one point, I asked if he ever got tired of talking about tires all day, and he said—this is a verbatim quote—"No! I can't believe you would even ask me that. No, tires are *so cool*. I *cannot express* to you the coolness of tires."

Anyway, one really smart thing that T.J. pointed out is that tires are the only part of your vehicle that is actually connected to the ground.

The major sign you need new tires is that the tread has been worn down to less than one-sixteenth of an inch. You can check this with a penny—stick Lincoln, head-side down, into the tread. If you can still see his whole face, then the treads are too low.

You *can* buy used tires if you're crunched for cash and it's an emergency, but you should just pony up for new ones. Lots of tire stores offer free rotations and warranties, so ask ahead. Ask specifically what the warranty and lifetime care covers: If you get a hole, will they patch it? How long does the warranty last? On more than one occasion, I've gone to Les Schwab, where I get my tires, with a flat and walked out without paying a dime. Figuring these things out now is a good way to ensure that you won't have to spend any more of your precious, exciting money on boring tires than is absolutely necessary.

CLOTHES

Think of someone you know who always appears capable. Think of someone you know who often has stains on their clothing. Chances are close to 100 percent you are not picturing the same person.

You don't have to spend a lot of money on clothing, as we established in the Money chapter, to look swell. You do need to take proper care of the clothes you have—wash them in the temperature and manner they want to be washed, with similar colors. If they were human, this would be racist, but since they're inanimate items, let it slide.

Some things to have on hand for proper care of clothing:

- A liquid laundry detergent that doesn't fade colors
- A stain remover (I find the OxiClean ones tend to work very well)
- A mesh garment bag that you put your undies and tights in when washing
- Non-wire hangers

Step 278: Don't be wrinkled

- **Get a good steamer.**

Not the handheld, travel kind, but the sort that has a reservoir base and a wand that you use to steam.

Steaming clothing is incredible. All the wrinkles fall out, it makes your clothing smell fresh and clean, and it just . . . it just *revitalizes* it. A steamer makes old clothing look new.

To steam, you want to just run the steamer slowly on the inside of the clothing, angling so that the steam rises up. You absolutely want to watch your fingers, because steam burns suck. One strategy is to hold an oven mitt in your non-steamer-holding hand, although know that the steam can and will go right through that. SAFETY FIRST WHILE STEAMING.

- **Get a basic, but not cheap, iron.**

Irons are great for when you want the crisp details: a beautifully starched collar on a white shirt, for example. Get one that has steam and spray functions, which most of them do.

When ironing, be sure to set it at the appropriate heat level for that garment. Do *not* go higher, or you can easily burn the clothing. Don't forget to move the iron slowly but constantly, and—not that you would—never leave it sitting, hot-side down, on the piece of clothing. Lots of people like to start with the smallest panel of clothing (the collar, say, or the cuffs) and work to the largest. But if you're going to iron, be sure to iron all of it, because any wrinkles will stand out clearly against the vast smoothness.

Step 279: Let your deodorant dry before you put on clothing

Put on your deodorant, and let a few minutes pass. Also, when you're done wearing the clothing, spray the pits with hair spray (see step 284) or your stain fighter of choice.

Step 280: Wash most things in cold water

Unless something is really and truly dirty, there's no reason to use hot water—it fades colors, can shrink some things, and isn't energy-efficient.

Step 281: Sort by colors to wash

This doesn't mean that you have to have a load of light-violet-only garments, but you should sort whites, darks, and colors, paying special attention to clothes that are likely to bleed. Newer items should always be looked at with more suspicion than those that have proven themselves colorfast. Highly saturated cotton clothes tend to give off color, as does tie-dye.

Step 282: Master hand-washing

Anything delicate can and should get hand-washed. It's not that difficult, and is in fact easier than hauling a load of clothes to the Laundromat.

You do it with those often-mentioned, rarely understood delicates: think lace, fine sweaters, bras, and almost all nice lingerie.

Here's how it's done: Fill your sink or tub with cold water, then add some washing detergent. If there's food or grease stains on the item, add some dish soap (more on that below).

Put your items in the soapy water and give them a good swish. Let them soak for at least thirty minutes, swishing every now and again, then let them drain. Fill up the basin again with cold water to rinse, then hang them up to dry.

Step 283: Don't throw everything in the dryer

Dryers do a great, great job of prematurely aging clothing. Dryers are like the American presidency. Clothing goes in looking youthful and vigorous, and emerges slumped and gray-haired.

Some things are just fine in the dryer: Jeans, socks, T-shirts, and other similarly rugged clothing items will have no problem with it. Things that rely on elastic or stretchiness—think swimsuits, and garments with lots of synthetics in them—and anything delicate should be kept out of the dryer.

Invest in one of those folding, old-fashioned drying racks, or string up a clothesline.

Note: Do not hang something very heavy when it's wet, because the weight of the garment can pull on the shoulders and stretch it out. Things like sweaters and heavy dresses should be set on a towel, then sort of tugged gently into shape to dry.

Step 284: Use hair spray to get stains out

Sam Hart has run LiL' Gypsy Vintage Boutique for twenty years, and because of this she is a pro champion at removing stains and smells from clothing.

Sam swears by cheap aerosol hair spray—"Whatever I can get at the dollar store"—to get stains out. She said she's found stain removers to be hit-or-miss, whereas just spraying some hair spray on does the trick much of the time.

If it's a food or grease stain, use some clear dish soap. That Dawn you bought back during the Domesticity chapter should do you proud.

"There's nothing that cuts food better," Sam said, adding that if it can get grease off your pans, it can get grease off your pants.

As soon as you get the food stain, get it wet and rub some dish soap in, then put it in the laundry. When you wash it, wash it on cold and do not put it in the dryer. Washing on hot makes the stain a permanent part of your clothes, but with cold there is still a chance to salvage the item.

Step 285: Use vinegar to get smells out

Throwing a cup of white vinegar into a full load of laundry neutralizes odors. Sam said a paste of vinegar and baking soda can also do a great job on stains, especially armpit stains.

Step 286: Get over your fear of bleach

I spent years living in bleach terror. How does it work? What does it do? If I have some in my house, will my clothes develop splotchy bleach stains by a process of osmosis? I imagined bleach fumes floating menacingly through my house at night, searching with slit bleach-fume eyes for potential sartorial victims, not unlike Hexxus, the evil spirit of pollution cloud voiced by Tim Curry in the seminal 1992 animated classic *FernGully: The Last Rainforest*.

Needless to say, this is not how bleach works. Bleach is simple. Bleach is your friend. Use it on whites, and whites only. Let the washer fill completely, without putting your clothing in it, then add three-quarters of a cup of bleach and make sure it's mixed well. Add your white clothes in.

Afterward, Sam said, it is absolutely wonderful if you can hang the whites outside in the sunshine to dry. This does an excellent job of getting them extra, extra white.

Step 287: If you are going to wear white, you must[1] commit to it

This also goes for baby blue, baby pink, spring green—basically, any color that would be at home for an Easter service.

Before you put on that white garment in the morning, ask yourself if you can refrain from the following until that item is safely back in your closet:

- Eating any sort of tomato-based broth? Especially the kind with that deadly orange grease floating on the top?
- Painting?
- Using Sharpies in any but the most subdued and careful manner?
- Consuming any food that isn't Nilla Wafers while driving?
- Any sort of interaction with your car other than delicately pumping gas? (Think tire and oil changing, or nearly anything that requires you to pop the hood.)
- Acknowledging the existence of mustard? Seriously, don't even look at it.
- Ground-sitting?
- Chili-cheese anything?
- Carnivals? Carnivals combine everything above, plus face painting, into one dangerous brew.

Also, if you manage to vigilantly protect your white garment from harm, *take it off when you get home.* Your house is safe for you, yes, but 37 percent[2] of indelible stains happen in the home.

Step 288: If something is delicate or squish-able, find a way to safely store it

Hats go in hatboxes. Purses can be lined up neatly on a top shelf in a closet but shouldn't always hang by their straps. Give purse straps

---

1. You don't *have* to commit, as every single white garment I've ever owned will attest, but you *should*.

2. I made that up but it seems right.

a much-needed break, because purse straps are the middle-aged wait-resses of the clothing world. They are working hard.

Bras should be gently nestled within one another. Do not allow stockings to invade your lingerie drawer, or they will get all twisted around your nice lingerie.

Step 289: Hang up or fold things, as they prefer

Things that get hung up:

- Nice pants and slacks
- Skirts, except the very most casual, un-wrinkleable kind made of synthetics
- Button-up shirts
- Jackets
- Anything else that is constructed through the shoulder—think shoulder pads or 3-D construction
- Dresses
- Coats
- Ties (do not leave them tied, either; untie them)

Things that get folded:

- Sweaters: This is important
- T-shirts
- Underwear
- Gym clothes
- Jeans

Step 290: Store jewelry like the expensive thing it is

Nice jewelry should be separated from its Forever 21 kin and deli-cately coiled individually in a jewelry box, ideally lined with velvet or some other similarly luxuriant fabric if it's something easily scratched or delicate. Remember that pearls are finicky and should never, ever have anything (like perfume or lotion) near them—they lose their lus-ter and sulk. Speaking of nice jewelry, if there is something you really, really love and wear every day and have the fake version of (for me, it was pearl stud earrings), go ahead and see how much it would be to get the real version. If you can, *get it for yourself,* because this is the most satisfying. Perhaps, like me, you'll enjoy putting on Destiny's Child "Independent Women, Pt. 1" and screaming the relevant lines: "The shoes on my feet? I BOUGHT 'EM. The watch I'm wearing? I BOUGHT IT," et cetera.

Step 291: Don't put tacos in your purse

A short list of things that should not be stored in your purse, backpack, or murse, even if you don't have anywhere else to put them and you can't imagine the worst that could happen:

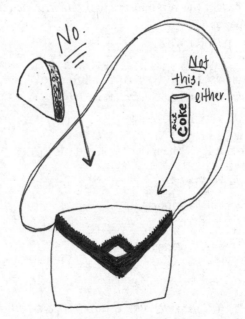

- Tacos.
- Cans of soda, or bottles of any liquid, really, unless you are extra certain that they are hermetically sealed.
- Leaky pens. In fact, once a pen has leaked (even once!) treat it as you would a boyfriend that slept with your sister (even once!) and throw that busted shit out. You don't need that in your life.
- Bright red lipstick when the temperature outside is over ninety degrees.

- Stainy liquid makeup in general (foundation, bright lip glosses, liquid eyeliner), unless it is zipped safely into a case that has proven itself reliable.
- Calzones.
- Any meat, really. Beef jerky is okay.

If you've ever arrived somewhere to find everything you own covered in shampoo, you understand the importance of packing such things in ziplock bags.

Step 292: Find a good tailor

Okay, don't do this for a little while, because it's easy to get addicted to tailoring. But if you have something nice—think a suit, or a really beautiful dress—that you've spent a lot on, there's no reason not to spend fifteen dollars more and make sure it fits you perfectly. If you work in an office, ask around. A good tailor, like a good mechanic, is someone that people are deeply dedicated to, but you are unlikely to find them on your own, and certainly not via the internet. Ask around the office, or your parents' most stylish friend, if they know anyone good.

Step 293: Before you write it off as ruined, take it to the dry cleaners

Dry cleaners are magical. They are sorcerers. They are a man on the moon. Something can seem completely unsalvageable, and not only do they fix what's wrong with it, but they make it look new again even though it was floppy and faded and sad when you dropped it off.

Case in point: One time, I got bright lip liner all over a camel-hair coat.[3] Every single panel of the coat had cruel coral streaks. I was crying in the gym locker room and complaining to anyone who'd listen that I'd ruined my one nice coat, which is *not* an effective problem-solving strategy, until a kindly naked lady took pity on me and suggested I take it to the dry cleaners.

I still have that coat. Because dry cleaners operate outside normal laws of physics, at least when it comes to stain removal.

---

3. Don't ask me how this happened. I still don't know.

HOUSEPLANTS

There is something quietly admirable about people who capably take care of plants. Plants are the ultimate passive thing: They never tell you what they want, they just sort of wilt and die if they don't get it, like tiny green Gwyneth Paltrows.

Despite this pathetic tendency of theirs, they are a lovely thing to have around. They make oxygen, they serve as a nice counterpoint to your animated self, and there is something deeply satisfying about watching something that only needs two minutes of your time per day flourish.

Step 294: If it's going to be indoors, get a houseplant, not the outdoor kind

There are many, many plants that love nothing more than to be inside, maybe on a northern-facing window with indirect sunlight. Before you go to the nursery, scope out your living space and see where they can get at least a little natural light. Is it sunny there for six hours a day? Two? Is it shaded, or is it direct light? This will go very far in helping the friendly nursery people figure out what will work for you.

Easy indoor plants:

- Succulents, including aloe
- Most small cacti
- Sago palm
- African violets
- Ficus trees
- Philodendron
- Spider plants

Step 295: Find out how often your plant wishes to be watered, and do not overwater it

It's really, really easy to drown a plant, whereas if they're underwatered, they just sort of look droopy and sad and Gwyneth-esque. But among the many endearing qualities of plants is that even if they're thirsty, they quickly cheer up once watered, usually within twenty-four hours.

Stick your finger in the pot. If you can still feel moisture, they probably don't need any more water yet.

If the soil is very dry and the water just runs out of the bottom of the pot, place a bowl or plate under it and add water. This allows the dry soil to rehydrate, and your plant will soak up the water from the bottom.

Step 296: Do not repot them right away

Just like people, plants find moving to be very, very stressful and don't want to do it unless things have become unbearable in the old place. It's possible that it'll be ready to move on immediately (see below), but if not, you're probably just stressing it out by repotting it.

After you take a plant home from the nursery, leave it in the pot it came in, at least for the moment. Chances are good this is a hideously ugly plastic pot, so by all means buy an attractive planter that's one size larger. They usually get larger in two-inch increments; if it's planted in an eight-inch pot, buy a ten-inch pot. Then put its current pot inside its future home, and maybe scatter a little moss around the top to disguise this arrangement.

Step 297: Repot when they become root-bound

Eventually, your happy plant will swell and fill its home with roots (if it hasn't yet when you bring it home). To see if it's ready to move on up, take it outside, tilt it partially upside down, and gently shake it out of the pot. If the roots swirl around the edges of the soil, it's ready.

Add a little of its soil of choice to the bottom of the new pot. Set the whole thing in gently, and pat soil into the sides. Give it a good, loving, and thorough watering.

PETS

So you've not killed a plant and are ready for a step up in the responsibility department! Yay! Pets are wonderful, and you should go for it . . . if you are ready and have the right motivations.

I got my beloved cat Marigny Treme Brown-Gervais just as soon as I moved out of the dorm room and into my first apartment. I'm ashamed to say that my thought process was not *Do I have the money to take her for yearly checkups? Who will watch her if I go intern somewhere for the summer? What will my life be like for the next fifteen years, which is how long she may live?* but more along the lines of *My life would be happier if there were a cat wandering around in this apartment.*

Eight years later, we still enjoy each other's company. But there are apartments I can't get because I have a pet, and pet-sitting to arrange when I go away, and vet bills when she gets a kitty ailment. I still wouldn't be able to spend thousands of dollars if she needed surgery, which makes me feel like a bad owner, but having four thousand dollars squirreled away seems an unreasonably high bar to pet owner-ship. She's 800 percent worth it to me, but these are things I wish I'd given more thought to.

And dogs are way more care- and cost-intensive than cats. Cats, I am pretty sure, are closer to houseplants than to dogs on the care-requirement continuum.

A couple of quick reminders:

• A pet is not a living safety blanket. It is a small being with hopes, dreams, and a frequent, ongoing need to poop.

• Moving is not an excuse to take a pet to the shelter. Chances are good that your pet will not be adopted, particularly if they're older, a mixed breed, or have any behavioral issues. If your options are to leave your pet by the side of the road or take them to a shelter, then obviously you should take them to a shelter. But their chances, once there, are not great.

Step 298: Free animals are not free

Especially when they're little. Brittni Lipscomb, who helps run Orchard View Veterinary Center, pointed out that kittens and pup-pies need vaccines every three weeks, and deworming every two weeks until they're sixteen weeks old. One benefit to adopting from a shelter is that your pet will already have lots of the necessary procedures under its belt.

But it's more than just the first few weeks: Pets are expensive.

First things first: Before your pet comes home, go to the bank and get a hundred-dollar bill. Put this in an envelope, then write [YOUR PET'S NAME] EMERGENCY FUND. Keep this around. This can't pay for everything, but it'll help.

Know that to do the bare minimum, health-wise, for your pet will be around three hundred dollars per year. Can you set aside twenty-five dollars per month? What if you didn't have cable? Or a gym membership?

Step 299: Find the right vet for you

Brittni said she thinks interviewing potential vets is a great idea. "Remember that you are hiring them to do a job for you. Visit the practice, tour the facility, ask if you can watch a procedure, check prices, ask what their philosophies are," she said. "Make sure you are going to a veterinarian you trust."

Step 300: Don't be afraid to talk to your vet about the most cost-effective options

First, vets are not out to screw you. They are not getting wealthy off their glamorous, dog-vomit-rich lives. And they understand that not everyone can afford everything. Saying, "I love my pet and I want the best for her, but I can only afford X" is a fair statement. Ask if there are less optimal, more affordable ways to solve whatever the issue is.

Step 301: Buy decent food for your pet

It doesn't have to be the super-high-end stuff they sell at the vet's, but some brands are more nutritionally sound than others. My vet recommends Royal Canin, Science Diet, or Eukanuba.

Step 302: Treat your pet for fleas, especially during the summer months

Vets recommend that you treat year-round, but if money's tight and you live in a cold climate, you may be able to get away with spring/

summer treatments. The key here is that there are a few things that are very effective, and a whole host that are not. Buying a four-dollar flea collar at Petco will do nothing for you.

You can certainly get prescription-strength stuff, but Vectra, Advantage, and Frontline are all over-the-counter and work well.

Read *all the instructions* before you apply the stuff. You are about to put some pretty serious poison on your beloved pet, so take the ten minutes and make sure you're doing it correctly. If your house is infected with fleas, get a bug bomb. Do not try to do any all-natural stuff. Just get a bug bomb.

Step 303: Pay attention for signs your pet may be sick

"Anytime your pet is acting differently than normal it can be a concern," Brittni said, adding that changes in eating or drinking, sluggishness, and having accidents in the house can all be signs that they're sick. One reason it's important to feed your pet the same amount of food at the same time is that you can immediately tell when they're eating less than usual. She also pointed out that many illnesses aren't obvious to the owner, so regular checkups are important.

Take your pet to the vet (or even the hospital) ASAP if any of the following is happening:

- Acute abdominal pain
- Uncontrolled bleeding or bleeding from the neck
- Coughing up blood
- Breathing problems
- Broken bones
- Burns or electrical shock
- Car accidents
- Collapse or fainting, loss of consciousness, seizures, paralysis or lack of coordination
- Diarrhea that goes on for more than a day (especially in young animals)
- Distended abdomen
- Eye swelling or injury

- Frequent vomiting, or unproductive retching
- Frostbite
- Neck injury
- Pale gums
- Poisoning
- Straining to urinate

If any of these things are happening, call your vet right away. Note: This is a non-comprehensive list.

Step 304: Consider pet insurance

It is a legitimate thing to own a pet even if you couldn't pay for a forty-five-hundred-dollar surgery, if it came to that. It doesn't mean you don't love your pet. But it is not a legitimate thing to own a pet if you can't afford the very, very basics—vaccines, spaying and neutering, and flea treatment.

AROUND THE HOUSE

Most day-to-day house maintenance is basic cleaning (see all of chapter 2). But there are a few things you can and should do that go above and beyond to keep things in good working order.

Step 305: Clean out underneath the burners if a lot of oil or food has spilled down there

Unless you like grease fires, in which case, you know, do what you do.

Otherwise: If you have a gas stove, this is pretty easy; if it's electric, you'll need to pull the burners out first. Grab them at the point where they plug into the stove, then wiggle and slowly pull them out. Use dish soap and hot water to break down the grease underneath, then a dish towel to dry it off.

If the saucers under the electrical burner get really funky, as they will every couple of years or so, every big-box store with a home-improvement section sells replacement saucers.

Step 306: Pay some attention to your fridge

Beyond just not letting the stuff in there rot into a nasty, dripping mess, there are a few things you should do every four months or so. They're easy and don't take long.

First, make sure the coils on your fridge aren't covered in dust. They're located either behind or under the fridge; if they're underneath, you'll have to remove the front panel. Dust them off with a broom if need be.

Then wipe off the plastic edges that create a seal with disinfectant. Make sure they aren't cracked or warped, otherwise the fridge will overwork itself to make up for the lost cold air. If a dollar bill falls down when you close the door on it, the seals aren't working well.

Finally, clean the inside and wipe it with white vinegar, which prevents mold. Put a new open box of baking soda in there to keep it fresh smelling.

Step 307: Don't put hair down your drains

Or oatmeal, or anything else likely to glob up into a gunky mess. But if you do notice that your sink or tub is draining slowly, do not wait until it's totally stopped up. Go get some Drano, and *read the damn directions.*

BODY

It's impossible to phrase this section in a way that doesn't sound like nagging, and people nagging you about your health is the most guilty squirm-inducing conversation there is. It's so easy to reach the "Fuck it!" saturation point. Because of course they're right: There is no more important physical thing in the world than the body you happen to inhabit. You only have one, and some things you do to it are not fixable.

But it's so fun (in the moment) to abuse them. It's more fun to eat Doritos than bananas. Diet Coke tastes better than water. Staying out late and drinking always seems like a great plan, at least until the next morning. Believe me, I get it: I used to be a chain smoker, and I *loved* it. I loved every single one of the hundreds of thousands of cigarettes I've smoked to date. But while I loved cigarettes, I hated myself a little every time I chose to smoke.

You have to take care of your body. You have to. You have to. You have to. Yes, right now if you're in your twenties, then it seems like nothing will ever be wrong with it, other than hangovers and non-reality-based concerns about your upper arms looking fat. But even if you can't feel or see the consequences now, they're there.

Plus, think back: There is probably at least one time in your life when you were being healthy—eating right, exercising, and getting enough sleep. You really do feel and behave better when you do these things. You don't have to be an all-organic yoga instructor to be good to your body. Just make one small, good choice every day, and you will slowly but surely become healthier.

My friend Elisabeth, who, when she is not being my friend, is a surgeon (seriously: She professionally cuts people up. That is her *job*.), was willing to chat about how she treats her body, which is pretty different from how I treat mine.

Step 308: Being healthy is actually pretty simple, if not easy

"Think about it this way: You have a couple of holes where things go in, a few where things come out, and you're surrounded by breathing, dynamic skin," she said, then added that the whole key to health is watching what you put in, monitoring what comes out, and protecting that skin.

Step 309: Never start smoking and if you have, quit

Elisabeth pointed out that cutting down on cigarettes is better than not cutting down, and suggests to her patients that however many cigarettes they smoke daily, the next month they smoke one less per day.

You can't quit unless it's your time. No one else, and certainly not a book, can pressure you into it, because that isn't a decision for other people to make. It's yours. But you can choose, in smaller ways, to turn your back. You can choose, next time you want a cigarette, to say, "You know what? I'm not going to have this one. I can have one later, if I want, but this one I do not need."

Step 310: Purchase real food

So, so much money and research has gone into making food that tastes delicious and makes us want more.

"Anything that tastes really good—think twice about," Elisabeth said. "Try to eat seven bananas, and your body's going to shut down and say, 'You know what? I'm done.' You can eat the same caloric amount of McDonald's and your body will want more."

Elisabeth mentioned the old trick of shopping around the edge of the grocery store, which is where the things that humans have eaten for thousands of years tend to be located: fruits, vegetables, meats, and a few carbohydrates.

The less a giant food company is adding to your food, the healthier you will be, the more energy you will feel, and the more you are likely to maintain a healthy weight.

Step 311: Keep an eye on weight gain

We are all differently shaped and sized, and a big part of being a grown-up is accepting your body for what it is, and not spending mental energy anguishing over something that's just a feature of you. If you have seriously unhealthy feelings about your body, obsess about food and weight (not health: weight), and base your self-image on how thin you look, that is called an eating disorder and generally requires mental health counseling to recover from.

That being said, obesity can cause some serious health issues. And it can sneak up on us: For hundreds of thousands of years, the human beings who survived were the ones whose bodies could effectively retain energy (read: fat) through the lean times. Then, in the past hundred years, that has gone right out the window. Don't blame your body for this tendency. It makes perfect biological sense, and it's not a reflection on anything except millennia of evolutionary selection.

But it does mean you need to find a way to maintain your body where it is, what your particular balance of exercise to calories should be.

"Let's say you were 140 pounds last year, and you're 145 this year," Elisabeth said. "If you don't change your habits, in four years, you're twenty pounds heavier, plus you've established four years of habits that lead to five pounds of weight gain per year . . . It happens so subtly. If you divide five pounds by 365 days, it's not something you'll see on any given day. But in ten years, you'll be fifty pounds heavier."

Step 312: Find a couple of healthy things you can cope with snacking on in lieu of the delicious stuff

Somewhere in this big wide world, there are at least two healthy snacks you can tolerate. Find them. Maybe they are frozen raspberries, or tangerines, or low-fat string cheese, or shelled edamame. These are the things that are allowed to live around your home in vast quantities, lying in wait for you to mindlessly eat a big bowl of (or, in the case of the string cheese, two packets, peeled very slowly).

It's easy to say, "Don't eat unless you're hungry! Don't eat if you're stressed! Don't eat if you're watching TV!" but for a lot of us, those habits are very deeply ingrained. Eating something that's low-calorie and good for you can be a nice compromise.

Step 313: Pay attention to portions

After putting on about twenty pounds, I decided to lose it. I didn't have to stop eating the things I liked (anything that includes animal fat and is favored by old Southern men), but I did have to start eating the amount humans are supposed to eat of the things I liked.

A twelve-ounce steak is not a steak. It's three steaks. Half a big bag of chips is not a serving of chips; it's a quarter of the daily calories you're supposed to eat.

The trick to smaller portions is (a) to eat them slowly, and (b) to wait a little while before going for more. A lot of times, you can be nearly as happy slowly eating your 14 chips; as you would eating 140 in the same amount of time.

Step 314: Find an exercise you like

Bodies need to move. That is their whole point, besides eating, pooping, and sexing; that is what we all have this extensive and beautiful musculature for. So just make sure your body is in motion, at least sometimes. Ten minutes a day is better than nothing.

You don't have to go to the gym to do it, either. There are yoga videos on Hulu, walking is free, you can go dancing, you can bike ride, you can jog around your apartment—even though that sounds like a direct path to madness to me. Do a bunch of things. You will feel stupid and out of shape when you do them. But eventually, you will do something that does not feel like working out. You will do something you enjoy, something that makes you feel more at home in your body than you did the day before. Keep doing that.

Remember, you don't have to go balls-to-the-wall to get the health benefits and lose weight. Tina, who is the group fitness coordinator at my gym, pointed out that if you're at that very, very high point in the workout—the anaerobic part, where you can't talk except in gasping breaths—you're actually not burning that much fat, because your body isn't getting oxygen effectively.

Also, remember that you don't need to spend money to find expert advice and help—there are tons of great online resources, like Couch to 5K, and apps for everything from counting calories to quitting smoking.

Step 315: Consider taking vitamins and probiotics daily

Yes: If you eat nothing but lean proteins, fruit, and leafy vegetables in all colors of the rainbow, you are probably getting all the vitamins you need. Is that how you eat?

Elisabeth pointed out that vitamins and nutritional supplements are not monitored or researched by the FDA, so it's worth your while to find ones where the manufacturers have done the studies and research themselves. She herself takes omega-3 capsules, a daily probiotic, and prenatal vitamins.

• **Omega-3:** "Take omega-3, not omega-6," she said. "This is actually proven by the FDA and drug companies to restore a good balance of triglycerides in your bloodstream...I take it to justify the fact that I'm also taking in pizza and beer. It's the least I can do for my body to make up for all the shit I put into it."

• **Probiotics:** These are the healthy strains of bacteria that make up your body's flora and keep tabs on all those malevolent bacteria.

"Between 60 and 70 percent of your immune system resides in your gut," she said. "So every time I take one of those, I have thirty billion more little bugs fighting in my favor."

Step 316: When you get a prescription, read all the enclosed information

Make sure that it doesn't interact with other prescriptions (or habits) you may have. Some antibiotics make birth control ineffective. Others will make you violently ill if you drink more than a glass of wine. Ask your pharmacist about it.

Finally, even though prescriptions seem safe despite the thousands of possible side effects, know that there are side effects and that this is a risk you take. A small pill that effects a systemwide change is not something to mess around with, particularly if you're taking other ones, too. Take it as prescribed, and if you have any concerns about it, call your doctor before you take it. Also, if you're taking antibiotics, take all of them, as prescribed, even if you feel better. Otherwise, your urinary tract infection or whatever it is may well retreat and come back stronger and crueler than ever.

Note: Carry around a little card in your wallet that lists any medications you take, as well as the dosage. This could save your life if you're in a car accident. You need to be able to tell doctors what is already in your body so they can make the correct decisions as to what will be safe and what won't.

Step 317: Don't time-travel on the weekends, especially if you do an eight-to-five schedule on weekdays

"If you don't go out until 11 PM, you get in at 4 AM, and sleep until 2 PM...and you go back to your eight-to-five schedule, that's like traveling to another time zone every time you do that," Elisabeth said. "If you think that jet lag is bad and messes you up, think about the fact that you're doing that every weekend."

This is not to say you can never go out. But think about if it's possible to do that in ways that aren't radically different from your weekday schedule.

Step 318: Wash your hands. Really. And don't touch your face

"All day long, I touch sick people. And truthfully, the one way to avoid getting sick yourself is to wash your hands frequently, and get out of the habit of touching your face," Elisabeth said. "You have a beautiful face. Look at it all you want, but don't touch it. Just say no."

A reminder that good hand-washing involves at least thirty seconds and vigorous scrubbing—that's what breaks down the cell walls of the bacteria. Also, if you can avoid touching things that a million other people have touched—if you can open the door with your hip, for example—you'll be better off.

If you don't get sick that often, then yay! Continue to not worry about it. If you do, and if missing a few days of work isn't possible, then get good at hand-washing.

Step 319: Keep hydrated, especially on airplanes

I used to get sick every time I stepped on an airplane, because airplanes are essentially germ canteens hurtling through the sky. But my uncle Tom suggested that I get a saline nasal spray, and it's worked wonders.

"You naturally secrete antibodies in all your mucous membranes," Elisabeth said. "And of course you can blow your nose and flush that stuff out. But when [the membrane] is dry and cracked, the germs stay there and flourish."

Side note: If you're blowing your nose and the output is anything but clear, that's a sign that you may have a sinus infection.

Step 320: Wear sunscreen (or stay in the shade)

Decide now which is more important to you: a tan or skin that still looks nice when you're fifty. Some of us don't have a choice, because we're genetically deficient redheads that can't be in direct sunlight for more than ten minutes. But even if you didn't lose the melanin lottery, it's still a good plan to put on sunscreen daily.

I have found my sunscreen soulmate in Elta MD Physical, which is sort of a tinted moisturizer that makes my skin clearer. Even if this is not for you, somewhere in this world there exists a combination moisturizer–daily SPF protectant that won't bother the hell out of you. Get used to putting it on every day, even (especially) when it's cloudy.

Step 321: If there is an optional choice you're making that's hurting your body, knock it off

Here, I think about cheap high heels, but this applies to all sorts of things. Pain is your body's way of registering that something bad is happening to it. If that pair of heels makes your feet cramp every time you wear them, then stop wearing them. It doesn't matter how cute they are. The whole point of maintenance is making sure that you're not permanently hurting or damaging something up through carelessness, and that includes active carelessness as well as the passive kind.

DISCUSSION QUESTIONS

1. Why are healthy things so boring? Why are comfy shoes so ugly? What is the meaning of all this?
2. What's the most responsible, dull expenditure you've experienced in the past month?
3. What is the most high-maintenance item that exists in the entire world? Do you think it's the Large Hadron Collider? I do.

Chapter 8
FRIENDS AND NEIGHBORS

You probably already learned this through any number of cheerful preschool songs, but friends are some valuable-ass people.

They don't need to hang out with you; they're not obligated to give you their affection; they don't have to have you in their life. *They choose to.* Most of them don't even want to have sex with you! So treasure them. Work hard to deserve their affection, and give them yours freely. Initially, you don't owe them anything, and they don't owe you anything. Once you've chosen each other, decide to care about them enough that you'll get up in the middle of the night to drive them home after they get freaked out by a regrettable hookup's bird-eating spider. Don't Google that.

When you're little, friends are like weather. Some are better, some are worse, but they're more or less always there. But it's harder than we expect to make and keep them once you're working and living on your own. As my friend Nancy pointed out, she could go to a bar any night of the week and find a man to sleep with her (**Note:** She does not actually do this. But she *could.*) Meeting friends, not so simple. Finding and solidifying a friendship isn't difficult, but it is daunting and ill defined, unlike the obvious course that bar hookups travel. But the rewards are great, and less likely to send you to the ob-gyn to figure out what, exactly, is happening in your crotch.

Also, know that when you get out of school, it's likely—not certain, but likely—that if you move to a new place, you will spend a while feeling very alone. One of the many shocks that come from graduating is that for the first time ever, we're not surrounded by a giant cohort of clear potential friends. Sure, there are work friends, but from here on out it is going to be a little trickier than it was in your hometown or at your college. You have to push through this— you can and will make friends. It just won't happen at summer-camp speeds where you meet someone at noon and by 5 PM they're your best friend ever.

Step 322: Assess honestly your own friendship needs and wants

Some people have the time, energy, and boundless affection to have thirty-seven really close friends. Some people want two close friends, and fifteen people they can call to go out dancing with on a random Friday. Some people want one really tight-knit group. All of these are 100 percent reasonable social needs.

Our model for someone who does well in friendship is someone with a zillion friends, who is never alone, who can conjure twenty people at a bar with nothing more than a mass text. For some, this is indeed what they want. But it's okay if that's not what you want—if you're a quieter, shyer person who would rather have a small handful of people you're genuinely close with.

Step 323: Decide that you are going to have an amazing group of friends

Sarah Von Bargen of yesandyes.org is one of the best friends I know—not in that we're best friends (although I would be delighted if that were the case) but in that she is great at being a friend, and as such had some choice insights.

The first step to making friends as a grown-up, Sarah said, is to decide you want it.

After grad school, she said, she found herself in a new city. "I literally was like, 'I want this sort of social life where I go to backyard parties and barbecues, and I want a group of friends that's smart and interesting and engaging, that does fun stuff, and I'm going to find a way to make this happen,'" she said. So how did she do that?

Step 324: Go to places that have the kinds of people you want to be friends with, then ask them on a friend-date if they're even vaguely promising

Friendship-making is not all that different from dating.

"You put yourself in situations where like-minded people are going to be, and then you talk to them," Sarah said, adding that she would do things like go to the all-women climbing night at the local rock climbing gym.

"I'd take an existing friend with me, and then we'd chat with other girls while we were waiting to belay, and then I'd say, 'Do you guys want to go get a beer with us?'"

Not everyone is as outgoing as Sarah, and this is stressful in the same way that asking someone on a date is stressful. Anytime you say to someone, even in a very veiled way, *I care about you. Do you care about me?* it's scary.

But almost everyone will be pleased that you took the initiative. And if they're not delighted by your straightforward friendliness, there you go! That is a bad friend candidate, and it's good you won't be wasting any more time.

Step 325: If you like them, announce your intention to become friends

Sarah suggested this, and it instantly made me burn with desire for someone to say this to me.

"If I really connect with someone, I just full-on say, 'We're going to be friends.' And 100 percent of the time, they're like, 'Yeah!' . . . I navigate life by saying the super-direct, awkward thing we're all thinking. I'll say, 'You're awesome. I want to be friends. Let's hang out.'"

So if Sarah had met this person, say, at a house party, she'll announce intentions to find them on Facebook, then send a message saying, "Hey, it was great to meet you. I know you're also into amazingly awful movies, and my friends and I are going to go see a screening of *Showgirls*. Wanna come?"

Step 326: Find friends through your other friends

If someone is smart and fun, chances are good their friends are similarly great. If there is a friend-of-a-friend you see a lot in group social outings, go ahead and grab coffee or a beer with them one-on-one and solidify that friendship.

"Take the initiative to hang out with them individually, to be friends outside the circle," Sarah said. " 'It's great to see you at these parties; I want to be friends for real.' "

Step 327: If you and your friends all want to expand your social circle, think of creative ways to do that

Sarah said that once every few months, one of her friends has a dinner party where she invites maybe five people, and asks everyone to bring someone new, often someone who has just moved to town or maybe recently broke up and is in the market for new friends. Which brings us to...

Step 328: Be nice to new people

Being new to a place or job is like being really sick. When people show you a small amount of kindness, it feels like a great deal of kindness, because you're so nervous/stressed/anxious/lonely/unable to swallow solid foods.

You don't need to go over the top, but stopping by to introduce yourself and issue an invitation goes a long way. If they're new at work, invite them to grab a cup of coffee that afternoon. If they're new in the building, let them know that you'd love to answer any questions about the neighborhood—where the best pizza is, which scary neighbors to avoid, and so on. You can even pull the old-fashioned, still-classy move of bringing the new neighbor a pie.

If you've ever been new in a non-friendly place, you know how awful it is. All of us, sooner or later, will be new somewhere, hoping there are decent people around. Be those decent people.

Step 329: Find a thirty-something (or older) friend

One of the distinct pleasures of being a grown-up is that all of a sudden, the age range of your friends widens drastically. You can actually be friends with someone old enough to be your mom, and not in the "You're my friend's mom and you like me as a secondary child" kind of way. Also, truism: People who are older than us are smart, and interesting, and know so, so much more about life than we gave them credit for when we were asshole teenagers.

A big part of my inspiration for this book came from a trio of friends I had at my first reporting job in Mississippi, when I was twenty-one. Nancy, Henrietta, and Rachel were all between five and nine years older than me, and they were *so fucking smart*. They would do things like (gently) tell me not to wear cocktail dresses to work, or why a certain relationship would or wouldn't work, or, in one Very Special Episode of Preparing Kelly To Fend For Herself, how to cook a chicken breast.

These things, in retrospect, seem obvious, but they weren't to me. Not because I was stupid, or ill prepared for life, even though I sort of was. There are just lots of things that someone who is twenty-seven knows, thanks to the five extra years of experience being on their own. There are even more things that someone who is thirty-two, and has ten years under their belt, knows. If you apply this principle to the workplace, it seems obvious that someone with years of experience will understand things a new guy won't. But we don't give others the same amount of credit when it comes to understanding general life preparation.

So if you can find a friend who will tolerate you, and take you under their wing, this is the way to go. And someday you, too, will patiently explain how a French press works to a bright-eyed but confused young thing. It's the circle of basic competence.

Step 330: If you haven't seen someone in a while and you miss them, spend the thirty seconds to reach out rather than angsting about the lost friendship

Getting in touch doesn't have to be a huge deal. Text them and say, "Hey, I miss you. We're overdue for a drink; let's catch up."

"You can think, *Why don't my friends do that to me? Why do I always have to be the one who does that?*" Sarah said, but then pointed out that a lot of people just aren't like that—they're busy or just aren't conscientious about that sort of thing. But they'll almost always respond if you start. If they don't respond two or three times in a row, then know that the burden of communication will probably always be on you. Some people are flaky but totally worth it. Some people aren't. Make that call.

Step 331: Do well in your long-distance friendships

Distance is what shows you whether or not something has long-term value. It's easy to fall away from someone who is out of your fishbowl, who no longer works with you, who every time you talk requires fifteen minutes of updates to be on the same page. But if this person is still a vital part of your life, they're worth holding on to.

A long-distance friend is like a cactus. They don't require a lot, but they do require some. Call on their birthday, or better yet, send a card. Be pen pals, because a postage stamp plus ten minutes of effort is a great way to make someone's day. Make sure you don't go more than three months without talking on the phone. Gchat. Keep someone in your life's orbit, and stay in theirs. Best of all, go visit.

Step 332: Be a fun-thing initiator

If you want to do more fun things, take some initiative. Usually, there's at least one social chair in any given group of friends—the person who seeks out fun things to do, then figures out who wants to come. Even if this isn't normally your role, step up to the plate at least once in a while.

Also, do not be discouraged if not everyone you invite shows up—people are busy. It doesn't mean they don't love you or don't want to see you.

Step 333: If there is something you want your friends to do, and it's important, spell that out ahead of time rather than being angry when people fail to read your mind

We are conditioned to minimize how important something is to us. But if it really is important, go ahead and say that—"You know, I know everyone's busy but it would mean a lot to me if you could make it."

If your feelings will be hurt if people don't show up to something, tell them that. It's an okay thing to say, so long as you're not doing it all the time. And, of course, so long as you are the kind of person who shows up for the things that are important to them, even if maybe they don't tell you that directly. A strong way to do that is . . .

Step 334: Pay attention to how your friends show affection

If you have a friend who fusses over you on your birthday, then fuss over them on their birthday. If you have a friend who is always, always ready to drop everything and talk to you when you're upset, do the same for them.

"If someone is really important to you, one of your closest friends, pay attention to how they show affection to you, because that's probably how they want affection shown to them," Sarah said.

For example, Sarah noted that she couldn't care less if someone came to watch her run a 5K, but for some of her friends, it's really important. And that's legitimate. Just because something isn't particularly important to you doesn't mean that it shouldn't be important to someone else.

Step 335: Tell the people you love why you love them

"My friend Darcie is the singularly most capable person I know," Sarah said. "And I tell her, to her face—'You are the singularly most capable person I know; you're great at everything.' I love her and I want her to know that."

I try, once a year, to write a letter to each of my closest friends and let them know why they mean so much to me, and why I am so damn lucky to have them in my life. Everyone wants to be acknowledged. Everyone wants to feel loved. There is no reason to withhold this from the people who are worthy of it.

Step 336: For goodness' sake, keep your friends' secrets

This is non-negotiable. If someone swears you to secrecy and you break their confidence, you are being a bad friend. I don't care how big your mouth is, figure out a way to keep it shut.

Remember that a lot of times, people sort of assume there to be a free and open exchange of information between significant others. So when someone tells you something, you can say, "Is it okay for me to tell Matt about this?" And if they say no, respect that. To protect yourself, if you are confiding in someone, be sure to ask them specifically not to tell their boyfriend or girlfriend if you don't want that person to know.

Step 337: Don't gossip about a friend with someone who doesn't love him as much as you do

I have a core group of five really close friends, and we've all known each other since we were twelve. If I tell one of them something, unless I swear them to secrecy, I'm sort of telling all of them because we're incorrigible gossips and spread secrets via osmosis. But the key here is that we all really love one another, and so when we talk about one another's actions, it's more a familial tightness than a need for idle gossip.

But I would never talk about one of those friends with someone who didn't love her like I did, because that would be disloyal. If her name came up in conversation with someone who wasn't as close to her as I am, I'd probably say something along the lines of, "You know, Amy is one of my very best friends and I don't feel right talking about her." Loyalty is one of the very loveliest of qualities, so do your best to show it.

Step 338: Don't freak out when friendships wane and wax, especially the long-term kind

If there's someone you've been dear, dear friends with since you were twelve, that is just *tremendous*. There is a very finite number of people in the world with whom you can honestly say that you've been friends forever, so that small handful of people is very, very valuable.

That being said, sometimes you'll go through periods where you have less in common, and see less of each other. It happens. Especially if you're in really different situations. If they just got married, say, or you have a kid, or one of you is in grad school while the other is working hard as an aspiring actor, you will probably have less to talk about. Don't throw it away or write the friendship off.

The value of the relationship is not in the uninterrupted continuity of same-level friendship, but in the fact that you can be friends at twelve, twenty, twenty-five. So don't freak out if you're not close friends for six months when you're twenty-three. You won't ever make any new old friends. Don't get mad at them, or yourself, if it's not exactly the same as it used to be. A lot of times you'll find that after a few years, you'll feel closer again.

Side note: Everyone knows that moons wane, but not everyone knows that they wax (get bigger). I move we reclaim the verb *waxing* from the painful hair removal sense, and instead use it to refer to the process of getting almost imperceptibly but steadily larger. This makes everything sound disgusting but also hilarious. "Y'all, my armpit fat is waxing something *tremendous* this summer."

Step 339: Monitor your friendships like you do romantic relationships

Friendships are more intuitive than romantic relationships, so we give them less scrutiny. But a lot of the same questions you ask yourself in a romantic relationship are valid in a friendship.

"When you're in a romantic relationship, people are proactive about communicating their needs and evaluating, 'Am I getting what I need from this relationship?'" Sarah said. "I don't think people do that with friendships, and they should."

To that end, she said, she pays attention: Has this friendship run its course? Is this person a toxic presence in my life? Are both of us getting what we need from this?

"If every time I hang out with them, I come away feeling down or like I'm just their unpaid life coach, what's the point?" she said.

Step 340: Do not treat your friends like your unpaid life coaches

It's just not fair. This should be a give-and-take, and if you are always taking, your phone will be quieter and quieter.

Your time together should be a heady brew of inside jokes, discussion of shared interests, interesting bits of gossip that are too juicy to share with the general public, and, yes, talking about things that are important to you. Discussing something that's forefront in your mind when necessary is one thing. Making every interaction into a soliloquy about Your Troubles is another. That shit gets exhausting. You know that.

Friends can and should be there for each other, and sometimes one party needs a lot more support and love than the other. But your friend can't be your psychiatrist, and it's not fair to ask them to be. If you have large, ongoing issues that take far more to work through than can be sorted out by venting over cocktails, it's a good idea to seek professional help (see step 463).

And if a friend always, always turns to you with problems that are beyond your friend-healing abilities, then it's fair to say—gently!—"You know, I know this stuff with your family is really, really hard for you, and I want to be there in any way I can. But I feel like a lot of this is deeper than what I can help you with. Have you maybe considered talking to someone?"

Step 341: Be supportive of depressed or heartbroken friends

Straight up: It is rarely as fun to be friends with someone when they are clinically depressed as when they are their normal selves.

But everyone, everyone, everyone goes through a hard time every now and again. Do not bolt when this happens. Do not interpret their silence or their sadness as a rejection of you. It doesn't matter that it's a pain in your ass; it's just what you have to do.

If they are struggling especially with depression or mental illness, it can be such a lifeline to say to them, "Hey, we've talked before about how you're going through depression, and I remember you said you wanted to get some help. Any updates there?" and then, if they say no, you can make some concrete, helpful offers: Could you look into what their insurance will cover or, if they're not insured, what low-cost services there are? Would it be helpful if you called around and got an appointment on the schedule? Do they want to just go for a walk? Et cetera.

Step 342: Celebrate your friends' big milestones with them (even if some very, very small part of you is jealous)

First, a note on jealousy: It happens. I get it. You are not a bad person for feeling that way, and oftentimes the envy comes when you're struggling and life is extra tough. You can't help what you feel...but you can help what you do about it. So, take a breath, remind yourself that comparison is the thief of joy, that this degree or marriage or first home was not the last one on the shelf and your friend grabbed it so now you will *never have one.*

Then, be so, so happy for them. Even if y'all hang out all the time, write a letter about how proud you are of them for earning that degree, or how happy you are about the engagement and what a wonderful person they're marrying.[1]

If you're especially close, a personalized gift can be so, so special. Etsy has a bajillion adorable and affordable necklaces that can have a date engraved on them or, if you're crafty, feel free to make something.

If it's a wedding, it's very kind to offer up help you can happily give and do well (see suggestions below). Housewarming gifts are always a nice touch even if they aren't having a party—my dear friend Kris gave me a hummingbird feeder and a recipe for the nectar they like and *now sometimes I get to see hummingbirds!*

A FEW QUICK WEDDING ETIQUETTE TIPS!

1. Do not ask if you are invited, and if you're not invited, you are welcome to feel hurt but do your best not to take it personally. Chances are pretty good that the couple would love to have you and not, say, every single one of their many, many great aunts, but it's not always up to them, and budgets are a very real thing.

2. If you are invited, yay! But if you know as soon as you get the Save the Date that you can't make it, whether you have a longstanding commitment that day or just will not be able to travel to it, it's nice to write the couple a sweet note saying how happy you are and how sad you are to report that you won't be able to attend. There may very well be someone they were dying to invite but couldn't, and now they can!

3. Technically, you have a year from the wedding to send a gift, but it's nice to get it over with. Also, there's no guideline on how

---

1. If you believe their beloved is the opposite of wonderful, well...just focus on how happy you are for them.

much you should spend. Take your finances into account and then get something you can afford. Also, you don't necessarily need to buy off a registry. If you are a creative and/or artistically talented person, you could either make something (a painting of the couple?) or offer something for the wedding (maybe serve as videographer?). If you are sending something, please actually send it to their house and don't bring it with you to the wedding.

4. YOU MUST RSVP. YOU MUST RSVP. THEY HAVE PROBABLY EVEN SENT A TINY ENVELOPE TO YOU FOR JUST THIS VERY PURPOSE. GOOD GOD, PLEASE RSVP.

5. Plus-ones! Sometimes you get one, sometimes you don't. If you don't (and if this is, indeed, a question of bringing a random date and not your significant other who wasn't invited), then for heaven's sake don't ask for one, because it implies that you will not be able to enjoy this very lovely and meaningful celebration without a human safety blanket by your side. Just ask the bride or groom ahead of time if there are any single folks you might be interested in. If you do have a significant other and they were left off the invite list, get in touch with a member of the wedding party and see if they can do a little sleuthing for you—it's entirely possible, especially if you live far away, that the couple has no idea you're in a new relationship. If they did know and your partner was left off the invite purposefully, well, perhaps that's something to consider when you're sending that RSVP.

6. An invitation does not mean you have to send a gift, but if you're RSVP'ing no, a note wishing them well is great. And if you do want to send a gift, by all means!

7. If you have questions in the days or weeks ahead of the wedding—what should I wear?, et cetera—ask a member of the wedding party or the family instead of the couple, who at this very moment has tens of thousands of questions to answer.

8. That's it! Show up looking nice (not wearing white or anything too showy), look appropriately moved and touched by the ceremony, make pleasant small talk during dinner even if you've been seated at the boring table. Stay at least through the toasts and voila! You are a hecking great wedding guest.

Step 343: Think long and hard before you agree to be a bridesmaid

Guys, or anyone who's been asked to be a groomsman, go ahead and skip this step because as far as I can tell, your only duties are buying a bunch of whiskey, showing up in a suit, and not throwing up *during* your toast (you may feel free to throw up during others').

But bridesmaiding? That can be very high stakes. Note that I said "can be," because of course there are many, many brides to be who are so relaxed and nonchalant about the whole thing that you begin to wonder if you should be getting stressed *for* them. (Answer: Absolutely *not*. Quietly and gratefully absorb their wisdom.)

But then...there are your other friends. The friend who has been *obsessed* with weddings as long as you've known her. The very, very highly strung friend who is a total perfectionist. There is the friend that—yay for her!—has a lot of disposable income and doesn't understand why you "never want to do anything fun," like go to a spa or super-fancy restaurant or small Mediterranean island with them.

It is this second set of friends you might want to pause before you squeal yes to. They are, I'm sorry to say, the ones who are more likely to ask for way more than you can give—or, when you can't write that eighth three-figure check for, say, catering at the second shower, imply that you don't care about them or their wedding.

Because fair warning: The same way breakups and moves can make people crazy, so can a wedding. Even if she or he is as down-to-earth as they come, there are likely a bunch of people weighing in on what they should be doing. There is the natural pressure of trying to warmly and thoughtfully host so many people you truly love. There's a giant interconnected web of dark forces implying that if he or she doesn't spend X on Y, then *is their love even real?* It shouldn't be this way, but it is.

So when you are asked by one of the less sensible ones—or, as is often the case, you just *don't* have the hundreds or thousands of dollars of disposable income to spend on someone's wedding—say sincerely and without hesitation, "Oh my God, Mia, I am so, so incredibly honored that you asked me. Seriously, this means so much to me. The only reason I'm not jumping up and down and screaming YES YES YES is that—and I'm a little embarrassed to say this—but money is super tight for me right now, and I'm worried about the cost of the dress and shoes *and* the flights to Majorca and Sardinia. I am so excited for you and Trevin and the last thing I want is for you to worry about this stuff, so I think I'm going to have to decline. But, may I..." and here, offer something that you *can* do.

Maybe it's help her out with addressing the envelopes because you have cute handwriting, or hosting a crafting party to make wedding décor. Maybe it's playing the piano, or singing, or offering to schlep stuff day-of so she and the wedding party don't have to worry about it. The idea is that you want to convey to her that you love her, you're so excited and happy for her, and you're eager to be a part of things (in a way that doesn't require you to buy a $350 [before alterations!] dress in a color best described as "membrane").

Here is something that I know, firsthand, to be painfully true: If you say yes when you mean no, and then feel resentful and angry at your friend for behavior that is bad but also 100 percent what you expected, it will hurt the friendship. It may even *end* the friendship if you are sufficiently resentful. It's hard to say no, but it's way better than saying yes and putting yourself in an incredibly frustrating situation.

Finally, if you are a bridesmaid, two words of wisdom:

1. Maintain your own boundaries. If you can't afford something, you can't afford something, and that's okay no matter what the mean-girl head bridesmaid in charge says.
2. During the wedding proper, *maintain a laserlike focus on the couple*. You will be tempted to gaze at the crowd. Do not do this, because the moment you do, a photographer will snap your picture and I guarantee it will be the one that ends up framed on the mantel where everyone looks lovely and you look like a golden retriever who just saw a squirrel.

Step 344: When your friends have kids, it will change your friendship

Real talk: It *should* change your friendship. If he or she has just as much time for you now as they did pre-baby, if they are totally down to meet you for happy hour with fifteen minutes' notice, these are signs that they should be focusing a little more on the "providing every single material and emotional need to a tiny, helpless human whose growth and development is almost entirely on their shoulders" thing. It's okay to mourn that, in some ways, this friendship may never again have the primacy that it once did.

It's also okay to have conflicting feelings, particularly if your friend does that "Oh my God, if you haven't had a baby, you *just have no idea what love is*! You can't even *imagine*! Before I had a baby, I *thought* I had things I cared about, but now? Oh my *God*. I'm pretty sure that only parents have emotions; everything before then is, like... okay, so you know the difference between looking at a postage stamp or standing in the Sistine Chapel? I'd say that's the difference, emotionally and spiritually. Also, once you're a parent, you care about the future! You have compassion for your fellow man! Because you can read their thoughts! You see up to twelve new colors!" thing.

It is totally reasonable to be (quietly) annoyed by this, but know that this is most likely temporary. Quietly relish your non-parental pleasures of sleeping in and almost never having someone throw up on you.

Step 345: But you can still have the friendship, even if it's a little bit different

For the first year especially, plan on visiting and helping them. Can you come by and drop off dinner? Would it be nice to have a quiet Friday in watching Netflix? Know that they are probably very sleepy, all of the time, and also know that they will not have a newborn forever. Babies really *do* grow up fast, and even if (like me) you are not particularly a baby person, it's rad to see a tiny human with your friend's beautiful smile. Plus, they only get cooler with time (the babies, that is, but now that I'm thinking about it, also the parents). Pretty soon, the baby will be talking and then making jokes and then calling you Auntie Kelly (or your name of choice), and pretty soon, your friend will be able to have non-baby social time with you.

Step 346: Remember that your new love interest is only moderately interesting to your friends

There are few times in life when you have So! Much! To! SAY! as when you've just started dating someone you're excited about. And since your friends love you, chances are that they are happy for you, too, and want to know all about this new person.

But remain aware that although this is a ten on your interest scale, it's probably a four on your friends', especially if you try to shoehorn your love into every topic they introduce ("Oh, you got a promotion? I think one time *Matt* got a promotion!"). Tell them about him or her and feel free to gush, but pay attention to their receptiveness/enthusiasm level. When it starts to flag even a little, it's time to change the subject. Life is long, and if it works out, you'll have plenty of other chances.

Here are some people whom you should not share your buoyant enthusiasm with:

- People who've recently filled their friend obligation of listening to you prattle on for one reason or another
- People who have suffered heartbreak and are unhappily single
- People who wish that *they* were the person you were now seeing

Step 347: Don't date your friend's ex

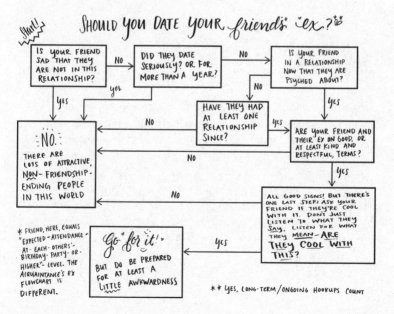

SHOULD YOU DATE YOUR friend's ex?**

Start!

IS YOUR FRIEND SAD THAT THEY ARE NOT IN THIS RELATIONSHIP? — No → DID THEY DATE SERIOUSLY? OR FOR MORE THAN A YEAR? — No → IS YOUR FRIEND IN A RELATIONSHIP NOW THAT THEY ARE PSYCHED ABOUT?

yes ↓ | yes ↓ | No ↓ | yes ↓

HAVE THEY HAD AT LEAST ONE RELATIONSHIP SINCE?

NO. THERE ARE LOTS OF ATTRACTIVE, NON-FRIENDSHIP-ENDING PEOPLE IN THIS WORLD

ARE YOUR FRIEND AND THEIR EX ON GOOD, OR AT LEAST KIND AND RESPECTFUL, TERMS?

yes ↓

ALL GOOD SIGNS! BUT THERE'S ONE LAST STEP: ASK YOUR FRIEND IF THEY'RE COOL WITH IT. DON'T JUST LISTEN TO WHAT THEY SAY, LISTEN FOR WHAT THEY MEAN—ARE THEY COOL WITH THIS?

Go for it! BUT DO BE PREPARED FOR AT LEAST A LITTLE AWKWARDNESS ← yes

* FRIEND, HERE, EQUALS "EXPECTED-ATTENDANCE-AT-EACH-OTHERS'-BIRTHDAY-PARTY-OR-HIGHER"-LEVEL. THE ACQUAINTANCE'S EX FLOWCHART IS DIFFERENT.

** YES, LONG-TERM/ONGOING HOOKUPS COUNT

Or do, but know Things Will Be Weird, almost no matter what.

Step 348: Tell your friends the truth about important things

When it comes to things of consequence, you need to be honest or you're not being a good friend. It's an issue of respect. They can handle it, and they deserve it. Be on their team. If your friend is dating someone who treats her badly, and asks your opinion of him, you should give it to her. If he wonders aloud about whether he has a drinking problem, and you think he does, say it. Once someone has ambled down an avenue of conversation, even if you think they will be upset by the answer, you should still give it. If they opened the Pandora's box, chances are they want a look inside.

These things are not comfortable or fun to say, particularly if you've been socialized to avoid bluntness. When you speak a painful truth aloud to a friend, it doesn't just hurt her; it hurts you, too. Because of this, it requires bravery, and it requires a vast ocean of love. Find them within yourself, for that person's sake.

SOMETIMES TELL THE TRUTH ABOUT UNIMPORTANT THINGS. SOMETIMES, DODGE

When someone asks you a question where the answer isn't, ultimately, important—Does this dress make me look fat? Do you like this new person I'm dating that you've met once?—sometimes they want a real answer, and sometimes they just want someone to tell them they're okay.

If it's the former, be diplomatic—"You know, that's not my favorite dress on you." If it's the latter, unless you feel like they are really and truly not okay, then say, "He seems great." If you're going to lie, lie convincingly and briefly, because the more you qualify, the more obvious the lie becomes.

Step 349: If a friend is fucking up their life, open your mouth and tell them

This may never happen, but if it does, you'll know because you will worry about them constantly and feel guilty about remaining silent. This happens rarely, because it's not particularly your job. This is a layer of responsibility above just answering honestly if they ask you about something. Unsolicited advice is rarely welcome and should rarely be given. If people want to know what you think about a given topic, they'll ask you.

However. However. If your friend is on the precipice of making (or continuing to make) a really, really bad, permanent decision, it's your job to tell them that. If they are throwing their life away to move across the country for someone who doesn't care about them, if they are about to marry a raging asshole, if they are missing work because they're too hungover from doing coke on a Wednesday, open your mouth, pass air through your vocal cords, and speak your piece.

This could mean an end to the friendship, at least for a while. This, too, will be painful, especially if your friend doesn't see the truth in what you've told them and doesn't make any changes. Know that sometimes, that stuff has to settle in, and that doesn't happen overnight. That can take months, or years, and they have to want to know the truth of what you've said. But eventually, hopefully, they will come around and realize that you did it out of love. Or maybe you were wrong, and you'll come around. Only time will tell, but if you don't say something and it will eat you up, then say something. If it's a really good friendship, it will survive.

Step 350: End a friendship, if need be

You are not obligated to be friends with someone, nor they with you, and sometimes friendships run their course. If you don't take pleasure in their company, if they always blow you off, or if they act too much like any of the frenemies (step 351), then you can end it without guilt. If you find that you're regularly not happy in their company, that's a deal-breaker.

If it's a casual friend and they call repeatedly, you can either do a boundary-setting get-together ("You know, I'd love to get a drink but

I really only have time for one because I have to be somewhere at seven thirty") or just avoid them.

But sometimes, people will poke at the wound, keep calling, wish to be absolutely and completely positive that you don't want them. If this is the case, an explanation may be in order. If you were close friends, an explanation will nearly always be in order.

If it boils down to "I just don't have that much fun with you," then that should probably go unsaid, since that will only hurt the person and not particularly do anything for them long-term. If there's something more specific, and sharing it will (a) not cause undue hurt and (b) have the potential to help them with future friendships, then phrase it diplomatically.

"Lisa, I feel like we spend a lot of time fighting and not that much time just being friends, and that our friendship seems to have this conflict always at the center of it."

"You know, you're always really down on yourself, and it makes me feel sad and down, too. It's hard."

Step 351: When faced with a frenemy, determine which type it is

Is this the undermining frenemy? The one who hangs out with you to feel better about her own life? The dear childhood friend who has become slowly but surely toxic in your life? A lot of times, we feel upset at someone but can't tell why exactly. Do your best to crystallize this to yourself, and your plan of action should become clearer.

The Seven Dwarfs of Frenemies:

- **Flaky:** Do you two have plans? How about now?
- **Flirty** (to your significant other): This girl needs you to accept the fact that she playfully jostles your boyfriend every few minutes because that's just who she *is*! She's just *friendly*! Oh my God, it doesn't even *mean* anything! You're not *mad*, are you?
- **Boasty:** This frenemy says something boastful but phrases it as a complaint about themselves so you're forced to comfort her, even though both of you know damn well that she isn't upset about looking too thin.

- **Crabby:** This frenemy can never, ever enjoy a single thing, but instead keeps up a monologue of misery and disdain. Never bring this person to a fun dance party, or a goofy movie, or to meet your new significant other. Spoiler alert: She won't like them. Because she doesn't like anything.
- **Backstabby:** This friend loves you soooooooo much! Except when you are between her and something she wants, in which case, fuck you!
- **Underminey:** No, that dress you bought looks…great! So you! It's awesome that you feel so comfortable with your body!
- **Doc:** This frenemy knows *exactly* what you're going through and has all kinds of advice. It doesn't matter whether or not you're actually going through this, because Doc has diagnosed so, so many things wrong with you. She's only trying to help. She's just doing this because she cares.

Step 352: Decide whether there are deal-breakers at play

There's better and worse things about all of us. And every single person you will ever engage with will have some less-than-ideal qualities. These are, as the brilliant Dan Savage put it, the price of admission.

So the question of whether or not this price is too high is a valid one. On one side, you've got whatever foolishness this person is pulling, and on the other you've got all their great qualities, difficult though they may be to see at this moment. And, of course, the difficulty and potential awkwardness of ending a friendship.

Step 353: Don't bicker on Facebook

Seriously, that is the worst. You know how, when someone is being unpleasant and nasty at a party, everyone else in the room is sort of cringing? Well, just remember that Facebook gives you the ability to make people all around the world cringe in unison.

Step 354: Learn to apologize

You know who loves apologizing? Nobody. Well, that's not true. There is a certain segment of the world that enjoys nothing better than a cringing mea culpa, and they will apologize all the damn time for anything. But the rest of us hate it.

But everyone must accept the fact that, at least on certain issues or certain actions, you will most assuredly be in the wrong. Many times! You're going to do something wrong today, I guarantee it. Which is okay, but if your wrongness hurt someone else, you need to acknowledge it, apologize, and try to do better next time.

How to make a good apology:

• Realize precisely what you have done wrong. You can't apologize in a meaningful way unless you actually regret what has happened. So tumble that in your mind. What did you do, what should you have done, what would you have done if you could do it again? These things all matter, and you can pick out themes to fold into the apology.

• You just need to be as humble as possible while at the same time not making excuses. You can explain yourself, but don't try to excuse yourself. That is their job.

• Be sincere in your regret.

So here is how a sample apology looks:

"Amy—listen, I just feel terrible about [action] because [reason why what you did is shitty]. I don't know what I was thinking, except [if there is a *very* pertinent bit of exculpatory evidence it may go here so long as you make it clear that this is not an excuse]. Honestly, if I could do it again [something that would have been better for everyone]. I'm very sorry, and I hope you'll forgive me."

Step 355: Graciously accept the apologies of others

It is so, so hard to cough them up. So when someone has gone through this difficult gestation, labor, and delivery, you need to be gracious about it.

Even if you are still really angry, you can say, "I forgive you." Say it with the amount of sincerity that you will feel about the apology in two months.

Step 356: Do not graciously accept apologies for the same transgression again and again

Remember in the step about apologizing, how you need to do better next time? Well, that holds for other people as well. Some things are human nature. Some things are people's nature and will not be changed. But if you keep getting the same actions, followed by the same apology, you need to accept that this is a thing this person does.

Step 357: If you really can't accept an apology, then let them know in a calm way

Some things, put simply, are indeed unforgivable. They are friendship-enders. There is no need to go through a list of them, although I think it's fair to imagine that at least 60 percent of them involve a significant other and/or the opposite sex.

Now. If you feel like you can forgive them eventually but are just really enjoying the groveling, then by all means, let it continue and enjoy. But if you know that no amount will make a difference and you are done with this person, then you need to say something like this:

"Listen. I know you're sorry, and I appreciate you letting me know that. I really don't feel like we can be close anymore, and I need you to respect that. If things change, I'll let you know."

Step 358: Find a strong, deep sea of insincerity to be sort of sweet to people you dislike

For the regular, run-of-the-mill enemies, you should conceal at least some of your distaste. You don't need to treat them like an actual friend. The key word here is *cordial*. Never be openly hostile. Exchange unenthusiastic pleasantries, then, sort of scoot away and you have fulfilled your decent-human-being obligations.

FRIENDS AND ENEMIES
IN (OR NEAR) THE HOME

Being friends with your roommates and neighbors is the absolute best, because not only can you get drunk together and then totter home down the hall, but you also always have a perfect pet-sitter. And vice versa (see step 33, on giving them a key).

But the incredibly close and, in many cases, unchosen proximity is a petri dish for the bacteria of chilly resentment. No one wants this—after all, one of the best things about being at home is that there is no one there to hate.

Step 359: The first time you see a new neighbor, introduce yourself

You don't need to be Welcome Wagon about it (although you should; see step 328). Just say, "Hi, I'm so-and-so. Did you just move? Oh, neat. Yeah, I've been here a couple of years; it's a great building. Well, if there's ever anything you need, just let me know!" Then, give them your phone number unless they seem crazy. This way, they can call you rather than the landlord when you're listening to music too loud.

Step 360: Follow standard escalation procedure with neighbors who are doing wrong by you

1. Don't make your first step the landlord. That's chickenshit. Give the offender the benefit of the doubt. Knock on their door and state your issue in a calm voice that says, *Hey, you probably didn't know this was bothering me, but it is. Would you mind helping to solve the problem?*

Sample dialogue for a neighborly problem:

"Hi! Sorry to bother you. I'm Kelly and I live upstairs in 4D. I just wanted to let you know that your music is pretty loud [**Note:** If it's sex noises, just say that there's a lot of noise] and I was hoping you could turn it down; I work early."

Then, when they apologize, smile graciously and say, "Oh, it's not a huge problem. I figured you didn't know," which lets them feel thoughtful and kind when they comply with your request.

2. If it happens again, write a note. Yes, notes are the most passive-aggressive form of communication possible. But at least they don't have to respond.

Dear so-and-so,
I have to tell you that the loud music is still bothering me. The walls are thin, and I work early. Could you please turn it down around [specific nightly time]?

Best,
Your name

3. If it happens a third time, get the landlord involved.

Hint that you are terrifically unhappy and will have to reconsider your living situation if the problem doesn't improve, and you know that you're not the only tenant bothered by this. You hate to get them involved, but could they please say something?

Step 361: Be a good, quiet neighbor generally

The music and sex noises of others are never as great as the ones you produce. It is nearly guaranteed that your neighbors feel the same way. So keep that in mind, and be reasonable about quiet hours.

Step 362: If there is an issue with a roommate, discuss it calmly and do not allow pressure to build until it explodes

If you're living with someone, chances approach 100 percent that there will be at least one thing you disagree on, and that is okay, and you can discuss it and find a solution like adults. But not if you first spend 11.5 months fuming and compressing your anger into a brilliant diamond of rage.

The third time you notice the thing that upset you, calmly put it out there in a non-judgmental way; say that it bothers you and you want to figure out a solution.

Example: "Hey, I feel like the dishes aren't always being done in a timely manner."

Step 363: Don't leave passive-aggressive notes for your roommates

That is for stranger neighbors only. If it's your roommate, you can say it to their face.

Step 364: Leave before things become unbearable

Moving is a total pain in the ass (see steps 55–66). But sometimes it's the only way. If you find yourself dreading your at-home hours, then consider whether the living situation is right for you. Don't ride it until the wheels fall off and the friendship is ruined.

Step 365: Be the kind of friend that you want to have

This is what it all boils down to. Listen when they bitch. Tell them they'll be okay. Go over and check in on their cat when they're on vacation. Call them on their birthday, or better yet bake a cake in the shape of their initial. Keep their secrets. Treat them like what they are— the rare person in this world who gives a fuck about you not because they have to, but because they want to. Give a fuck about them.

DISCUSSION QUESTIONS

1. If you are going on a friend-date, is it appropriate to try to hold hands during scary parts of the movie? (No. [Unless they're a super-cool friend, in which case they'll be down with it and HOLD ON TO THEM TIGHT, FOREVER.])
2. Which is a more important friend quality, honesty or someone who wears the same size shoe as you and is willing to lend and forget?
3. Agree or disagree: The most amazing friend move of all time is to make someone a homemade Pegasus-Unicorn piñata on their birthday and hang it above their desk. I love you, Ruth.

Chapter 9
LOVE

Oh, love. It's great, except when it's awful. Let's talk about how to maximize greatness while minimizing the terrible.

OVERARCHING DOWNER LOVE THEMES

Love is so complicated, so chaotic. But there are a few ways to responsibly approach what is, in the end, the point of humanity (or at least the future; if everyone stopped having sex tomorrow, eventually there would be no more people).

Step 366: Accept that heartbreak is inevitable, and realize that the only way to be a full human being is to experience it at least once

Let's get the bad news out of the way right up front so we can move on to the delightful aspects of romance. There is nothing you can find, read, or do to guarantee you will find true love or prevent you from experiencing pain in the course of its pursuit.

But if you are paralyzingly terrified of heartbreak (and her sister, loneliness), then you will never really experience the good stuff, because you'll be too consumed by the specter of the bad.

No one likes pain (emotional pain, anyway), and everyone feels it. The quicker you accept that your heart *will* get broken at one point or another, that you will *not* die from it, and that it will in fact make you a fuller, more compassionate human, the better off you'll be. You don't need to dwell on it, just like you don't need to constantly think about your own mortality. But you need to be at least somewhat cool with it.

> *Terrible Awareness-Society Idea:* The Mortality Awareness Association (MAA), dedicated to reminding people they'll eventually die. This will be the least popular cause ever, and everyone will dread when it's pledge-drive time. ("Hello, this is Kelly calling from MAA. Can I speak to you for a moment about the ever-present threat of death? Did you know someday, no one will ever remember you existed?") Granted, so far this chapter has been a little MAA-ish, but it'll get more positive soon, I promise.

Step 367: Don't unnecessarily cause others' heartbreak; don't perpetuate or cause your own

Don't casually hurt people who love you, even if you don't love them. This is not good for your soul. And yes, lots of times the best way not to hurt someone (or to minimize the damage, anyway) is to break up with them.

On the flip side, you need to have enough dignity and self-worth to walk away from something (or, more likely, someone) that is bad for you. If you stick around and accept less than what you deserve, that's on you. You cannot rely on others to do what is best for your heart. It's yours, not theirs.

Step 368: Love is still, always, worth it

You know this. I don't have to tell you what love means. The pain-to-payoff ratio could be four times worse, and we'd still do it.

On to the steps! We'll start with singleness, then move on to dating, relationships, and (sigh) breakups.

Step 369: Be cool about being single

A few people really love being single. You don't hear it much from them, because people who are *actually* happy with singleness don't spend a bunch of time telling everyone how great it is. They are too busy going out dancing and having exciting sex with attractive strangers. Or they're the kind of self-fulfilled, joyful people who have an all-consuming yet productive hobby, like yoga or parasailing or bonsai. They feel no need to defend themselves, because we're all jealous anyway.

And then there's the fairly large mass of people who are single who aren't super-duper excited about it, and that's just fine. Don't let all the jokes about sad single people get to you. Not having a significant other and wanting one doesn't make you a sorry cliché or traitor to feminism.

It's reasonable to feel lonely if you're single and don't want to be. *Sometimes.* But you should also take pleasure in the freedom to flirt, and have the adventures/misadventures that will happen before you find your favorite. Ahead of you lie not only first kisses but also first-make-out-against-a-wall-for-twenty-wonderful-sloppy-enthusiastic-minutes sessions. Those are *great* and rarely happen after month three of a relationship.

Step 370: Learn to enjoy your own company

The valid solution to sad singleness is not an end to the singleness; it's an end to the sadness. Buck up and learn to enjoy the pleasure of your own company. Remember, you could find the world's most perfect dude or lady, be insanely happy with each other, and then he or she could get run over by a bus tomorrow. Be a full, intact person on your own.

The best part is, when you're okay being alone, you *choose* to be with someone rather than *needing* to be with someone. And choosing is key. When you fall in love, you choose them and they choose you. No one is stuck somewhere they don't want to be. Strive for that, not partnering up out of desperation so you don't have to be alone with your thoughts.

Bonus step: Have dance parties for one when the fancy strikes. Ideally, your soundtrack will be a bunch of songs about how great you are, like Daft Punk's "Harder Better Faster Stronger" or pretty much anything by Beyoncé.

LOOKING AROUND FOR SOMEONE

Step 371: Ask someone out

This goes for both ladies and men. The process itself is pretty simple if terrifying, sort of like giving birth. But it gets easier with time.

If you're interested in someone, and you think they're interested in you, the only way to find out is to ask them out. Then you'll have your answer. Don't spend a bunch of time pining for someone who's either unavailable or too dense to pick up on your fine, fine qualities. The key here is to not be ambiguous, even though that makes it even more nerve-racking, because the intention in asking someone out is to clear up any remaining ambiguity. And, mainly, to get you a date.

Here's how it should work:

"Hey. I think you're great. Do you want to go get [coffee/drinks/dinner] sometime?"

Don't qualify it with *if you're not busy* or *you know, just a casual thing*. No need to undersell yourself or anticipate rejection. Just put a period at the end of that statement. A metaphorical period, obviously, since it's a question.

A SHORT LIST OF PEOPLE WITH WHOM IT IS 99.5 PERCENT GUARANTEED TO END BADLY:

- Someone you find physically but not emotionally attractive (or vice versa)
- Someone who is married
- The significant other of a close friend or family member
- Someone you have already broken up with at least twice
- Someone more than seven years behind or ahead of you in Emotional Maturity Years
- A person you find insanely attractive but is so-so about you

- Someone who is mainly attracted to a gender that you are not, but is making a rare exception
- Scorpios

Step 372: Don't be friends with someone you're romantically interested in, hoping they'll change their mind

I've been on both sides of this equation and can safely report that it will result in nothing but frustration and/or hurt feelings.

When you are the object of affection, it introduces unsettling questions about whether someone genuinely enjoys your company or is just hoping that if they persist for long enough, they'll see you naked. Guys, y'all do this a lot and it is *not* a great strategy. It forces straight women to give every intergender friendship the side-eye.

When you're on the other side, those tiny bright bursts of happiness you get from seeing this person will never equal the slow trickle of anguish that comes from pretending they'll come around.

If you like someone, say it. And if things don't go your way, then at least you aren't throwing good feelings after bad.

Step 373: Just because someone rejects you does not automatically make them a bad person

It's counterintuitive, but just because someone doesn't want to date you (or continue to date you) does not mean they are an awful person with no taste who will likely die alone.

So while rejection always hurts, pay attention to the *way* you were rejected or broken up with. Was the culprit decent about it? Were they straightforward? Did they behave in a way that implies that they understand you are a person, with feelings and pride?

If the answers there are yes, yes, and yes, then that person is a fine individual who, for whatever misguided reasons, doesn't want to be with you. Forgive them for it (in time) and accept that they aren't some kind of heartless monster. It will help you get closure (see step 431) insofar as that even exists.

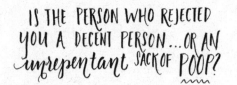

IS THE PERSON WHO REJECTED YOU A DECENT PERSON...OR AN unrepentant SACK OF POOP?

IN OUR MINDS:

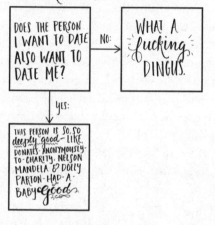

DOES THE PERSON I WANT TO DATE ALSO WANT TO DATE ME?

NO: WHAT A *fucking* DINGUS.

yes:

THIS PERSON IS SO, SO *deeply good*—LIKE DONATES-ANONYMOUSLY-TO-CHARITY, NELSON MANDELA & DOLLY PARTON-HAD-A-BABY *good*

IN REAL LIFE:

DOES THE PERSON I WANT TO DATE ALSO WANT TO DATE ME?

yes: MAYBE SHE/HE IS A COOL, DECENT PERSON; MAYBE THEY SUCK. ONLY TIME WILL TELL.

NO:

Step 374: Don't be unkind to someone because they're interested in you

If they like you and you don't like them, they don't deserve scorn; they deserve kindness. (Please note that kindness does not equal giving false hope. In fact, that is the opposite of kindness.) Don't laugh in their face; don't automatically hate a club that would have you as a member. Be flattered, be kind. But don't lead them on.

ONLINE DATING

Full disclosure: I met my current boyfriend on Tinder; our first date was at a truck stop the night before Halloween, because life is short and why the heck not?! In my defense, it was halfway between our cities and I *thought* that it was the World's Classiest Truck Stop per billboards I'd seen (turns out that was a *different* truck stop).

At the time, I'd come to the *entirely reasonable* position that after I got unmarried, I would never find love, or indeed any sort of romantic relationship, ever again. I would live out my days triumphantly single; I would establish a Gynocratic Palace where my best girlfriends and I would raise our children together and sometimes men would be allowed in for sexytimes.

I was excited to get to use Tinder and such, as I'd totally missed this era of dating. I assumed this was a gritty, bodily-fluids-soaked way of finding sexfriends who would be quickly discarded. Then, a couple weeks into it, I swiped on a dude who didn't have much of a profile and who looked waaaaaaay too outdoorsy for my taste and here we are and things are just so comfortable and easy.[1]

Almost everyone meets on the internet (and apps) nowadays. There is absolutely nothing wrong with online dating; just think of it as a big big big big party with all the single people in your area.

Buuuuuuuut! Even though it can really feel like a game, it's not, and the rules of decent human engagement still apply. Off we go!

Step 375: Meet in person ASAP

The rest of these steps are more or less chronological, but this one is so very important, beloved pelicans: Meet in person *as soon as humanly possible*. Do *not* build a texting/chat/whatever relationship with this person until you've laid eyes on them. Chemistry is a frustrating and impossible thing, and it will be terribly disappointing to both of you if you've built up something that twists of biological fate will not support (see step 396).

---

1. On our anniversary, we explore a new truck stop, because we are so classy and also I love doing all my Christmas shopping at truck stops.

Maybe that face that looked so good in pictures looks alarmingly like your uncle in person. Maybe their lips make a smacking noise that isn't okay even once, let alone every few seconds. Maybe they are three clever hedgehogs dressed up as a human. You won't know until you meet in person.

Step 376: Say something (but not tooooooo much) about yourself in your profile

It doesn't have to be brilliant. It shouldn't have dumb jokes you copied off the internet. You can say what you're looking for—if you aren't looking for anything serious (or if you *are*), it's good to let other humans know that so everyone goes in with necessary info.

Do not focus on what you don't like; focus on what you do. Actually, that's a good principle in nearly all our affairs, but *especially* dating profiles. Do you want someone to go backpacking with? Or, like me, are you seeking someone who wants to watch an entire season of *BoJack Horseman* while eating Popeyes? Do not lie about who you are, because the goal is to find someone who wants to date you, not a weirdo alternate universe version of you where you're really into gardening and reading Pynchon.

You can put up some filters. My dear friend Kim has a picture of herself holding a very... *frank* sign at the Women's March on Washington, because that's who she is. If someone is turned off by that picture, well, they're not a very good candidate for her.

Step 377: Don't disparage the app or the process in your profile

You don't need to say that this is dumb, or you're going to delete it in a second, or that you have low expectations as to the quality of person you're going to meet—even if you truly think those things. Remember that not everything you think needs to be said aloud.

Even if you do feel that way, potential dates probably don't. Plus, as my friend Adam once pointed out when someone told him that he was always at X location—you're here, too. If your distaste for the entire process absolutely overwhelms your ability to express anything else, maybe just delete the app?

Step 378: Don't fret if there's a lag in communication

I know that it's frustrating. But people have actual lives and may have things like work or social engagements or anything in the world that's not a random stranger chatting into the void.

Hopefully if they're not interested, they'll let you know that kindly (and you should do the same). But this is a pretty low-stakes interaction before you've met in person.

Step 379: Be flexible, not flaky

The basic courtesies of human interaction still apply: If you make a date, you should keep it. Be on time, be positive, don't be late. I know that lots of people do not do this. Their bad behavior doesn't have to be yours!

Step 380: Meet for something quick, IN PUBLIC, and have an out

A first online date can and should be a low-stakes affair, particularly because it is very, very possible that as soon as you sit down you will know this person is not for you. And that's okay!

Coffee or beer dates: a good choice. Meeting at your/their house, or going backpacking together in Murderous National Forest: not good choices.

You can pull a move from my friend Cat, who always says she has an appointment in an hour—then, if she really likes the person, she'll say, "You know, I made that up in case there wasn't chemistry, but the truth is that I'm having a wonderful time and would love to keep hanging out, if you can."

Step 381: Be present with your date

It may be that this is clearly not a match, and that's okay. But no matter what your future romantic prospects are, this is a human who, like you, is vulnerable and has feelings and maybe spent a lot of time figuring out *just* what to wear on your date that you would think is cute.

Don't be on your phone, don't be dismissive, and whatever you do, *do not stack up additional dates behind this one.*

Step 382: Pay your half on the first date

There could be a whoooooooole discussion here on notions of money and power and patriarchy and ownership and blah blah blah but let's all skip it. Go dutch on the first date, bringing cash to make this transaction easy and seamless.

Step 383: Be honest but kind if you're not interested

I know that—especially for us ladies!—this can be really hard. But if you're an unambiguous FIRM PASS, it's the right thing to let them know.

Stay for the duration of your drink, then say, "You know, Cart,[2] it was lovely to meet you, but I don't think we're a good match. Thank you so much for your company."

Step 384: Those apps can make possibilities feel endless, and like no one person matters all that much. This is not true

On the one hand, it's a good thing that there will always be more matches, that if this one conversation peters out or there isn't a connection with the person you're sitting across from, well, that's okay! There are *so many more*!

But while there may be vast numbers of humans on this app, website, whatever, they are all, in fact, humans. Give people chances and, if you find that you connect with them, nurture that. Yes, there's lots of people in the world. But also, every single one of those people will be imperfect in at least three dozen ways for you. Human connection is still valuable and rare. While you can and should move on when something you were hopeful about doesn't materialize, don't forget that the humans matter.

---

2. If there is anyone out there who is actually named Cart, I'm sorry. That's tough, friend.

HOOKUP ETIQUETTE

Let's acknowledge that not all sex is in the interest of finding a soul mate. Sometimes, we don't have time for a relationship, or we're still hurting from a past one, and we just want to get laid. *There is nothing wrong with this*, so long as you're doing it in a way that isn't destructive to you or the other person.

Step 385: Friends-with-benefits situations can work, but only if the following conditions are met:

1. You genuinely like and respect them as a person and vice versa but
2. You have no desire to date them and
3. They have no desire to date you but
4. This doesn't hurt anyone's feelings.

This doesn't happen all the time, but when it does, it can be fantastic. Chances are good that within a few weeks or months, someone's heart will change and this will be washed away, a sand castle into the sea. So enjoy it while it lasts.

Be honest with yourself if emotions get involved, and talk to your partner if you see heartbreak on the horizon. If you don't feel comfortable talking honestly to them about what it is, ask yourself why. Are you secretly in love with this person and hoping your magical vagina will eventually bring them around? If so, that's not fair to them. Open your mouth and say what's actually up.

Step 386: It doesn't have to be a walk of shame. It can just be a walk

The morning after can be rough. Even if the person's being great, even if you had a good time, even if you're not even slightly hungover. If you're feeling bad, take a minute and remind yourself that you probably won't feel this way in a couple days. It is what it is, which is Not the End of the World. You did what you wanted to, you had fun, and that's that. If you feel this way over and over, skip to step 390.

Step 387: If you hooked up with someone the night before and they're being anything besides gracious and awesome the next day, fuck 'em

Should you find yourself greeting the morning in an apartment both unfamiliar and unwelcoming, there is no reason to slink out. I mean, you don't need to high-step, but whatever, you've done nothing wrong—they're the one who is being a jerk.

Gather your things—double-check that you are not leaving any beloved items behind, because the last thing you need is for this unworthy person to think you're fishing for a reason to contact them. Then square your shoulders back, thank them frostily for the nice time, and march on out.

Step 388: If you've been sexual with someone, treat them with respect and kindness

No need to have flowers delivered or anything, but you should be cordial and kind. This means acknowledging when you see them around, not shit-talking their performance or allowing your own complicated feelings to translate as unkindness.

Step 389: Don't kiss and tell (except with your closest friends)

It's just not terribly dignified. Adults don't brag about their sexual conquests. If someone asks, smile coyly and say something vague like, "Oh, yes, Seth is a wonderful guy. I'm very fond of him." Period.

Step 390: If hooking up makes you feel bad about yourself, don't hook up

There shall be zero slut-shaming in this book, because allowing others to experience their sexuality however they see fit is important. There are some people who hook up with minimal emotional attachment and they *love* it, and if you're one of those people, enjoy the hell out of it with like-minded people, and skip these next few paragraphs.

But there are other people for whom hooking up—that is to say, messing around with someone without commitment or the sort of closeness that comes with a relationship—is just no good. And generally speaking, you won't really know which kind of person you are until the morning after you hook up.

People in the latter category think to themselves, *This time*. *This time, it will be different, and fun, and I won't feel guilty, like all those other times*, but then, sure enough, they feel guilty. If you're one of those people, then acknowledge that about yourself and don't be self-destructive. Wait for the right thing. It'll happen.

Step 391: Don't use your sexuality as a weapon

Sexuality, obviously, can be super constructive. It leads to love and pleasure and intimacy and all sorts of other things. But sex can also be a wrecking ball. You can use it to damage others, to swing back at someone who hurt you, or to punish yourself.

If the way you are behaving sexually causes you or others anguish, then examine that and do your best to knock it off.

Step 392: Don't be a piece on the side

Think back on friends who have been the other woman or other man. Think about how many of them have said that the experience was *awesome*, it worked out *exactly as they were hoping*, and, once they finally had the cheater in their grasp, they found his or her character *totally changed*.

If you like someone who's in a relationship, it's okay to tell them, loud and clear, that you're into them. ONCE. Don't touch them while you do this. Then you must *drop it and move on* in the hope that they'll extricate *themselves* from a relationship that they were maybe not totally into.

Someone cheats on a significant other they're really into if they are a cheating kind of person. Hence the no-touching policy. But no one's going to break up with a significant other they're really into for the chance to date you.

Do not purposefully break up someone else's relationship. Not only is it a bad idea in the abstract karmic sense, but it will also be bad for you in the immediate term.

If you get involved with someone who is attached and accept a secondary, secret role, you establish yourself as someone who doesn't respect yourself enough to demand all of someone's affection. Also, make no mistake that you are getting involved with a cheater. People who cheat with you aren't doing it because they find you so irresistibly hot. Maybe you are, but they are the kind of person who finds *many* people irresistibly hot because they have poor boundaries and self-control.

If you don't want anything serious, don't care about how the third party feels, *and* the idea of bombing someone else's relationship really doesn't bother you, then fine. But it's silly to consider a future with that type of person.

Step 393: Don't date someone you're not crazy about, or who isn't crazy about you

This bit of advice came from my friend Max, and I honestly couldn't have put it better.

People project their feelings onto others since the feelings in their own head are the only emotional condition they are ever *fully* exposed to. So when we are just so, so burningly into someone, it feels like they must be so burningly into us, too.

But that isn't how feelings work. There is not an even exchange rate going there, so the best you can do is to look for someone who at least has a similar exchange rate to you. If your feelings are euros and theirs are vouchers for buy-one-get-one McFlurries, get out.

When you stay with someone you adore, and they don't adore you, you run your heart through a can opener. Constant tiny punctures until it's eventually a pulpy mess.

If the exchange rate is reversed and they are so super excited about you but you aren't excited about them, do the right thing and let them go. Do it for yourself, too, because it is painful to know you are slowly dashing someone's hopes and making them sad.

Note: This does not apply to the first couple months of a relationship.

You do not need to be batshit crazy in love the first time you hang out (though that is nice).

Step 394: Don't get into something you already want out of

During an episode of VH1's seminal *I Love the '90s: Part Deux*, celebrity dreamboat Michael Ian Black was discussing *Titanic* and unintentionally gave a perfect metaphor for these kinds of relationships.

"I was on the edge of my seat through that whole movie, saying, 'What's going to happen? *What's going to happen to this boat?*'"

What's going to happen to this boat, indeed?

Step 395: Don't try to feel something that isn't there

This one is big. Most of us have met someone who would be *perfect...* if only we were into them. It can be so frustrating to meet someone who seems ideal on paper, but who sparks in you little enthusiasm, like tofu. The temptation can be to date them in the hope that something will develop.

And you can do this... for a while. But if nothing grows, eventually you need to break it off. You will likely hurt this person who has been nothing but wonderful to you, and you will feel like a big piece of poop.

Your guilt is natural and indicative of the fact that you're not a sociopath. But the heart is complicated and doesn't ever fully explain itself. If you could have those feelings, you would. Don't beat yourself up if you don't.

Step 396: Chemistry matters

It shouldn't! It is so terribly unfair that it does!

But... it does. A lot. Once, I met someone wonderful who I was so, so into. Then, the first time we kissed, it was... underwhelming. And yet I persevered, because even if I'm a tiny bit repulsed by how he tastes and smells *today,* maybe I won't be... next week? Someday? There might be a time when I look forward to physical intimacy? Please, God, please let this little brick fall into place for me so I can marry this wonderful, smart, kind, lovely person?

How do *you* think this turned out? Go ahead and doodle your answer.

Yep. If it's not there, it's not there, and chances are good it won't *be* there. This isn't to say you need insane scorching chemistry to make love work. But there should be some biological drive there, particularly if you're a sensuous person.

DATING

Yaaaay! You like them and they like you and now it's time to *date*.

Step 397: Try to go on at least a couple of actual dates

Here are things that are not dates:

- Meeting up at a party
- Going to someone's house to watch movies
- Getting stoned and watching *Arrested Development*

All those things are fun, but they are also not, technically speaking, dates. Now that you are a grown-up, your goal is to get to know each other, and hopefully you don't need too many substances to enable that interaction (though a drink or two is permissible).

Things that are dates:

- Meeting for coffee one-on-one and then chatting happily for a few hours
- Strolling around a park, making entertaining observations about other people you see
- Going out to dinner, then sitting at a table for two and trying to impress each other by ordering the jellyfish

Step 398: Don't get drunk on the first date

Limit yourself to a few drinks. A drink, even. If you're too drunk to take a Breathalyzer, you're too drunk for a first date. No matter how much you love the booze, just take it easy for a couple of dates.

This also makes you less likely to have sex on the first date, which is, generally speaking, another bad plan.

Step 399: Hold your cards close to your chest, at least at first

The older you get, the more backstory there will be with the people you date. They will have been in love before, had their heart broken, gotten an STD, or experienced a serious loss that they still hurt from. And so will you. The trade-off, of course, is that as you get older you also get better at love.

But the first few dates are a time to circle each other, sniff cautiously, make sure no one is planning on making a suit out of anyone else's skin, and *then* commence the process of really getting to know the other. No need to reveal your deepest, darkest bits on the first few dates. Try to establish that you're both reasonable, levelheaded people first.

Note: You really should disclose any relevant health (read: STD) issues before you have sex. That is the decent, grown-up thing to do. To do this with accuracy, you need to get tested at least every six months.

In return, when and if someone reveals them to you, don't flip out. Lots of people have them, and if you're safe and cautious, they can be a total non-issue.

Don't drop this card on the table right before you have sex, either. People aren't good at processing important things when they're naked.

Step 400: Do be yourself on dates

Yes, you should be a good-behavior version of yourself, but don't make up a new persona. It's a fine line but you must, must be yourself. You can't fake being someone else forever; it just won't work. You don't want someone who is into a contorted projection of who you are; you want someone who is into you. So make sure they have a chance to see that. Remember, if you fake it, they will not think, *Oh my God, an incredibly hot astrophysicist who shares my love of curling! WHAT ARE THE CHANCES?!* They will think, *There is something off about this person and I don't know what it is.*

Step 401: Do give the necessary disclosures before or concurrently with any discussion of exclusivity

Here are some things that someone you are dating—really actively dating, and into, and maybe headed toward a relationship with—deserves to know:

- Any past marriages
- Any children
- Any chronic health conditions that may affect them, including mental health stuff

Things that you are never, ever obligated to reveal:

- How many people you've slept with
- Things you liked better about exes
- Unchangeable things about their personal appearance that bother you

Step 402: Don't discuss past loves overmuch

It seems so relevant. You're romantically involved with this person! You *were* romantically involved with *that* person! Maybe this would be a great time to introduce them into the conversation.

But it's usually not a great time, especially not on the first few dates. Bringing up an ex broadcasts that that person still looms large in your mind. More often than not, the other person will interpret your comments to mean that you are still not over your ex, and grown-ups don't date when they're still hurting over someone else (see step 436).

Step 403: Don't assume you're dating exclusively unless there's been a discussion

If it's been a month or so and things are going really well and you decide you *want* to be exclusive, then just say, "Hey, are we exclusive? I want to be." Chances are good that this will be a relief to both of you and the other party will appreciate your initiative.

And if they're not wishing to be exclusive, well, there you have it.

Step 404: Beware the dangers of New Boyfriend Narnia, and limit your own disappearance

It's so easy to disappear down a rabbit hole the first few months of a new relationship. If you're newly in love, it just doesn't make *sense* to do anything besides lie in bed together for days, gently stroking each other's faces and behaving in ways that are so uncool and so fun. It's the best, and lucky, lucky you. But remember that, although you may be so, so deeply and significantly in love in ways that no one else could ever understand, outside obligations do not disappear.

Your friends still want to see you; your mom still wants you to call; your work still wants you to show up; your cat still wants to be fed. Do all of those things you usually do, so that you may sail away on your dreamboat without guilt once those duties are met.

Step 405: Your significant other is not your best girlfriend

This assumes that you're a girl dating a boy, although this could also go for boys dating girls and girls dating girls and boys dating boys.

There are lots of things that are *fascinating* to you but maybe not so much to your significant other, and vice versa. Acknowledge that just as you might not want a blow-by-blow of the Giants game, he may not want every single detail of the latest interaction with your work nemesis, who is an unrepentant trout-mouthed bitch.

One person can never be everything to someone else. So talk about the things that interest both of you, feign semi-interest when the other one goes off on something unbearably boring, and eventually, gently re-route the conversation. And pay attention when they are re-routing you. If they are not giving responses when responses should logically be given, that means they are hoping you'll move on.

Step 406: Be cool doing things on your own. Actually cool, not just saying you're cool

Let's say you're a part of a couple like my friends Sarah and David. Both are social, outgoing people-people, but Sarah has a pretty firm window on how long she wants to be at a party.

Toward the beginning of their relationship, she let him know this.

"I said, sometimes we're going to go to a party, and after a few hours I'm going to want to go home. I'm telling you right now, it's not a trick; I'm not saying, 'No, it's fine!' when it's not fine. I'm going to go home and fall asleep in your bed, and when you come home I'll ask you about the party. I'm not going to be angry. You're enjoying yourself; why should you not stay and enjoy yourself?"

Do not take not wanting to spend every second pressed to each other's sides as evidence you're not a good couple. The best couples are cool when they're together and cool when they're apart. Wanting to do the same thing at every moment is a sign of nothing except a lack of imagination.

Step 407: Do not date someone because of what dating them says about you

When you think of significant others as status symbols, you likely think of trophy wives and Botox. But there's more to it than that. Sometimes you'll date someone because of how hot your friends think he or she is, or their status in the community, or how rich they are, or whatever outside rubric applies. This is not the right thing to do.

Date someone because of who they are and how they make you feel, not because of the external stuff. And trust: If you base your self-image and -worth on the fact that you are dating Mr. X, things will almost invariably go poorly for you. Remember that thing about the possibility of Mr. X getting smushed by a bus at any moment?

Step 408: Treat good-personhood as a basic dating qualifier

…which means, of course, that bad-personhood should be a deal-breaker. If someone treats other people poorly, eventually that behavior will extend to you, too.

This means different things to different people, so I can only speak in generalities that mean something to me. But is this person a good person? Are they kind to people regardless of whether that person can do something for them? Do they value honesty? Do you feel they are guided by an internal compass that is at least mostly in line with yours?

These qualities aren't necessarily the sexiest, and they don't reveal themselves immediately. You can look at someone and tell right away if they're hot. You can't look at a person and know what their internal architecture is like. Those are things that will reveal themselves, in ways big and small, and you *need to pay attention.* Because no one is hot when they're eighty. But some people will still be internally beautiful, and others will still be assholes. Which do you want?

Step 409: Ask yourself if you could happily chat with this person when you are eighty

This tip came from my friend Emily. As noted above, eighty-year-olds don't care as much as we do about boning. But when scorching chemistry is gone, you know what will remain, and even improve? Your

companionship. How happy you feel lying in bed next to this person, each reading a book the other has zero interest in. Your ability to work together to overcome obstacles. Your ability to understand and forgive each other, to accept the other's quirks, to chat happily over dinner. So assess those qualities. They are the important ones.

Step 410: Before you get in too deep, make sure you want similar things

Falling in love with someone who isn't right for you is as easy as falling down the stairs, and they both end pretty much the same way.

While the Big Questions of what you want—Marriage, or no? Kids, or no? Monogamy, or no? Living in Manhattan or a small town?—don't need to come up immediately, they definitely should at some point. And if it turns out you two are fundamentally incompatible, then you need to move on, painful though it may be.

Step 411: Don't date someone who is mean to you

Another one of those clichés that is true is that it's a cruel, cruel world we live in. But it's tolerable, because we find and surround ourselves with people whom we love and who love us, and together we function as a cushion against that cruelty.

But if the person you date is contributing to, rather than subtracting from, the sum total of unpleasantness and cruelty in your life, it's time to move on. Then maybe take a little while and figure out why that behavior is acceptable to you.

Lots of times, we act out dysfunctions we picked up when we were young in relationships. We all have buttons, good and bad, that people push. So if you're into someone, and you realize that you're into them *because* they push your fucked-up buttons, then take a minute and work on yourself.

Step 412: Know that it's not always easy or fun

Here is a list of things that are always easy:

- Lying in bed
- Watching reality television
- Eating a bunch of delicious pastry

Here are things that are always fun:

- Jet Skiing
- Looking at puppies frolic happily
- Eating a bunch of delicious pastry

You'll note that "long-term relationships" doesn't appear on either of those lists. Because yes, sometimes they're easy and sometimes they're fun and they should be both of those things much, if not most, of the time.

But if you bail the second it's not one or the other, you'll wind up lonely. Being in a real, grown-up relationship means deciding every day to love another person, even though sometimes they will annoy the everlasting shit out of you.

Everything needs maintenance. Loving someone is not a onetime thing, something earned once then secured forever. It's more like a human six-year-old, something delightful but also in need of vigilance and attention lest it fall out of a tree and break its wrist.

Step 413: Don't try to change people

If you need an improvement project to take on, then start a garden or take up woodworking or volunteer. Do not make someone your project, unless you are really into endless amounts of bitterness and frustration on your part and theirs.

Accept the person you are dating for who they are and who they are not. If that's not acceptable to you, then break up with them.

People can and do change. When *they* want to. You cannot do it for them. You can give them some Real Talk. If you love someone and care about them, romantically or otherwise, this is a responsibility you have to them. But you can't, in the end, make them into what you want them to be. It prevents actual growth on their part.

Step 414: It's about you two, and what you want, and that may or may not be what we traditionally think of as a relationship

Lots of people want to be monogamous—some people don't! Some people want openness, or flexibility; others never want to have sex. Some people are in three-way relationships! What the heck, build a deck!

The point here is that you should model your relationship on what makes you and your partner happy and fulfilled, and you don't need to judge that against some Platonic Ideal Of What A Relationship Should Be.

The important thing here is to *be honest* and make sure you're on the same page. Talk early, talk often! Know that if you do go with a non-traditional relationship (and it's new for one or both of you), there *will* be some awkwardness and some Weird Feelings. This doesn't mean that you're doing the wrong thing. It's very, very common that the first time we do something, we make mistakes and have feelings about it. The second time, you'll make fewer mistakes and have fewer feelings. Just because something is new and unfamiliar doesn't mean it can't work for you.

That said, do *not* ever agree to something that your gut cries "Nooooooo!" to in order to keep that person. *What's going to happen to this boat?*

Step 415: Don't undervalue the importance of sex in a relationship

Good sex isn't a valid reason to stay in a relationship, but bad sex is a valid reason to leave one.

There are certainly people for whom sex doesn't matter that much, but for most people it's pretty central, perhaps since it's kind of the point of human existence. It doesn't make you a shallow or carnal person to view sex as an important part of a relationship. The main thing that concretely distinguishes this relationship from every other relationship in your life is that either you sleep with this person or are planning to. If you are promising to just have sex with one person, maybe for the rest of your life, *it should be good sex.*

If you have a high sex drive and they have a low one, that is an issue that warrants discussion, just like it would be if you are someone who loooooves to spend money and they're a saver. It's a facet of incompatibility, and while you can certainly overcome it, you can't overcome it by being too squeamish to even bring it up.

Step 416: Say what you want in bed, without shame or fear

If this person is a decent guy or girl who cares about you, they will want to know how to make you happy in bed. If they don't care about what kind of time you're having, that's a good sign they do not deserve to be in bed with you.

But the only way they'll know what you want is if you tell them, either non-verbally or, if it's something a little more complicated, verbally. This can feel reeeeeeeeally awkward and terrifying, because our sexuality is this very private, quiet part of ourselves, and the idea of someone rejecting it is so painful.

But again: A decent partner will want you to be happy in bed. And unless what you're asking for is really, really out there, they'll probably be excited to try something new.

Step 417: Have frank discussions about possible consequences of sex with the people you're sleeping with

You should be able to talk about the fun stuff in that previous step, but also the not-so-fun stuff. You must be able to have a rational, non-squirmy (or at least minimally squirmy) discussion of contraceptives, STDs, what would happen if someone got pregnant, and so on.

Don't talk about these things in bed, either. Talk about them when no one's mental energy is consumed thinking about the fun sexytimes that are about to be had.

Sleeping with someone *is* a big deal. It's easy and fun and you should do it when you want to, but it's a big deal. This will be the most mom-ish sentence in this whole book, but sex is one of those arenas where there can be consequences, and those consequences can be life-altering. Make sure you're on the same page.

Step 418: Fight like a grown-up

Those people who say they never fight with their significant others are semi-full of it. It is in fact possible not to fight, although it's impossible to never disagree on anything unless one person is so doormat-ish that they refuse to have opinions.

Here are some ineffective fighting tactics:

• Yelling, name-calling, or anything else that brings to mind overprotective parents arguing with a Little League coach
• Bringing up past, unrelated resentments
• Not admitting what is really wrong, and what you feel the solution is
• Refusing to accept a sincere apology

Here are some effective techniques:

• If it's the heat of the moment and you are too furious to talk without yelling, take a break. Say, "I love you, I'm going for a walk, let's talk in half an hour." Then call one of your friends, or a parent, and vent to them. Get feedback, too.

• Stating, clearly and concisely and with minimal judgment, what you are upset about, and why.

• Listening and being open to what the other person has to say, and not going into the argument with a winning-no-matter-what mentality.

• Not raising your voice. This is a person you love, not a dog that you're scolding.

• If you're going around in circles, drop the banana (see step 148).

Step 419: Hold off on the big stuff (in ascending order: living together, pets, mortgages, children) until you are really and truly positive

Sometimes, if things are rocky, it feels like maybe making a Grand Life Gesture is a way to prove to the world (and yourself) that things are okay. This is the worst possible thing you could do.

In the grand scheme of things, most problems aren't really problems, and most mistakes aren't really mistakes. But having children or buying a house with someone you are iffy about is a Problem and a Mistake (so much so that they become proper nouns, capital letters and all), and you shouldn't do it.

Living with someone prematurely isn't quite as big a mistake, but you know what is? Making your lifestyle dependent on a relationship that isn't written in stone. Or, even worse, committing yourself to a lifetime of compromises, complicated logistics diplomacy, and forced togetherness because of shared offspring.

COHABITATION

Living together! The idea is pretty exhilarating—just the two of you, nestin' so hard, livin' and lovin' in sin. Moving in can be great, a successful trial run demonstrating that you can dwell together without descending into madness. Or it can be calamitous. If it's calamitous, then, hey, at least you figured that out now. But there are some things you can do to smooth the way.

Before you do it...

• You should probably date, *very successfully*, for several months after the honeymoon phase ends before moving in together. *Successfully* in this case can be defined by the things that aren't happening: No big ugly fights, no almost breaking up or *actually* breaking up and then getting back together, no nagging feelings that this relationship is doomed. Moving in together will not solve any of those problems.

• Make sure you're on the same page when it comes to the home itself. Is it always going to be sparkling clean, or are socks draped over a lamp shade par for the course? Can you compromise on decor (or, ideally, have one person with zero opinions on color schemes)? Is your house loud and full of guests, or quiet with an early bedtime? You probably know a lot of these things about your boyfriend or girlfriend already, but an ounce of discussion ahead of time is worth a pound of yelling at each other to pick up those goddamn shoes.

• Are you doing this for financial reasons? Sure, you can save a lot of money, but if you're setting yourself up for ruin in the event of a breakup, that's a bad call. A much more adult decision would be to get your finances in order so you don't need to depend on a relationship (see chapter 6).

During...

• Make sure you have a good system worked out for paying bills. One great idea I've heard is to have a joint checking account for rent, bills, and groceries that each of you can deposit money into or pay from. If one person makes a lot more money than the other, does she or he contribute more toward expenses?

• Figure out an equitable, or at least fair, way to divide up chores. Nothing breeds resentment like someone shouldering more than their fair share. That shit is the petri dish of anger, and before you know it, colonies of slow-burning rage will crop up everywhere.

• Do you prepare and eat meals together? Who cooks? Who cleans? Who grocery shops?

• Will your pets be cool together? I'm just saying. Pets have feelings, too.

After...

• Should things go south in the relationship, try to have an exit strategy in place. Is there someone you could move in with temporarily? Could one of you continue in the lease if the other one leaves? If not, give that yearlong lease extra scrutiny.

REASONS NOT TO GET MARRIED

Here's the thing about marriage (well, *one* thing, anyway): It's big and scary and based on a promise we have no way of guaranteeing, forever, to keep. There's a huge kerfuffle and everyone is sooooooooooo excited and happy for you, and if you're *not* getting engaged, well, what's wrong with you? Is your relationship even real? Because if it was real, you would 100 percent want to get legally bound to each other in a huge public gesture that sort of requires your friends and family to get you nice sheets.

But here, now, are some Reasons Not To Get Married:

• You feel like you should, like it has been enough time, and, well, here we are!
• *They* really want to get married, and *you* really don't feel like having another fight, or vice versa.
• You're tired of people asking, "Soooooo! How are things with you and So-and-So?" and you *know* they're just asking if you're engaged yet or what.
• All your friends are engaged and/or married. Why not *you*?
• You want people to take your relationship seriously.
• You look really, really good in ivory.
• You're feeling pressure from your family, or your friends, or their family or their friends, or society writ large, or a religious institution, or...well, any pressure, other than thinking "I want this person to be on my team forever, and I want to be on theirs."
• You have many important ideas about Mason jars, and ways they may be dispatched for maximum ambiance.

- You can't help but notice that everything—aside from the relationship itself—is so very perfect. You love their people; they love yours. And such a meet-cute story! And you should be really happy. But when you close the door at the end of the day and it's just you two, there's something missing...so the problem must be with you, and in time, you can shove all these feelings down into a small, dense ball. Sure, a spoonful weighs a ton, but just *don't ever think about it,* and everything will be okay.
- You're pregnant, or she is!
- You're a product of the South and despite strong feminist feelings and the knowledge that marriage is an antiquated institution, it has been slowly and methodically drilled into your head that your left ring finger is the one to focus on. That finger, and its nakedness *or* sparkly adornment: That is your goal. For once you have that ring, it says to everyone: I have been chosen. Someone wants me. Here it is, this thing that you all have told me I need! This bit of metal and mineral—with this, I am whole.

REASONS TO GET MARRIED:

- You truly know this person, through and through, and accept the good with the bad, knowing that you, too, are imperfect. You're willing to give 60 percent to their 40 percent. You want to build a life with them—it's hard to imagine one without them—and the fact that you can have a party, sign a piece of paper, and get significant societal and social benefits, well, that's just gravy on the cake.

Step 420: If you do get engaged, do not announce it to the important players over Facebook

Before the social media press release, you need to tell families and close friends yourselves. Social media, in general, is not a reliable means of broadcasting important news, and you will be guaranteed to hurt feelings in the process. But once they know, feel free to tell the whole world. Hooray for you!

ENEMIES IN LOVE

That title doesn't refer to actual enemies in love, though that sex would be pretty, pretty hot. Instead, any time you have a significant other, they will probably tote along at least one person you don't care for.

Step 421: You don't get veto power over their friends, sadly

Ideally, this is a dumb friend from high school or someone whom she or he doesn't see that often and you can just sort of not hang out with. Guys need lots of time alone with their friends anyway, and most men aren't super-duper sad if their buddy's girlfriend can't come along for the night.

Don't talk shit about this person to your significant other. He or she will probably be able to pick up on your dislike, anyway. Knowing one person you love dislikes another person you love feels like two stones grinding against each other in your stomach, especially if there's nothing you can do to improve the situation.

Step 422: Make peace with the closest friends and family members

If this person is a major feature in their life—a best friend or close family member—then just accept and make peace with the fact that you may really dislike each other, but you both love your significant other. Mustering up all your inner strength and serenity is the price of admission.

Step 423: All of the aforementioned must go both ways

This must go both ways. This must go both ways. This must go both ways. This must go both ways. She or he must accept and be gracious about your dear people whom they are less than fond of. This must go both ways.

WHEN IT IS OVER

This is not meant to imply every relationship ends in failure. Many lead to marriage or long-term partnership; many dissolve in a way that is natural and leaves both parties feeling relatively happy, with fond memories of the other.

But let's face it: Lots, at least in the early twenties, end in sucky, sucky breakups.

There are two distinct (though sometimes overlapping) roles in a breakup: the breakupper and the breakuppee. Sometimes, you've gotten to the point in a relationship where neither person gives a shit that it's over (or never cared much in the first place) in which case your only job is to not shit-talk (see step 437). But for the most part, after a breakup, one person hurts and one person hurts a lot more. Let's start with the slightly hurt party before we move on to the really hurt.

Step 424: Don't stay with someone because it's emotionally convenient

When you realize something is over, you need to end it. It will never get easier. There will never be a time that severing a relationship that has lasted years will be no big deal.

Think of it this way: When you're in a relationship with someone, you sort of grow into each other, like two closely placed trees. The farther you go, the more entangled you get, and the more impossible it becomes to extricate yourself without cutting away big swaths of yourself.

Signs that it's over:

- You're less interested in sex.
- You have a deep, unshakable feeling that there is something just not right.
- It is hard to remember why you liked them.
- Even endearing things they do annoy you.
- You want to or are having sex with someone else (in which case, come on, stop being like that; be a grown-up and end it).

Step 425: Start an emotional distancing process a little bit ahead of time

When you start to feel like it might be over, then you have permission to start withdrawing a little bit—for a while. No more than a few weeks, though, because really what you're doing there is buying time to get over it while this person suffers through uncertainty and dark premonitions.

That said, it's the mark of a sociopath to go from being 100 percent into it to over it within a few days. Take the time, start putting a little space between you and your partner, start getting your things out of their apartment, and then pull the plug.

Note: If you are in an abusive relationship of any kind, this does not apply. Ditto for breakups involving obvious fault (substance abuse, cheating, and the like). You can and should bounce immediately. If you live with this person and think they may harm you, then get out right now. When they leave for work, call upon all your friends and move your stuff out now. Seriously. Do that now, read the rest of this book later.

Step 426: Break up with someone in a kind yet direct way

Here are the sorts of things you should not say when breaking up. They may seem kind but are actually awfully cruel, as they leave the heartbroken in a terrible holding pattern, thinking that something will change and they will get clearance to come back to the relationship.

- "I just don't want to be in a relationship right now." (So someday you might want to? I shall languish in heartbreak purgatory until you decide.)
- "I just want to be friends." (Yesss, very good. We will stay friends, until I can trick you into falling in love with me again.)
- "I need some space." (But if you need space *now*, then I'll bet you won't need space *later*, so I'll just be right here.)

If you want to break up with someone, break up with them. You don't want to cause unnecessary hurt, but saying things that make you feel temporarily better and them much worse is not the way to go.

Here's how a grown-up breakup should go:

- "Listen. I know this is really, really hard. But I want to break up."

Don't listen to begging, don't equivocate, don't give this person false hope.

Step 427: Do give an ultimatum, if that's what matters

If you really and truly *would* be willing to stay with this person if that one thing changed, then by all means, tell them that and set concrete guidelines for success.

"I can't keep dating you while you're drinking. If you want to stay together, you need to quit and I need to see that happening *now*."

This can happen once every five years. An ultimatum is supposed to be a game-changer, not a dysfunctional pattern to be repeated endlessly.

Step 428: But if it's truly over, don't give reasons

Your reasons for breaking up with someone, unless there is obvious cause, probably boil down to "this just isn't right," and "we both deserve a better fit." Which you do. Your not being into them automatically qualifies you as a bad mate for them, and that is something that cannot be changed.

Yes, maybe there are specifics, but unless sharing them will really and truly help this person grow and be successful in their next relationship, don't share them. Knowing that you can't stand the way they chew their food or that their spit doesn't taste right won't help them; it'll just be the cherry atop the emotional agony sundae.

Step 429: You do not need to worry, right now, about whether or not something is abusive—if you have those questions, you can and should get out

This is not, in any way, to undermine the seriousness of abuse in a relationship—it's real and it happens and it's corrosive. Part of why abusive situations are hard to recognize is that making someone doubt their own perceptions and thoughts is one way abusers assert power and control.

But here's the thing: You don't *have* to figure out if something is abusive. There is, in life, no Abuse Court where a judge will bang a gavel and Then You Will Know. Nor do you have to!

Maybe it *is* abusive. Maybe it's just deeply, deeply toxic on both sides. If you're wondering about this, you do not need to wait for a Truth And Reconciliation Panel. You can just go. Toxicity is reason enough to go. If they've become someone you don't recognize—and, especially, if you have—well, that's enough, right there. You do not, in this moment, need to be able to say what, exactly, was wrong—just that something was, in fact, terribly, terribly wrong.

Note: If you think a relationship is abusive, there are some really fantastic resources out there, and you can and should seek them out. Google these things, and Google local help. Please just go ahead and call any crisis lines you may find. It's okay, no one is going to bust in and sweep you away, Elián González–style, and if it turns out it's not "abusive," per se, you will not be laughed at and hung up on. There are very kind and lovely people out there who are here just for this. For free! Lots of times, when we need help in life, it is sadly lacking. This isn't one of those cases.

Step 430: If someone is breaking up with you, do your best to walk away with your dignity intact

Quick: Take a moment and go over your personal-worst-moments highlight reel. Chances are decent that at least one of them involved a breakup. And yes, during the actual breakup you have permission to dissolve into a trembly, snot-drenched mess.

But. When you leave that terrible room and conversation, take a moment and decide how you want to comport yourself. You are broken up. So now, even though everything is shitty, you can stay on that steady level of shittiness *or* you can lose your dignity to boot and add a new, shitty dimension.

You don't have your boyfriend or girlfriend anymore, but you do have your dignity...right now. If you spend the next weeks and months calling, texting, begging, pleading, driving by their house like a crazy person, et cetera, then you won't have that, either.

Step 431: Don't expect "closure," ever, on anything

We all want "closure." But that doesn't make closure any more of a real thing than, say, a kind and gentle Pegasus who is eager to read your unpublished novel.

Because what you mean when you say *closure* is "magical verbal bullet that will make me not feel like shit, even though I've just been dumped." And that, sadly, is not something that exists. In real life, closure comes from months or years of perspective, reflection, and insight. Or it doesn't—some things close, some things don't. But there is no closure to be found via an excruciating conversation with a very recent ex.

Here is how you imagine a conversation that will provide "closure" would go:

You: Why did you break up with me?

Person Who Broke Your Heart: Because you were too incredible, and way funnier than I am, and I felt like you could fly ever higher once you weren't weighed down by me. I loved you so much that it felt selfish to spend one more second with you, because you have already brought me five lifetimes' worth of joy.

You: Oh. Well, when you put it that way.

But if someone were going to be honest about the reasons they broke up with you, here's how an actual "closure" conversation would go:

You: Why did you break up with me?

PWBYH: Because I knew I couldn't stand a lifetime of that humming noise you make when you chew, and I'm tired of having sex with you and want to have sex with other people—people who *aren't* you, and who *don't* make that humming noise. Also, my mom doesn't like you.

You: Oh. Well, when you put it that way.

Really, your ex's reasons probably can't be verbalized, and if they could they wouldn't be nice. Think about the last time you broke up with someone without obvious cause (cheating, substance abuse, or the like). If that person demanded an explanation, could you give one? And would you want to? No and no. This answer, if it even does exist, will not bring you peace. It will just allow you to spend a lifetime hating something about yourself that a future love interest may find endearing (or at least not mind).

So wait for closure if you wish, but you will save yourself a good deal of time and angst by accepting that it doesn't matter *why* it didn't work, only that it didn't.

Step 432: Do not talk to someone who has broken up with you

This advice was in *It's Called a Breakup Because It's Broken* by Greg Behrendt and Amiira Ruotola-Behrendt. I *cannot recommend this book highly enough* to those who have recently had their heart smushed. It is so, so helpful, although also embarrassing when someone spots it on your bookshelf. The authors argued that you should absolutely not talk to someone who's just broken up with you for two months, minimum. No calling, texting, passive-aggressive Facebook status updates—nothing.

This will start the painful but necessary process of accepting your life without them. When you're in a relationship with someone, you mold your life around them. Then they're gone, and there is this raggedy, raw edge where they used to be. What you need to do right now is smooth out that edge and make yourself a complete person without them. *Because they are gone.* It's just you. So be alone, try to heal, and stop prolonging the pain with contact. Remember being satisfied with the pleasure of your own company? Draw on those reserves of self-sufficiency.

Step 433: If need be, have your friends spread news of the breakup

There are people who should know about it, but if you can't bring yourself to have the same anguish-inducing conversation fifteen times in a row, ask a friend to do some PR on the breakup, saying that it happened but you don't really feel like talking about it.

Step 434: Forgive yourself if you go a little crazy

Heartbreak can induce insanity in the very sanest of us. It's okay to be so, so deeply sad. You can feel sad for years, if need be. What will not help is berating yourself for having that sadness. If you could wave a wand and make yourself not feel it, you would. Constantly reminding yourself how pathetic you are doesn't need to be a part of it.

That sadness is evidence that you had something good, even if it ultimately wasn't right for you. You won't feel it forever, but it's okay to feel it for now. It's okay to feel it next week, next month, next year. Just know that no matter how endless and constant it seems, eventually it won't be there. Someday you'll open that emotional drawer, and it will be empty.

Step 435: Remember that your ex will never, ever again be a source of that feeling you felt

In my early twenties, I was batshit crazy in love with a dude. Just ridiculously head-over-heels, wouldn't shut up, couldn't believe my luck, et cetera. One time, I remember, we'd been talking on the phone and after we hung up, I sat down on my couch and just screamed and screamed, like a twelve-year-old at a Beatles concert.

And yet, I was not happy in this relationship because he didn't really love me. Or maybe he did, but he didn't love me enough, or in the way it counted. He was unsure about me, and *it eroded me in the most painful way possible.*

And guess what? Yeah. We broke up.

Afterward, every time I ran into him at the grocery store, every time I saw him across a crowded room, I felt a tiny flash of what I'd once felt followed by crushing pain. I was like the rats in a study on addiction. Sometimes, when a rat pushed a lever with its little rat foot, it would be rewarded with cocaine, and sometimes it wouldn't.

And what the scientists found was that the rats would push, push, push push push push push that lever indefinitely, thousands and thousands of times, for the rest of their lives, even if the cocaine never came again.

And thus, the experience of being recently but no longer in love.

I finally realized that when I pushed that emotional lever with my metaphorical rat foot, I got nothing. Eventually, I accepted that I would never, ever feel that feeling again, at least not from him. The sound of his voice through my cell phone would never make me scream on a couch again. *There was nowhere in the world I could go that would make me feel that way, least of all parties where I knew I would "accidentally" bump into him.* And I needed to stop pushing the lever.

Step 436: Don't rush to replace someone if you're still really hurting

People are not bits of watch machinery. They are not interchangeable; you cannot simply go out and find another one exactly like the last one and expect things to work the same. If you are really, really missing someone, then miss them. Don't hurt a bunch of other people by imagining they can seamlessly plug the chunk that was scooped out of your heart. It won't help you and it's not fair to them.

Step 437: Don't shit-talk your ex in public

This doesn't apply to close friends, with whom you have complete permission to shit-talk, but rather strangers, acquaintances, nosy co-workers, and so on.

It can be *so tempting.* But don't. Whether you broke up with them or they broke up with you and you're indifferent/crushed/delighted, here are the talking points:

- Actually, so-and-so and I aren't together anymore.
- But they remain a dear friend (optional, and you have permission to use the term loosely).
- Period. Use vocal tone to imply the finality of what you've just said, then move on to another topic.

No matter why you broke up, reasons valid or not, here is the Official Reason:

"S/he is a really wonderful person, but we just weren't right for each other."

This is unassailable. "Not being right for each other" could be anything! Cheating! General boredom! Horrific screaming fights! Hating their family! Really enjoying the relationship but having the unshakable feeling that something is not quite right!

No matter which it is, this is someone you once loved, and airing whatever happened to satisfy a random person's desire to rubberneck is poor form.

Step 438: Be cool with your ex continuing to exist

Guess what? Your ex, despite your wishes, will continue to exist. You are entitled to feel the natural, logical desire that they move to a chilly Afghani mountainside and adopt a new life as a hermit who collects dried yak poop for fun and profit. But for your own serenity, you need to accept the fact that they will most likely stay on this plane of existence. And eventually, date someone else.

Step 439: Someday, try to be friends

This can only happen when both of you are really and truly okay with it being over, hence the need for separation, at least initially.

But this is someone who meant a great deal to you and vice versa, and some of the most wonderful friendships can come from exes, as long as you're honest, with yourself and each other. And never ever share details of your current sex lives.

Step 440: Be on each other's team

This doesn't have to do with breakups, but it's critical and therefore a good chapter-ender. When you are dating someone, you should be on their team and they should be on yours. Take their side, even if they're maybe wrong. If you find yourself unable to be on their team, that's a good sign that it's not meant to be, but at least give a good-faith effort.

Believe genuinely in them, and let them know it. Be the drum major leading the Him Parade, or Her Parade. Life is often dark and cruel, so give each other the warm, portable ember of knowing that someone is always in your corner. That alone can serve as proof that life is not that dark, or that cruel.

DISCUSSION QUESTIONS

1. What is the most ridiculous place that you've gone by yourself in the hope that someone cute would come talk to you?
2. Which do you, personally, feel is worse: heartbreak or colon cancer?
3. What was the most petty reason you ever broke up with someone? Were you right or wrong? You were probably right.

Chapter 10
TIMES WERE TOUGH

There's not a funny way to say this, because it isn't funny, but it's true: Sometimes sad, inexplicable things happen. These are the big ugly surprises lurking in the shadows of an otherwise normal Friday afternoon or Wednesday morning, waiting to jump out and change everything.

Sometimes these unexpected things will be small, short-term pains in the ass, like your car breaking down on the freeway when you are en route to a friend's wedding, or spilling coffee on your shirt before a job interview. Sometimes they will be enormous, long-term sorrows, like ongoing illness or the death of someone you love. But no matter what it is, you can handle it... or, at least, act adult in the face of it.

Like heartbreak, these unpredictable crises are not something you should live in fear of. Perpetual fear won't protect you. Fear is not a citronella candle; scary life happenings are not mosquitoes. They happen in ways we can't predict, control, or understand. The only guaranteed outcome of feeling scared all the time is that you will *feel scared all the time.*

These events are the true litmus tests of adulthood, and when you pass through to the other side of one, you will find yourself changed. As my mother would put it, these experiences are an AFGO (another fucking growth opportunity, pronounced *aff-go*).

If nothing else, and if it's not too terribly sad, someday this rough patch might be a great Times Were Tough story. Times Were Tough stories are a beloved tradition among my friends. You share a particularly unbearable experience—a middle school head-lice inspection or a bicycle trip home in an ice storm, perhaps—then you finish the story by saying, in a solemn voice, "Times were tough." And then everyone listening says, in equally solemn unison, "Times were tough."

LEGAL DISCLAIMER

Before we begin—and this may come as a shock—this chapter is not intended to serve as binding medical or legal advice, okay? It's just rough, general guidelines, which is why there will be no step 536: Master a defibrillator with these simple moves! If you're wondering what to do in a real defibrillator situation, call a doctor. Don't consult a book written by a twenty-seven-year-old journalist.

Step 441: Keep your cool, and don't fall apart (at least until afterward)

An emergency can pretty much be defined as a time when it feels impossible to be cool, but it's also when you need that calm exterior most. Whatever is going on, pause a second, take a deep breath, and remind yourself that you can handle it.

Turning off the "HOLY SHIT WHAT AM I GOING TO DO?!" air-raid siren in your brain will make it much, much more likely that you'll move forward in the right direction. Unless someone is actively having a heart attack, you have more time to think and deliberate than it seems. The decisions you make rashly are usually the bad ones.

It's easy to look at something enormous, or even something middle-size, and feel that there is just no way you can possibly face it. Luckily, you are capable of handling many, many, many things that seem impossible. You have no idea how good you are at, say, holding it together during a medical emergency, or packing up to move cross-country, until you actually do it. As a wise upstairs neighbor told me, when the ground is moving, stay still.

Step 442: Most things that feel like an emergency or a disaster at age twenty-one are not, actually, an emergency or a disaster

There's nothing wrong with feeling overwhelmed when facing something you've never had to before. The good news is that for 100 percent of the problems you will ever experience in your life, at least one other person has already experienced and lived through it.

Maintaining perspective is crucial. Whatever is happening is a temporary state of being. Time will keep moving forward, and eventually you will be on the other side. So before freaking the F out, take a deep breath, do a little research if possible, and remember that most things just don't matter in six months' time.

Things that are not, technically speaking, disasters:

- Car breakdowns
- Anything having to do with clothing, unless some of yours actually catches on fire, in which case, maybe
- Cat vomit
- Person vomit
- Any kind of vomit, usually
- Being broke in a temporary way, even if you did overdraw your bank account
- Anything involving your fingernails or hair (again, unless they're on fire)

Step 443: Keep a few items always available for wardrobe malfunctions

The best offense here is a good defense. Having these three things in your car or purse can salvage many clothing "emergencies":

- A stain-removing pen
- Clothing tape (tape your bra straps in place, say, or use if a button has popped off)
- A couple of safety pins

DISASTER PREVENTION

Remember a few paragraphs ago where I said not to live in fear, because it wouldn't do any good? While that's still the case all these paragraphs later, there are simple steps you can take to prevent some disasters, or at least cut them off at the ankle, if you will. Just imagine how sad that disaster will look, hobbling around on stumpy ankle-feet.

Step 444: Own at least basic first-aid supplies

Here are some things that should be in your medicine cabinet:

- A couple sizes of Band-Aids
- An Ace bandage (for sprains)
- Neosporin (be sure to put on before your bandage for safer, less-infection-prone healing! If you're sensitive to Neosporin—if your cut looks angrier the next day—go for bacitracin instead)
- Hydrogen peroxide (for cleaning out wounds after they have first healed; use soap and water on a fresh wound)
- Rubbing alcohol (for sterilizing)
- Tweezers, for splinters and such
- Benadryl cream (for bug bites and other itchy things)
- Gauze and first-aid tape
- An ice pack
- A thermometer

And essential over-the-counter remedies to have around:

- Aspirin (for headaches)
- Ibuprofen (for muscle aches)
- Pepto-Bismol (for stomachaches)
- Benadryl (for allergies)

Step 445: Actually clean your cuts. Don't just suck on them or wipe them on a napkin

Cuts should be washed out with gentle soap and water, then spread with a thin layer of Neosporin or bacitracin and bandaged. Sunburns can be relieved with aloe; I like to keep one of the gels that mix aloe vera with a topical anesthetic in the fridge so it is delightfully cool when I smear it on angry red skin.

Remember that if you are bleeding, pressure is your friend. Get some gauze and apply pressure to the area, which allows the skin to start its healing process and stop the bleeding. Once bleeding has stopped, bandage it.

Step 446: Deal with little burns

This assumes small second- (blistering) or first- (just red) degree burns, not serious burns, which are known as third-degree. As my friend Elisabeth pointed out, burns and murder are not analogous in grading. First-degree murder will get you life imprisonment; first-degree burns just need aloe.

Hopefully this is obvious, but if someone is seriously burned, or the burn covers anything other than a very, very small area of their body (not counting sunburns), they need to go to the hospital immediately. If the skin is taut, white, and without feeling after a burn, it's possible that it's third-degree and needs to be looked at right away. Even second-degree burns can be serious if they're bigger than three inches.

But smaller, run-of-the-mill burns? The molten-steam-rising-out-of-a-Hot-Pocket kind? You can deal with those at home. First, and as fast as you can, run the affected part under cold water. Then Neosporin and bandage it.

Step 447: Put together a little emergency kit for your house

A kit can be prepared slowly: For the next few weeks, just pick up a gallon of water whenever you go to the grocery store. Then put that gallon in a closet, and know that if your water were to go out, well, that's one day that you wouldn't have to worry about. Repeat this until you've got a week's worth of water, figuring one gallon per person, per day. Also, put a gallon in your car.

You can slowly supplement your water supply with other useful items such as non-perishable food (but first take a moment to consider how you'd feel eating this food cold—I don't suggest clam chowder for this very reason), a flashlight, a little emergency radio, and also something to relieve the terrible boredom/anxiety that you'd likely experience in the event of an emergency. Buy a special emergencies-only board game. That way, if everything else is awful, at least you have the tiny pleasure of this new board game.

Step 448: Think about a little fireproof safe...

This can be had online for $30; you'll only ever have to buy one and you will feel so, SO responsible. Look for one that's fire- and waterproof, and then put the following into it:

- Your birth certificate and Social Security card, plus photocopies of both
- Your passport, if you have one
- Photocopies of your driver's license and insurance cards
- Photocopies of any other insurance policies you may have (like RENTER'S INSURANCE, heyyyyy!)
- A piece of paper with the following phone numbers written on it: your immediate family, your close friends, your doctor's office, your vet if you have a pet, the local non-emergency number, a friend that lives nowhere near you (in case there's an earthquake or a hurricane and the cell towers are down);
- Another piece of paper noting any prescriptions that you may have with the dosages
- Anything truly irreplaceable and small that you don't wear (the thing you'd grab if your house was on fire, but if you have a fireproof box, no bigs!)
- A few blank checks
- An external hard drive with your computer backed up on it
- Your credit and debit card numbers written down, with expiration dates and security codes and whatnot
- Any leases you may have
- Last year's tax return
- Names and addresses of previous landlords, along with the dates you lived at each place
- Ideally, some cash

I can hear you sighing deeply. I know. It seems like a LOT of stuff to gather. Please know that having some of these things is way better than having none. This is more or less a one-time thing, and there *will* be non-catastrophic times when you need to take every single scrap of paper that proves you exist to the DMV, or utilize most of these documents for a job application. It is nice to know that these things are always in this one, safe place.

Step 449: If the opportunity arises, take a first-aid class

Yes, even if you took it in eighth-grade health class ten years ago. Note that I said "if the opportunity arises," like maybe if your workplace is offering it. I'm not going to suggest that you sign up for it at the senior center, although if you are the kind of amazing safety go-getter who seeks it out yourself, hats off to you. First-aid class is one of those opportunities that does present itself. Unlike most opportunities. So take advantage.

Step 450: Have some basic provisions in your car

Again, a gallon of water, some non-perishable snacks, a flashlight, and a warm blanket can live happily in your car, a cozy little stockpile of things that you will probably never need but would be infinitely grateful to have if you did. Also, buy a ten-dollar first-aid kit at Target or something, then stick it in your trunk.

ADVANCED ADULTING: HAVE SOME SERIOUS PROVISIONS IN YOUR CAR

Here is an amazing list of things above and beyond those mentioned above. Mary Henderson, a former park ranger and all around badass woman, put together this list for me. Some of these things are more important for those who live in rural areas, but hey—you never know when you'll be on a road trip. And road trips attract emergencies like mobile homes attract tornadoes.

• **Fold-up shovel:** For digging out of the snow, or the mud, or the muddy snow. Outdoor supply stores have these.

- **A pocketknife or multi-tool:** So small, so useful, so happy to live in your glove box.
- **An ice scraper:** Everyone who lives somewhere cold already has one, but if not, don't be like me and use CD jewel cases.
- **Windex wipes:** When your window is all fogged up, you *will* smear the inside with your hand and leave big hand grease marks everywhere. Windex wipes protect you against yourself.
- **Jumper cables:** "Oh, do you need a jump? I have cables" is such a grown-ass man or woman thing to say.
- **Tire gauge:** Know it. Love it.
- **Commercial window breaker:** This is also known as the Life-hammer, as popularized by *MythBusters*. You will probably never, ever use this. But fifteen dollars is a worthwhile price to pay for something that could save your life. Not only does it allow you to shatter windows, but it also has a seat-belt cutter. Put it where you can grab it fast.
- **Paper goods:** Paper towels and toilet paper are cheap. But when you need them and don't have them, you would pay a lot for them. A roll of each goes in the trunk.
- **Cell phone car charger:** Self-explanatory.
- **Some nice-ish shoes and a black synthetic dress (or its sartorial equivalent):** Sometimes, you'll think you're dressed appropriately and then you're not. While these items will not help you if, say, everyone decided to climb a glacier, it will smooth the way if you're terribly underdressed.

Step 451: Do not roll around with less than a quarter tank of gas

My little gas light is on so often that I worry about whether the bulb can burn out. I do not know why it is so difficult for me to just go ahead and fill up the tank. This is the same principle as toilet paper—my car will need that gas eventually, so why not just put it in there now?

But the fact is people who always have at least a quarter tank of gas and refill the tank as soon as it dips below that line will never run out of gas on a backwoods mountain road and have to be rescued by a kindhearted trucker. Or murdered by a non-kindhearted trucker.

Also, on the subject of emergencies: Remember to fill up your tank at the first hint of an emergency; otherwise you will wait for hours at a gas station.

Step 452: Get AAA, or some sort of roadside assistance

Knock knock.

Who's there?
An eighty-dollar towing job on top of the many hundreds of dollars it will take to repair your car.

Knock knock.

Who's there?
Walking three miles down the interstate to the gas station.

I could continue with these chilling knock-knock jokes for seven or eight more pages, but the point has been made. AAA, or roadside assistance from your cell phone or car insurance company, will cost perhaps five or seven bucks per month that you will not miss and will be so terrifically worth it.

Step 453: Get renter's insurance

Again, this is relatively very cheap—I pay maybe fifteen dollars per month to be covered for twenty thousand dollars' worth of damage in the event of a fire, flood, or earthquake. Be sure to read the fine print here—many policies don't cover for floods, and some will require specific information about the construction of your apartment.

Step 454: Take pictures of your nice things

You can opt to have extra coverage for certain categories of things—computers, for example, or jewelry, or musical instruments—but you need to be able to prove that, at one time, you owned them. Take thirty minutes and wander around your apartment, documenting all the nice things you have that hopefully nothing bad will ever happen to...but if something did happen, you would want replaced.

Then send these pictures to yourself, or put them in the cloud—just make sure they don't exist solely on your computer, because what if your computer burns up?

Step 455: Keep your cool in a car accident

This is a hard situation to be cool in, but you must be. Otherwise, things could go terribly, terribly further awry for you.

If you get in a car accident, your first step should be to get out of traffic if the cars can still drive. Pull over to a safe place.

Assuming no one is seriously hurt, make this as cool and business-like as possible. Do *not* say it was your fault. Do *not* apologize in a way that implies you are at fault. Ask people if they're okay. Be kind and decent, but get their information. That means name, address, cell phone number, driver's license number, insurance info and policy number, license plate, and description (make, model, color) of each car; give all of yours, too. Call the police. If there are witnesses who weren't involved, get their numbers as well.

As soon as you can, write down all the details you remember, because the insurance companies will have about a billion questions. Even shit that seems completely irrelevant should be noted because insurance companies are completely insane. Before you go, take pictures of all the cars and the road itself.

You need to call the police, even if they don't come out in person, because many states require you to file an accident report. Don't call 911 unless someone is seriously injured or traffic is blocked; Google "police [city name] non-emergency number" and call that one. Then call your insurance company and let them know what happened.

Also, go to the doctor even if you feel okay. You never know when things will surface down the road, and it's best to get checked out.

NUMBERS TO PROGRAM INTO YOUR PHONE

Spend the fifteen minutes on Google that it takes to get all these in your phone, because generally speaking, the times you'll call them are the times you least want to lose any time:

- The non-emergency number for the police department in your town
- Your insurance company's phone number (if you have more than one kind of insurance, put all of them in)
- Someone labeled IN CASE OF EMERGENCY
- Poison control
- A number to a local animal hospital, if you have a pet
- Your doctor's phone number
- Your pharmacy's phone number

Step 456: Understand your health insurance, and what you are covered for

Pop quiz, hotshots: What's your deductible? What is a deductible, anyway? Do you have an HMO or PPO? What's your coinsurance? What is coinsurance?

Health insurance is a wretched institution and you will probably get angry just by reading the fine print. But this righteous anger is not helpful; you will strike zero blows against the health care monolith by remaining ignorant as to what, exactly, you are covered for. Look at your policy, then Google any words you don't understand.

Step 457: Know what some serious medical warning signs are

This is by no means a comprehensive list, but there are some things that indicate you need to seek help immediately. This means the emergency room or, at the very least, an urgent care clinic. Such symptoms include but are not limited to:

- Any seizure, unexplained loss of consciousness, or serious trouble with your normal mental processes

- Ongoing bleeding; blood coming out of any orifice
- Serious shortness of breath
- A sharp, stabbing pain in your lower-right abdomen (this could be appendicitis)
- Paralysis
- A high (over 102 degrees) fever that persists for twenty-four hours or more

Again, this is not a complete list and there are many, many situations when you will need to go to the hospital for other reasons. But these things are nearly always big red flags.

Step 458: Know when to call an ambulance

Severe bleeding, serious trauma, shortness of breath, unconsciousness, and people who need more than minimal help to get to the hospital all warrant calls to 911. If you are wondering, *Should I call an ambulance?* the answer is probably yes, because that would be a terrible thing to be wrong about. Remember that in most places, there is no charge to call an ambulance, only for transportation (which is, indeed, very expensive). So when in doubt, call them and when they get there, ask. They won't lie to you.

Step 459: Keep perspective when you get injured

Whenever I get hurt, I sort of subconsciously assume that this is how it will be forever, that my toe will always remain stubbed and that now there is nothing to do but stoically accept this new life of pulsating toe pain. *Why me, Lord? Why me?!*

But here is the interesting thing about pain: It usually evaporates. You can't necessarily sense that evaporation, but the next minute, or day, or month, or year, you go looking for that feeling or sensation and it isn't there anymore.

Note: If the pain doesn't leave, then you should absolutely seek medical treatment. That also goes for emotional pain. You must feel it, but if you feel it and feel it and can't stop feeling it, that's the time when you need to care about yourself enough to seek professional help.

Step 460: Please, please, please be careful with opioids

This goes especially if you are physically and logistically limited by your injury. When the pain is acute—say, for the first day or two after the injury—that is a good time to use them *as directed*, because what you don't want is breakthrough pain. Of course, follow your doctor's instructions but also say to them that you are wary of opioids, and how long do you need to be on them? Could you do a lower dose, or a less intense form of painkiller?

They are so easy to get addicted to and, when you're sleepy and depressed and bed-bound, they can feel like a relief from what is an objectively awful and frustrating time…which is why it's always a good idea to look at alternatives. When I had no arms,[1] I ended up using medical marijuana (specifically, CBD topical ointments and inhalers). They were wonderful and, I think, a better choice than being on two months' worth of heroin's cousin. Some insurance covers things like therapeutic massage, which can be great. Mindfulness meditation is proven to improve pain symptoms and quality of life (plus, bonus: it's good for your mental health, which is extra necessary when you're injured).

Also, I hope this goes without saying, but don't use them recreationally. Do not. No. Go smoke some weed instead. If you're thinking, "Hey! Know what might be fun? Some Vicodin!" then do yourself a big ol' favor and watch any one of a thousand equally horrifying documentaries about *people who also maybe thought Vicodin would be fun.*

Step 461: Reach out to someone who has gone through a similar injury or sickness; grab a book on the subject

This can be helpful in all sorts of ways. One, it's just nice to have someone to talk to about it who understands. Two, they probably have some good advice or strategies that you haven't thought of (and may

---

1. It was *the worst.* My right elbow was broken and in a cast up to my armpit; my left shoulder was fractured and dislocated and had to be immobilized for six weeks. *Times were tough!*

even be able to lend you some medical gadgets that made their life easier). Three, just knowing that other people have gone through this, and felt the same way you do, makes it so much easier. Online support groups are also wonderful for this, especially if you're physically limited.

Step 462: Keep an eye on your mental health while you heal

Again, it's easy to see why people can get addicted to painkillers, because it is so, so hard to maintain a positive attitude when, say, you can't drive, go to work, clean, exercise, or do *nearly any of your normal activities,* particularly those that make you happy and keep your endorphins up. It can be really lonely. You're probably lying down much or all of the time and, if you're me, watching cable news nonstop. (**Note:** DO NOT DO THIS, as it will just make you feel worse. Pick a buoyant, low-stakes comedy that you've already seen and love instead; I suggest *30 Rock* or *Parks and Rec.*) Every little thing is frustrating or even impossible, and you'll probably find yourself crying in frustration when (just to use a personal example) *you can't even put the goddamn Hot Pocket, which is the easiest food there is, into its crisping sleeve* because that, like everything else in the world, requires arms.

If you've been on antidepressants before, this may be a good time to revisit them with your doctor or therapist. Reach out to your friends and tell them what you need, even if that's just their company or a ride to SuperCuts because you can't wash your own hair (maybe, if they truly love you, they'll wash and dry it for you? Or even put it in French-braid pigtails? I love you, Nikki!). Try not to be hurt when people aren't reaching out to you, because they probably have no idea what you need and assume that inviting you to things you can't attend will bum you out. This is a great time for mindfulness and meditation, if that's something you're into, and if you're not, look into it.

Step 463: If you need counseling but can't afford traditional methods, there are other resources available

You can, completely anonymously, call a crisis line and say, "Hey, I'm really depressed but I don't have health insurance or a lot of cash. Is there anywhere you can point me toward?"

You don't have to give this person your life story if you don't feel comfortable, but know that there is low-cost or free counseling nearly everywhere, everyone from psychiatrists doing pro-bono work to community mental health centers to spiritual counseling (which, p.s., you do not necessarily need to be a part of that religion or church to take advantage of). If this is something you need, then don't let money dissuade you from it.

OTHER PEOPLE'S DISASTERS

We all need each other all the time, but there are certain make-or-break times when you really need to step up and give a person you care about as much help and decency as you can muster. Often, these will be the times when you feel least comfortable around them and least able to provide help in a meaningful way. But don't underestimate your helpfulness. Think about the last time something hard happened. Think about the people who really showed up and supported you, or were at least present, versus people who disappeared into the woodwork. Which kind of person do you want to be?

Every single one of us will have someone close to us die. Not to be a downer, but it's true. I once interviewed a funeral director who said that, on average, people are "touched by [his] industry" three times in their life. If you stop and do this nightmarish calculation, it seems right.

But more often, we're on the periphery of grief—a friend's mom dies, say. And then we don't know what to say to that friend, how to be around them.

Whatever you do, don't let fear of saying the wrong thing prevent you from saying anything at all. You don't have to reinvent the wheel, or try to talk this person out of feeling bad. You mentioning it won't remind them, because chances are really good they hadn't forgotten until you brought it up again.

People who are grieving such a loss can feel very alienated because no one quite knows what to say and gives them their space... and then everyone is giving space when maybe that's not quite what's needed.

Step 464: Say the right things when someone has suffered a loss

Let's start with the DON'Ts:

- Don't tell them you know how they feel, unless you have experienced something *very* similar. If this person's parent or sibling has died, don't mention the time your great-aunt passed away.
- Don't try to minimize their loss, or feel like you need to cheer them up, or say anything along the lines of "This is for the best."
- Don't avoid them because you feel uncomfortable. Your discomfort is very small compared with theirs.

See? That's not too many things to remember. Let's go on to the DOs:

- Do tell them that you're so very, very sorry for their loss.
- Do create space for this person to talk about their loss, to say the same thing over and over if needed. Listen and don't feel a need to fix their problems, because in this case, you can't.
- If this person lives far away, do call *and* send a condolence note. In fact, send one if they're close by, too. It's not hard.

Step 465: You don't really need to know what to say; you can just listen

There is nothing you can say that will undo their loss; grief is beyond words and logic. The very kindest and most loving thing you can do is just be there when they need it. Listen to whatever they want to say. Encourage them to say whatever they like, tell the same old story for the fifth time, et cetera.

Sharing your stories about the person they lost is also a great gift. It's a way to underscore that even though their loved person or pet isn't here on the earth with them, they existed and they mattered to you, too.

Step 466: Write a decent condolence note

It's simple, and not a communiqué that requires creativity, innovation, or personal flair. It's a note that conveys a few things: I love you;

I am so sorry; I am thinking about you. They can be short and sweet, and sharing a memory you have of the person who has died can be particularly moving.

> Dear So-and-So,
> I am so very, very sorry to hear about your mom. She was always so kind, gracious, and charming, and an all-around wonderful human being—I'll never forget the time she counseled me until three in the morning about why I should dump the jerk I was dating, and she was so right. I love you and am thinking about you. Please call anytime, day or night, if you want to talk.
> *Love,*
> *You*

Step 467: When someone is in grief, let them be in their grief

Unfortunately, when someone close to you is in deep grief, you can't do much to help, but you can do things to hurt. When someone close to you is going through this, you have to let them go through it. Sometimes, providing a distraction—a stupid Will Ferrell movie, a trip to the beach, whatever it may be—can be welcome. But for the most part, this person is inside something so large in scope that they can't see anything else.

They may be full of things they want to say but keep inside because they're worried about dragging you down. Let them say whatever they need to say; be quiet while they say it. Read between the lines as to whether they want to talk about something but aren't saying it, and if so, encourage them. Let them say it for a fourth, fifth, sixth time in a row, because sometimes when we face something big, we have to repeat it, out loud, a few times before we believe it.

Extroverts want to process and process aloud, then circle back and process another seventeen times. Introverts may want to be by themselves, and find the expectation to talk to others exhausting.

Don't be afraid to ask them what they need and how you can help. The things you need in grief may be completely different than what I need. Do they want a distraction? A hug? Someone to hold them while they cry? Some space to themselves? Whatever it is, do your best to give it to them even if it's not what you would want.

Step 468: If someone invites you to a funeral, you need to have a really compelling reason to skip it

Funerals aren't for the dead; they're for the people left behind. If someone asks you to be there, even if you didn't know the person who has died, it is a good-person move to go. Imagine how you would feel if someone you loved very much died and there was almost no one around to mourn them. This would be a special new shade of pain added to the miserable rainbow you are already looking at.

Step 469: A miscarriage should be treated like a death

A miscarriage is one of the deep pains that people carry around with them. It's not as public or obvious as a death, but you should treat it the same way: Your friend is in anguish, and they have lost something very significant. The same principles apply. Write them a letter to let them know you are thinking of them, that you love them and that you want to be there. Then create spaces for them to talk about it, if they want to, or enjoy a distraction if that's what they need. Do not tell them it's for the best. Do not undersell, to them or yourself, what they have gone through.

Step 470: Same with an abortion

Please, please be so gentle with your friend when she's going through this. Offer to drive her, look up online how to make her comfortable afterward, allow her to say whatever she needs to say. If you truly can't support her in this decision, please don't harp on the point. Quietly call a close mutual friend who might be more helpful and, without revealing details, ask them to check in on her.

Step 471: Be cool when your friends are in the hospital

A hospital stay is not nearly as bad as a death, but it's a similar dynamic:

- Something bad that no one wants has happened;
- This is not a day-to-day situation, and so you probably feel uncomfortable and freaked out in addition to the regular sadness; but

- The emotional needs of the person who is sick or injured take precedence over your own.

Don't excuse yourself with an "I don't like hospitals." This is like "I hate funerals." Oh, really? Do you? Most people just adore being in the hospital; they'll be *thrilled* to take up the slack you create. No, no, no. You need to harden up and be a good friend.

First, try to ascertain if they want visitors or not. The best way to do this is just to call and ask. For some reason, people always sort of assume that anyone in the hospital has regressed to very early childhood and is no longer capable of holding conversations or deciding things for themselves.

Before you visit, call the hospital to find out what the visiting hours are, and if there are any restrictions on what gifts you can bring. For example, lots of times flowers aren't allowed in burn units because they may have bacteria, and someone who has recently undergone surgery may be on a restricted diet.

Step 472: When a doctor or nurse comes in, leave immediately

You don't need to *go* go, but you do need to step out into the hallway. It is quite possible that this person has been waiting to talk to the doctor all day about something specific or embarrassing, and really doesn't want to discuss something like their bowel movements in front of you. Spare them the humiliation and also the anxiety that could come if they don't say anything and then lose their chance to get to the bottom of their pooping issues for the next twelve hours.

Step 473: Be actually helpful to your friends, rather than vaguely helpful

Rather than saying, "What can I do?," anticipate a specific need and offer to fill it. People usually feel a little uncomfortable saying what they actually need because they don't want to be a burden, so they'll say, "Oh, nothing." Whereas "Can I watch your pet?" is much easier to say yes to.

YOUR GRIEF

I sort of wish none of us ever had to grieve anything, but we love people and pets and then we lose them and the immense grief is a testament to our ability to connect with another being. So... worth it? But God, it's terrible.

Your grief, when and if it comes, does not have to look like any particular thing. It will not be constant, but rather will come in waves, where one minute you are feeling normal and the next you're silently shaking and sobbing because you don't want anyone to overhear and comfort you; you want to be with and in a sadness that is as big as the sky.

It won't be linear, solved by x month with y strategies in z stages. Some losses will be surprisingly okay, and some will knock the wind out of you for a long, long time. There is just one way and that's through it. But as you are trudging, so slowly, through those dark woods, here are some things that will hopefully help.

Step 474: Breathe slowly

This sounds so simple, and it is. You can just focus, for a minute, on slow inhalation and slow exhalation. It might help to imagine your feelings as waves, rising up and then passing over your little island self.

Step 475: You can feel whatever you need to feel; some people will get it and others won't. Talk to the first group

About two weeks ago, my beloved Marigny the Cat died; we had fourteen years together. I'd always assumed she'd die in a knife fight with bobcats, but instead she went gently and stoically as I held her at the vet, ugly-crying.

The week before, I lost my last grandparent, Grandma Brown, who had a very, very hard life and who had been in constant terrible pain for several years leading up to her death.

For Grandma Brown, I felt mostly relief that she was finally free of the pain and depression that marked the last ten years of her life; I knew that her faith sustained her and that she was eager to be reunited with my grandfather, who had died almost thirty years earlier. I did not cry as much as I felt I should. For Marigny, I sobbed for days.

It's not a logical thing. I could not bully myself into feeling more or less sad than I did (which, for the record, was and is: Very). I could tell myself it was just a cat who honestly *didn't even particularly like me*, and it changed nothing. Nor does it need to.

This doesn't make me a bad granddaughter or a crazy cat lady. They're just big feelings that you're processing however you can. They're okay even when they hurt.

Step 476: You will almost certainly have a lot of guilt, and you can acknowledge these feelings without giving them the weight of truth

When my Grannybarb, who I was very close with, died, all I could see was what I hadn't done. She would have absolutely loved to go see this, and I always meant to take her, and never did. I could've called more; in this moment, I would give anything to hear her sweet voice. Why didn't she ever see my cute little house? She'd caught a glimpse of the outside and said it looked like an enchanted fairy house—*why didn't I bother to invite her inside?*

Grannybarb, happily, was a Zen Buddhist and made it very, very clear to everyone that her karma was in order and she was ready to go and, after she was gone, she didn't need or want anyone to feel guilty.

"Everyone has said what they needed to say and done what they needed to do, and so have I," she said on multiple occasions. She lived to be eighty-seven, and we had as uncomplicated a relationship as is possible between two humans, and she died a beautiful death, and *I still managed to find things to feel guilty about.*

But when I had those feelings, I could step back from them a tiny bit. Yes, of course, there are things I could've done that I didn't do. There are things that I *should* have done that I didn't do. But that is what it is, and I needed to make peace with it. So when those thoughts came up, I would hear the thought, then say to myself: *I love Granny-barb and I was the best granddaughter I could be,* which is a nice play off her mantra: Everyone does their best, and some people's best is shitty.

If your relationship was more complicated and convoluted, well, you did the best you could do. We all do. For better or worse, you *have* said what you needed to say, but you can always write a letter, or just go whisper in the wind, whatever is burning your tongue.

Step 477: Try to eat and drink and sleep, even (especially) when you don't feel like it

It feels as though the world has ended, and yet here you are, still breathing and digesting and perhaps growing toenail fungus.

Attending to your own basic well-being can all of a sudden feel like a monumental task, but please neglect it as little as possible. If you're not hungry, figure out how to get the right amount of calories in (I leaned heavily on white chocolate–raspberry protein bars). Drink more water than you think you need. Try to sleep; try to exercise. It's tough enough for your brain to just be; don't dehydrate it on top of everything else.

Step 478: Follow your gut when it comes to commemorating and celebrating them

Personally, it makes me very happy to have lots of things around that remind me of people that are no longer relaxing on this particular terrestrial plane with me; your mileage may vary. But if it feels good to make a little shrine in your backyard, or donate to a cause in their name, or wear that piece of inappropriately large costume jewelry every single day, *go for it*. Comfort is hard to come by in grief, and whatever brings that grace to you is probably a good thing.

Step 479: Watch for signs of complicated grief

Grief is—I'm going to use the scientific term here—so *phenomenally* sucky. You may feel totally gutted; you may feel rotated by the loss, subtly but permanently different than before. You might not sleep, or sleep all the time; never eat, or eat all the time; cry constantly, or feel like a robot trying to simulate human emotion. All of this is well within standard operating procedures. Again: not linear, not orderly.

But if your grief is enduring and indeed getting bigger, if you can't accept the death, if after many months you feel constant hopelessness, despair, or depression, it's possible you're in complicated grief, and you should find some help.

Unfairly (but also not surprisingly), people who have issues with depression, addiction, anxiety, and PTSD are more likely to suffer from complicated grief. If your loss was sudden, unexpected, violent, or preventable, this, too, can trigger it.

If you think you might have complicated grief going on, you can and should do some research and seek some professional help (for more on finding low-cost mental health resources, see step 463). If you don't know? Well, maybe go ahead and look into it, anyway. It can't hurt.

Step 480: Nothing needs to be past-tense about your relationship; it endures

It's inaccurate to say that I *loved* Grannybarb. I *love* her, present tense. I do not have access to her like I did when she was alive, but nothing about our relationship was undone by death. She will always have been my grandmother, just like Marigny will have always been my cat.

Step 481: If it's you who's having a hard time, accept that love and help graciously and gratefully

Just like the proper response to a compliment is not to try to tell the person why they're wrong about you, the proper response to offers of help that you need is not to say you're fine.

You can sense the difference between a sincere offer and someone saying it because they have to. Let the latter off the hook, and take the former up on it. People who love you sense so clearly your pain. It hurts them, too, and they want to alleviate their own pain, at least, by trying to do what they can for you. Let them.

THE LAW

Hopefully this goes without saying, but committing felonies is a decidedly non-adult move. Yes, even white-collar ones. Do your best to keep your nose clean, and if you do regularly flout the law, then be subtle and quiet about it. Don't be dumb or obvious about any recreational activities that the law might frown upon.

Step 482: Don't drink and drive, and yes, tipsiness counts

Duh. If the horrific potential safety consequences don't convince you, think about a suspended license, losing your job, having your name published in the crime blotter in your local paper, and spending thousands of dollars on a DUI attorney who—newsflash—may be able to alleviate some of the punishment but can't get you off entirely.

Step 483: If you need legal help, ask around for a good recommendation

Usually lawyers are willing to give just a tiny, tiny bit of their time for free, but they are more likely to do this if you come as a referral. "Hi, I'm John, I'm Susan Calabridi's son, and I had a quick question I was hoping to ask you."

Some lawyers, if they're really decent, will just answer your question, then let you know if you need further counsel.

Step 484: Know that there is often legal aid available

Many states have a lawyer referral service through their bar organization and can help recommend a lawyer who may be able to lend help for a minimal fee. Others have legal aid societies set up for issues of justice—say, for victims of domestic violence or people experiencing civil rights violations.

Another good option to find affordable law help is to call law schools in the area and see if they have a clinic in the type of law you need assistance with. If they say no, ask if they know any schools that do.

Step 485: Pick your battles with the police

You never need to admit anything to a police officer—no, you have no inkling of how fast you were going—and if you truly feel like your rights have been violated or the charge is unfair, then you should pursue it in court.

But if it's just a speeding ticket, chances are good that you were indeed speeding. Call the court, and say, "Hey, I have this speeding ticket and I'd like to plead no contest and I was wondering if you could reduce the charge if I just paid it in full now."

Other times, there may be the option of either doing community service or taking driver safety classes in order to have the charge dropped. Depending on how tight money is, this is always worth looking into.

Step 486: Know how to share bad news

It's an awful position to be in, but sometimes you will need to inform people about bad news. It's best to do this in person if you can, but don't keep people in suspense, because they will imagine the very worst thing possible.

Be direct, be clear, give as much information as specifically as you can, and tell if and when you'll have more. Be sympathetic, and also be prepared for a variety of reactions. Some people will dissolve, others will appear unmoved, and this is in no way an indication of how they actually feel.

"Hi, Megan, this is Kelly. I'm so sorry to say this, but I have some terrible news." Brief pause to allow this to sink in. "Amanda died in a car accident last night."

If the person in question is not dead, then you need to say that immediately, ideally before you state what bad thing has happened.

"I'm so sorry to let you know this, but I have some bad news. Amanda is in the intensive care unit at such-and-such hospital because she was in a serious car accident last night."

Then fill in the details as well as you can.

Step 487: Discuss will and estate issues with your parents

No one wants to talk about this. A conversation that hinges on the premise "What will life be like when you're dead?" is awkward and painful and generally the opposite of the things human beings enjoy in a conversation.

But not discussing death doesn't change reality, which is that chances are good that your parents will, at some point, no longer be alive. Figuring this stuff out in advance is infinitely easier than trying to muddle through after the fact. If they don't have a will, ask them to make one. This does not make you a cold person who won't care when their parents die. It makes you someone who will not have legal issues to grapple with on top of all the other mountainous awfulness that is losing a parent.

Step 488: If there are serious complications or squabbles within the family, you may want to hire an attorney

No one wants to fight about money issues with family, but an attorney can help defend your interests and can also provide a buffer against anger in the future. ("That wasn't me; that was the attorney.")

Step 489: Make a will

Yes, it seems unnecessary, and chances are it is. But if you're asking your parents to make one, it's only fair.

Discussion Questions

1. Does this chapter make you feel more or less depressed about life? Explain.
2. What is the ratio of kindly logging truckers to murderous logging truckers, do you think?
3. What is your worst Times Were Tough story?

Chapter 11
FAMILIES

Some of you reading this have super-happy, super-close families who gather each Sunday to eat, sing, laugh, love, and play everyone's favorite board game, during which no one fights and everyone wins. Some of you have chosen never to speak to your mother again. Most of us are somewhere in between, veering at various times closer to one side or the other of that continuum.

You can't change your family, but you can change how you deal with them. You can choose to emulate their good behaviors while rejecting any chaos or dysfunction that may come along with it.

As a grown-up, it's your job to establish new adult relationships with your family members. It's your job to draw boundaries with them. It's your job to figure out how to be a good family member, and how to love them the best you can. These, as you can imagine, are all sizable tasks, far more difficult than remembering that sweaters get folded, not hung up. But the payoff is much, much larger.

A brief note: A lot of this chapter is about the tough parts of being in a family. That's because no one has to tell you how to have a blast drinking with your cousins, or how to enjoy eating the kind of birthday cake your mom has made every year since you were little. Part of the beauty of family is that great things are so natural, so easy, and so self-evident. But because it's such a big and important part of our lives, the challenges are much larger and trickier.

A SHORT LIST OF THINGS YOUR PARENTS ARE NOT

- An ATM
- Caretakers of the place they think of as their house but is actually your pied-à-terre, where you drop in with no notice and behave however you want
- Gods
- Monsters (most of them, anyway)
- Responsible for picking up after your mistakes
- What stand in the way of you being a whole human being

Step 490: Bring as much grace to bear as you can when you interact with them

Before I get into this—which isn't just for families, but also for friends, significant others, co-workers, and the world at large—I will pause to introduce Laney Kibel, a licensed clinical social worker who has more than twenty-five years' experience with individual, family, and couples therapy.

"I like the word *grace*—in terms of being graceful in your interactions, being graceful in your interpretations, expecting the best, and assuming there's no malice in what people are doing to you," she said. "When in doubt or when your feelings have been hurt, ask for an explanation and an apology."

Give people who love you the benefit of the doubt. Chances are good they're not doing whatever it is to spite you. Chances are good they're doing it because they're just sort of pains in the ass. But they still love you.

Okay. On with the chapter. First things first: proving to your parents that you are, in fact, an adult, and deserve to be treated as such. This does not happen via a big hissy fit that culminates with you screaming, "YOU ARE NOT THE BOSS OF ME ANYMORE!"

Step 491: Remember that you're the one who's changed, not them, and the burden of proving that growth is on you

Your parents have been adults who more or less take care of themselves as long as you've been alive. You are the one who is now different, and you're the one who has to demonstrate that to them.

If you've been off at college, you've continued growing but they haven't been there to witness it. They were there when you started walking, but they weren't there on the first day of your real, grown-up job.

To me, I'm a grown-ass woman with a 401(k) and a regular fitness routine. Usually, that's how my parents see me, too. But they can still see me as an infant who, without their divine intervention, would've quickly suffocated under the weight and volume of her own poop.

And that's okay. The alternative to having people who view you that way is, I imagine, an undignified poop-smothered end. It's okay for them to see me that way, sometimes, and it's okay for me to push gently and respectfully back.

Step 492: Understand that as much as they want it for you, they also may need to mourn your independence a little bit

You being a grown-up means you are no longer the child they nurtured from infancy. They love you as an adult, too, but it is painful to see something you made and love more than anything spiral away from you. Those feelings are theirs to sort out, not yours. But accept that they probably have them.

Step 493: Be aware of what it means to them to be an adult, then highlight those elements of your life as proof you are a grown-up

If your dad always hammered at the importance of having a regular job, next time you're feeling the need to assert your adulthood, mention the fact that not only do you hold down a regular job, but you also just got a promotion. If your mom is obsessed with healthy living, let her know that not only are you eating well but you've even been working out recently. Reassure them that the lessons they tried so hard to pass on to you have indeed been learned.

"Sometimes it's difficult for parents to see adult children as adults if they're not doing the things [the parents] value as adults," said Sheila Walty, a licensed clinical social worker. "One of the things you can do is...find out what they value, then connect it with whatever part of that adult value you agree with."

Step 494: Do not accept money regularly from them

It's hard to prove you are independent if you depend on your parents for things, since that is in fact the opposite of what independent means. This happens especially with money. Accepting your parents' money makes them shareholders in your life. And they probably see themselves as the kind of shareholder that gets a vote when big decisions are made.

Do your very, very best to find a job (chapter 5) and get your finances in order (chapter 6) to live within your means and only very rarely request a withdrawal from Parental Interstate Bank.

"Taking handouts from your folks shouldn't be routine," my friend Nancy quite wisely said. "You should be able to conduct a reasonable life without their financial assistance."

This is especially important if your parents are the type who give money with strings attached.

Crystal Mattox, a licensed marriage and family therapist, told me one of her clients was getting married, and the bride's mother refused to help pay for the wedding unless the couple agreed to get married at a specific location. The bride, quite reasonably, refused the money and got married where the couple wanted.

This kind of controlling behavior, Crystal said, is a slippery slope.

"If they help with the house, do they get to pick the color of curtains?" she said.

Step 495: There is a difference between turning to your parents and relying on your parents

Your parents will always wish to feel like they are a part of your life, and they will always wish to feel wanted and valued. That's the key: want them, don't need them. Asking your mom for her thoughts is different from not being able to make a decision without her weigh-in.

"It doesn't mean that you should start viewing your parents as use-less; it's just a transition from benevolent dictator to trusted adviser," Nancy said.

Step 496: Pick up the tab sometimes at restaurants

Once you can afford it, of course. This is undeniably grown-up, and makes two statements: One, you're doing well enough to buy din-ner, which in and of itself is a great sign. Two, you are aware that this parent-child relationship is no longer one where all the obligation lies with one party.

BE GOOD TO THEM

You can't ever repay what your older relatives have given to you, and you're not obligated to. It's not a debt that you have to spend the rest of your life repaying. But all parents, except in rare and abusive cases, deserve your gratitude and appreciation. They gave their life to you, willingly. The least you can do is call on their birthday.

It's not just that they deserve it, but that you should want to give it. It's depressing but true that you will only ever have less time with your grandparents and parents, never more. They will, someday, be gone, and you will go on without them. So be good to them and love them now. Tell them that you love them.

Being good means different things to different people, but here are some general strategies for coming to appreciate and demonstrate your love for them.

Step 497: Your parents have first names. They have secrets you will never know. They do not just exist as an extension of you

"Imagining my mother as a child was unfathomable," Laney said. "I could see pictures and see she actually was once a child. But it was impossible to imagine what my mother was like as a teen or in the workplace."

But as we grow, she said, we should see our parents as whole people. I asked why that was important.

"I'll put the question back to you: Why is it important to you for them to see you as a whole person and not just a daughter?"

Step 498: Get to know them as people

What did your dad want to be when he was a kid? Who was your mom's first crush? What do they look for in a friend? What is the saddest they've ever been?

When you get to be an adult, you can actually be friends with your parents, and it's so, so satisfying. Get to know them not just as your parents but as actual people, and in time they will come to regard you as someone they can confide in, someone with whom they can share details beyond the "Aunt Susan is coming to visit next week" sort. One of the proudest days of my life came when my mom called me to ask my opinion on a problem she was having at work.

Step 499: Remember, when you talk to them, that you are not the only person with a life

Obviously, you should call on their birthdays and respective Hallmark holidays, but ask—and listen to—how their day was. Write them a note wishing them many years of love on their anniversary (and, even better, put a couple of lines in there about what they've taught you about love, by their example). Learn of their triumphs, and congratulate them. When possible, go celebrate their milestones in person, rather than expecting they'll always come to visit you.

Step 500: Call as much as you can

This has been a public service announcement from someone who really, really wishes she could call her Grannybarb.

Okay, maybe not as much as you can, but there is no reason you can't call every week or so. They love you and they miss you and chances are good that when you left, you took a big old chunk of them with you. If you don't live in the same town, then phone calls are all they have to sustain them between the occasional visits.

It doesn't have to be an hour-long conversation. If your mom or dad tends toward long-windedness, let them know at the beginning of the conversation that you're on your way somewhere, or someone is about to stop by. A ten-minute call is way better than none.

Step 501: While you can and should assert your independence, let them know their input and opinion still matter to you

"I am learning that letting them be part of important decisions and asking their advice helps maintain the intimacy of the parental relationship, and lets them know I still need them, just maybe in a different sort of way," was my friend Rachel's great response to the question of how to involve your parents in your life.

Step 502: Send them cards, maybe with a recent photo of you and your friends inside

This costs maybe three bucks total (fifty-cent stamp + fifty-cent photo + two-dollar card) and will give your mom or dad twenty-five dollars' worth of pleasure. Write a pen-pal-style note inside, maybe explaining the photo ("Molly and I went to see Boyz II Men at the casino!") and let them know you love them and miss them.

Step 503: Let them live vicariously through you, and share your triumphs freely

Basically, there are two people in the world who will almost never, ever tire of the subject of How Great You Are. Your friends are happy for good things that happen to you, but no one else cares about the blow-by-blow of how great you did on your work presentation.

"Include them, so they get to see the fruits of what they've done," said counselor Sheila. "Their pride is often based in how their kids are doing."

Remember: You are their life's work (although, as we established above, you're not the only thing in their life). They spent more time trying to make you into a decent, functional human being than they probably spent on anything else. It's nice to let them know when their efforts have paid off.

BOUNDARIES

Boundaries is one of those words that you shouldn't use too often around casual acquaintances. Frequently referencing your boundaries implies you're the intense oversharing type who talks a lot about your dreams and unexpectedly drops raw details about your sex life.

But boundaries are everything when it comes to families. There is a Venn diagram at play here: things your family wants from you, and things you can provide. Hopefully these circles very nearly overlap, but the farther apart they are, the more extensive the boundaries to set will be.

A VENN DIAGRAM
of familial
→ BOUNDARIES! ←

- Thrice-daily check-ins
- Veto power over job/partner/location choice
- Coming home for Arbor Day
- Docility
- For your hair to look nice, for once.

THIS IS WHERE BOUNDARIES GO!

- Weekly phone calls
- Presence at some holidays
- Kindness, consideration & respect
- Etc.

- Never calling except to ask for something
- Sleeping through Nana's 90th b-day
- Getting sullen & angry that they are just being SO THEM!!!
- Explaining, in depth, your polyamorous dabbling.

Things your family wants you to do

Things you can do without feeling resentful or insane

Step 504: No one, ever, will set your boundaries for you. So learn to set them yourself

This isn't even an issue of other people not wanting to. They are simply not capable of it. No one in the world, except you, is inside your head. No one in the world can take your emotional temperature with the perfect accuracy that you can. No one knows what's fine with you versus what feels like a nail file grating your stomach.

Step 505: With a given relative, figure out what you can and can't do

This, Laney said, is the first step: Figure out what your boundaries are.

"The first thing you need to do in setting a boundary is checking in with yourself," she said. If you decide you do not want to do something, then you can offer an alternative, though you don't have to. If a relative who stresses you out wants to go on a trip together, you can decline but also figure out a way to spend less time together with an easier escape route, should things go south.

Yes: You should do things you don't feel like doing for your family. Sometimes, I didn't feel like calling my grandmother as much as I felt like lying in bed watching episodes of *Mad Men*. If you don't feel like something but know it would make a relative of yours more happy than it makes you sad/bored/neither sad nor bored but also not getting to do something you'd slightly prefer, just do it. It's good karma. Seriously, call your grandmother right now.

But there is a fine line between not feeling like something and not wanting or being able to do something. The things that you truly can't or won't do, for your own sake: Those are the boundaries.

Step 506: Graciously deflect them when they're overstepping their bounds

Crystal said that it's important to remember that chances are very good the reason they want to give so much input is that they care about you and just want you to make (what they are certain is) the right decision. You can and should say, "I know you want to help me, and I know you are trying to support me." But you can shut the conversation down when overstep happens.

"You can say, 'I hope you hear that I can figure this out myself. I appreciate your concern.'"

If they won't drop it, then let them know there will be a consequence.

"Dad, if we can't let this topic go, I'm going to have to hang up and we can talk later."

Step 507: Your family does not get veto power over your life decisions

Sometimes, you just have to say, "I'm sorry you feel that way. This is what I'm doing." Then do it. This, of course, is much easier to say if you're not dependent on them for money.

Step 508: Use "and" instead of "but"

The problem with saying something like "I love you, but…" is that the *but* sort of invalidates the first part of the sentence, and sets up whatever you are about to say as being in direct opposition with your love for them.

It feels off at first, but you can use *and* instead.

"I love you and I need you to respect that this is the decision I've made" sounds very different from "I love you but I need you to respect that this is the decision I've made." Yet they're saying the same thing.

Step 509: You don't always have to pick up the phone and deal with things right then. You can take a little bit of time to figure things out for yourself

Sometimes, you're equipped to deal with shit that your family needs you to talk about, and sometimes you're not.

VISITS AND HOLIDAYS

Holidays are so f'ing *fraught*. There are so many moving parts, so many things that have to happen, so many things that must not, under any circumstances, happen, so many opportunities to hurt so many feelings. Holidays, in short, are a time to summon every bit of adulthood you can bring to bear. Holidays are a time when you can screw up spectacularly, or—*or!*—you can come out, in the immortal words of Britney Spears, stronger than yesterday.

Step 510: If you're staying with them, do not regress

It is especially easy to slip back into old habits and emotions whilst in your childhood home. It smells like you are sixteen again, the clothing from your regrettable goth phase is hanging in the closet, there's your old bed with the comforter you thought was the height of sophistication when you were a sophomore and...you know what? Maybe you *should* stomp off from the breakfast table and fling yourself onto your old bed, sobbing that no one understands you. That is a luxury you don't have in your current apartment!

Your mom—whom you love *very much*—is right there doing her Mom Thing, and your dad is matching her shot-for-shot in Dadness. Your siblings, whom you love and cherish, are a little bit tougher to deal with when you're all squished into the extra bedroom together.

It's enough to just be aware of this tendency and, when you find yourself getting irritated or flustered, take a minute to examine your feelings. What is actually upsetting you right now? Rather than have an argument that probably won't help anything, is there a good coping mechanism you could employ? Maybe even just offering to run to the grocery store, and then sitting in the parking lot for way, way too long?

Step 511: Take everyone's wishes into account, then set your own schedule

Particularly if you live far away, this may be the only part of the year your parents get to spend quality time with you. If you live far away, this also is perhaps your only chance to see your old friends.

Ask in advance when it's really important for you to be with the family, then decide how much time you should/want to spend with them and let them know when you'll be around and when you won't. Maybe you'll be with the family in the earlier evening, but leave at 9 PM to meet your old friends...and maybe make out with that guy you thought was so cute in high school. There is nothing like a boozy December 23 impromptu high school reunion.

Step 512: If you are a child of divorce, do not twist yourself into knots to make everyone happy

If you can make it to both Thanksgiving dinners, great! If you don't want to, that is your right. You can go to both, or one, or neither. You're a grown-up. Grown-ups get to set their schedule and make decisions for themselves. The paradigm for decision making does not have to be "What will leave everyone feeling least hurt?" It can be "How can I show love and respect to my family while also maintaining my own sanity?"

Step 513: Figure out how to make yourself an adult part of the celebration

Bring something for Thanksgiving dinner, something you make a killer version of, something that people will happily anticipate in the years to come. Arrive for Christmas with all your presents already wrapped, so you don't have to hit your mom up for wrapping paper. Don't pick fights with ornery relatives (see step 530). Go with the flow, and make people happy you're there.

Step 514: Be a good houseguest when staying with relatives

Being a good houseguest goes a long way toward establishing that you are not, in fact, your time-traveling high school self.

Pick up after yourself. Offer to help with dishes. Go get some groceries, then cook breakfast. Be mindful of not interrupting routines. Don't hog the shower; don't leave wet towels on the bed. Before you leave, go buy some fresh flowers for the kitchen table. These are actions that implicitly acknowledge that you are not permanently entitled to a bedroom in your parents' house—which, in turn, implies that they should not treat you like the teenager who was.

Step 515: If they drive you nuts, get a hotel room or stay with a friend

In both cases, you can plead convenience—"There are so many people staying there right now, it'd probably be easier for me to just stay with Steve. He's got a guest bedroom." If you're traveling with a significant other, say they're allergic to the pet.

You could even, controversial though this may be, tell a gentle version of the truth: "You know, Dad, I feel like every time I come stay with you, we end up fighting. I really want to see you, and I think this is a good way for us to spend time together while still having our own space."

This can go a long, long way toward restoring your sanity. It also subtly reminds your relatives that you are not just there to visit them; you are there to visit lots of people.

Step 516: If you know you need it, build in some time and space for yourself

If you are an introvert, if you are used to having a lot of quiet downtime and all of a sudden there are fifteen relatives every time you turn around, if—much as you love them—just being with your family causes you a lot of stress, then figuring out where your quiet, calm times will be is extra important.

Again, it may just be offering to run to the store.

MOVING BACK IN

If you live with your parents, you need to be working hard to move out. You just do. If you are living with your parents, moving out is priority one in embracing your adulthood. It is nearly impossible to feel like you are standing on your own two feet when your mom grocery shops for you.

But it happens. People lose jobs; people get out of bad relationships; people graduate and take nine months to find work. View this as a temporary, non-ideal situation, but one in which you can still act maturely and conscientiously. Much of that mature conscientiousness should be dedicated to figuring out and working on whatever your next move will be.

Step 517: Before you move in, have a long, difficult conversation about what you expect, and what they expect

Ideally, you'll start this discussion with an end date—"I will have figured out another living situation by [month]." Six months is a good upper end to things; three's even better. This tells them—and yourself—that this isn't a permanent state of being. You're there because you're in a hard spot, and hard spots don't evaporate overnight. But inertia is so easy to come by, and having a solid deadline keeps you on track to get out.

You also want to discuss money—can you contribute any?—and chores, and expectations. The problem here, of course, is that as my friend's smart dad Alan put it, if you're accepting someone's help, you also have to accept their advice. But the more you understand what is expected of you, and the more you can articulate your (inherently restricted) boundaries, the happier both you and they will be.

Step 518: If you are living with your parents, they control what happens under their roof. They do not control you

Being in your childhood home does not mean you are a child again. You must stick to the expectations they've set out for how you conduct yourself in the house. They might be unreasonable. They might be unpleasant. All the more incentive for you to get your life together and go.

However, you should remember that you are still an autonomous human being. You still get to make decisions for yourself.

Say your parents hate your boyfriend. While they are within their rights to say they don't want him in the house, they are out of line in insisting you break up with him. Every time you step out the door, you regain the autonomy you give up when you step inside. Use it.

Step 519: Do non-monetary things to help out

Showing your parents that you appreciate what they're doing for you goes a long way, and a great way to do that is to figure out things that they can't or don't really want to do around the house, then do them.

"It's not that you owe it to them, but that you want to do something to show your appreciation," Sheila said. "Everyone is way more willing to give when they feel appreciated."

Step 520: Get out

Really. Find roommates, find a job, find a way to make it on your own. You can. Seriously.

NEW RELATIVES

Family is not a static thing. Yes, you're born with some, but all along the way you gain and lose people. Happily, there are more gains than losses. People marry each other, babies are born, and graying black sheep return to the fold.

While people always enter into a family due to love, it's not necessarily *your* love for that person that brings them. But while you may not adore them right off the bat, you will probably grow to. In the meantime, you can be decent.

Step 521: *When someone is in the process of becoming family, make them feel especially welcome*

Even if you've never become part of a family by marriage, you've surely spent a holiday at a friend's house. Some families are just *delighted* that you're there and for the day, you are family. Some don't include you in anything because they don't notice you. You are an afterthought.

Get to know this new person. Welcome them, let them know that anyone who Cousin Sarah loves is all right by you. Tell them a little bit about the family itself—not deep dark stuff, but the inside jokes, the traditions, who maybe will get a little bit too tipsy, who to avoid sitting next to unless you want to hear the latest Limbaugh talking points.

Step 522: *Trust the judgment of the person who is bringing them into the family*

Here I will introduce Molly, a particularly insightful friend of mine who grew up in a family that blended, unblended, and reblended several times over. She maintains great relationships with father figures from her childhood but also has recently gained a new stepfamily.

So let's say one of your parents is getting married.

"Your job is to be supportive of your parent, to try to trust them and trust their judgment," she said.

But what if you don't like the spouse-to-be?

"I felt that way about some of my mom's boyfriends at first, but they've all grown on me over time," she said, adding that there's a difference between someone you just don't super care for versus someone whom you actively think is bad for your loved one. "The thing that's really important is that this person makes [my mom] happy, and is kind to me. Everything else is secondary."

Step 523: It's okay to feel apprehensive, but try to be enthusiastic about new people, at least on the surface

Having grown up as an only child, Molly said, it was weird for her to gain three stepsiblings at age twenty-seven.

"I'm lucky in that both my two stepsisters and my stepbrother are really enthusiastic—they're excited about me, and having me be a part of their family," she said. "I was a little caught off guard by their enthusiasm, partially because I'm an only child, but I was so touched by the warmth with which they received me. It comes back to having an open mind and giving myself a chance to appreciate this as a good thing, and not more complication."

Step 524: You don't have to be Best Friends Forever with someone else's new significant other

There is no need to make them a friendship anklet, or go on a one-on-one road trip, or anything. They're not marrying you, after all. You just have to be cordial and kind.

Step 525: If you do have serious concerns about the person, voice them to your relative

You have to do this kindly and respectfully, but this is the same as telling a friend when they are doing serious, perhaps irreparable, damage to their life (see step 349). Remaining silent is not the loving thing to do.

Step 526: You can and should remain in touch with former step-relatives, if you want

If you consider someone a relative, even if it's by marriage, they remain your relative when the marriage is over. Just because your dad divorces his wife doesn't mean you do.

Molly keeps in close touch with her former stepdad.

"I think, coming from a kind of non-traditional, blended family, I have recognized that if you've got a dad, even if he's not your 'real dad,' you shouldn't take that for granted," she said. "If they want to be a part of your life, and you want them to be a part of your life, then just keep working on it."

Step 527: When you are the new guy or girl of the family, do some chores

That is a gross simplification for step-title-writing purposes. But you could take a page from one especially clever aunt I know.

When she started coming to family celebrations, she would always find a chore to do—washing dishes, say, or setting the table. Not only does this demonstrate that you're a helpful, thoughtful sort of person, but it will also goad other people into coming and helping you, and then you can just chat happily away.

Step 528: Suspend judgment on the family you're entering into

A good 60 percent of families are an acquired taste. When you first show up, there is so much backstory, so many traditions, so much invisible social matter that you can't see and then accidentally bump into. It's easy to feel lonely and lost in the mix.

Maybe this is the kind of family that loves to holler at one another. Maybe they sit quietly, and that's their togetherness. Whatever it is, chances are decent that it's not what your family does.

But this is how it will go: The first few times, everything will be sort of confusing. Visits four through ten will still feel a little probationary. But sooner rather than later, you will understand the physics of this family and feel welcome. If you don't feel welcome, summon your maturity and slog through it. Every family visit comes to an end.

TOXIC RELATIVES

You know if you have a relative who is a toxic presence in your life.

When I was a reporter in Mississippi, I covered several towns that had maybe eight hundred people in them, the sort of place where people neither left nor arrived. And if two dudes in their seventies were fighting during a town hall meeting, you knew this was not the first problem they'd had. Their differences likely went back to a girl problem that happened in the 1930s. There is a similar dynamic at play with unreasonable family members. Whatever you're fighting about this moment isn't the fight you're having. It's just the latest skirmish in a long war.

As Molly put it, "Part of being an adult is knowing the difference between the relationships that you can grow from, and the ones that are going to hurt you."

There is, of course, the nuclear option. You can write someone off. You do not owe them your presence in their life. Sometimes, you have to do that. But more often, you need to figure out a way to limit their presence in your life while hopefully improving the relationship.

Step 529: Decide, consciously, that their dysfunction and their chaos are not yours

There are some things that aren't your fault but are your problem. Relatives who make your head and heart hurt are high on that list.

You can't control them. You cannot cure their substance abuse issues or their deep-seated anger. All you can control is yourself and your reaction to their behavior. When you internalize their self-destruction, when you allow yourself to be manipulated and abused and squished to fit around their issues, you do yourself a great disservice.

You can—and should—say to yourself, *I don't have anything to do with this. This is not my deal. This is her problem, and I can't solve it, and I'm going to detach with love.*

These are hard, hard things to do. These are things that likely require therapy, or Al-Anon, or similarly extensive work on yourself. You need to do that work on yourself. That is the other side of the "can't control them, can control me" equation.

Step 530: If someone is constantly passive-aggressive, act dumb and take them at their word

This was a brilliant strategy from Sheila.

"Even if someone's lying to you, act like they're telling the truth," she said. "If they say, 'I want to do this for you, and it's a gift from me, and I don't want anything in return,' even if you don't think that's true, act like it is and hold them accountable."

This, she said, gives you a watertight alibi if they try to guilt you later. "Then, if they say, 'I did this for you; why won't you do that for me?' you can say, 'That was a wonderful gift you gave me.' If we hold them accountable, it puts them in a position of being uncomfortable because they didn't speak their truth, rather than us being uncomfortable because they didn't speak their truth."

Step 531: When a family member hurts your feelings, do not strike back with the same

You all know this already, but it's the kind of thing we know but never remember when it counts. The solution to someone hurting your feelings is not to hurt them back. That does not unhurt your feelings; it just makes it so unlikely that anything useful will be accomplished.

How responsive and open are you to what someone has to say immediately after they hurt you? There you go. You cannot control what that person has done or said; you can only control your response.

"Rather than fly off the handle and assume there was intention, be graceful and think, *Okay, would they really want to be hurting me?* Maybe a conversation could help clear this up," Laney said.

Step 532: If they won't have a conversation, disengage

Sometimes, people are willing to have a conversation. Sometimes they're not. It may or may not be a permanent thing. But for whatever reason, right now they don't or can't hear what you're saying, especially if they're really angry.

"When you finally have established *Okay, we're not going any-place*, then it becomes a matter of self-protection," Laney said. "You're not going to convince your mother to be different than who she is, so on your behalf, you have to come to the point of *I'm not going to expose myself to hurt anymore.*"

Step 533: Before you write someone off completely, make sure you've had a serious talk first

I asked Laney how to make an exit when you just could not deal with someone anymore, be it friend or family member. What should you say?

"Why didn't you say something to them earlier?" she asked. "Half of people out there come from divorced families...and what you don't learn is how to resolve conflict. Resolution never comes, because we go away from each other and that's the resolution. We leave families, we leave friends. But it is so much more valuable when we are willing to fight the good fight to save the relationship."

Step 534: You do not owe them your presence

"I don't think, because someone has brought you into the world, or is related to you by blood, that it entitles them to mistreat you, or fail to operate under the standard that you want people in your life to live by," Crystal said.

If you have given a good-faith effort to make it work—if you have clearly outlined what it will take for them to repair the relationship with you, if you have offered to go to counseling together, if at the end of the day you both look at the same situation and see vastly different things, then your life may be better without them, at least for now.

You don't have to write them off forever. You can say, "You know, I think we both need some time to ourselves. I'm still willing to do X, Y, and Z. Until those things are done, I can't be in your life."

Step 535: Recognize that family is like love—a huge pain in the ass that's worth it a million times over

The concept of family isn't even about what it means to be a human. It's about what it means to be a mammal. It is a deep and powerful and primal thing. It connects us to one another, to the past, and to the future in ways that cannot be replicated elsewhere. So when you feel the stress of obligations, or frustration with this or that person, remind yourself that whatever is bothering you is a small facet of something very large and valuable. You are, in the eyes of the world, small and insignificant. But to a select few people, you are big, and important, as they are to you. So seriously. Call your grandmother.

DISCUSSION QUESTIONS

1. What's the most powerful guilt trip your mom has ever laid on you? On a scale of one to crying, how guilty did you feel?
2. Who is the black sheep of your family? What, precisely, makes them the black sheep? Can someone please, please organize a Black Sheep of the World conference, complete with Creepy Uncle Muscle Car Show and Crazy Aunt Spirit Healing Seminars? Please, someone, do that.
3. Have you called your grandmother yet?

Chapter 12
CONCLUSION

You are already way more of an adult than you think you are. Truly. Please be gentle with yourself, and give yourself credit where credit is due. Be good, be decent, be responsible, be kind. And don't forget to send thank-you notes.

ACKNOWLEDGMENTS

Without the incredible advice, support, and feedback from the following people, this book would be maybe fourteen pages long, and no one would ever have seen it for self-evident reasons.

Thank you first and foremost to Meredith "Editor" Haggerty, for brilliant edits and kindly phrased suggestions and a *lot* of glorious .bmps, and Brandi Bowles, a literary agent who is fearsome in the very best way, and the second most talented editor ever, after Meredith.

Thank you to Bill Church and Michelle Maxwell, who were so very, very endlessly patient with me, and Dana Borowitz and Adam Biren, for similar reasons.

Thank you, Ruth Liao, for the idea that became this book. Thank you to Jessica Maxwell, David McRaney, and Dana Haynes, for sage advice born of experience with this terrifying process.

Thanks to Will Bragg for so many super photos, and thank you to everyone at Grand Central Publishing, including but not limited to Carolyn Kurek in managing editorial, Giraud Lorber in production, flawless copy editor and ruthless mistake-finder Laura Jorstad, and Brigid Pearson in art.

Thank you Nancy Kaffer and Rachel Norman, for setting such wonderfully adult examples for me and for generous, near-constant feedback. Thank you to those willing to weigh in with edits, including Sarah Moore, Joce DeWitt, Megan Crandall, Andrew Ghetia, Shadra Beesley, Erin Sarin, and Elisabeth Frei.

Thank you to everyone who took the time to explain to me how to be an adult, including Bonnie Trumbull, Alan and Carol Kaplan, Jillian Kramer, Charles Price, Conrad Venti, Ron Kelemen, David Rosales, Carol Currie, Marissa Van Dyke, Karen Cristobal, Bharat Sharma, Susan Owre Gelberg, Jason Seibert, Shantrell Austin, Chris and Steve Hightower, Molly Woon, Stacey Dycus, Shane Rosenblatt, Brittni Lipscomb, Christine Lipscomb, Christina Olson, Tina Earhart, Sam Hart, Cindy Jackson, Sarah Von Bargen, Mary Henderson, Ben Lundin, Jared Mason-Gere, Laney Kibel, Crystal Mattox, Sheila Walty, Kyle Sexton, and Dana Michaels.

Thank you to the wise, if occasionally inebriated, patrons of *f/*Stop, plus Mark and Tiffany Bulgin at IKE Box and pretty much everyone in Salem. Thank you to all the wonderful and smart blog readers, who provided so many clever tips and suggestions that ended up in here. Thank you to Dave Gluck, who made this book inestimably better. Thank you to my friends (many of whom were named above) for not only understanding why I was being a neurotic hermit but also for loving me anyway when I emerged.

Four years later, I'd like to give all the thanks in the world to Davey Shlasko, Lelia Gowland, and Lois Mulrooney for their wonderful thoughts. To the wise and judicious Editrix Morgan Hedden, so gentle yet appropriately firm during what was, objectively, one of the most difficult periods of my life. To Kimberly Fanshier, Caitlin Carlson-Burkhart, Elizabeth Schulte; I am so grateful to have y'all as my coven and as part of the Sapphic Laughter Home. To Brooke Jackson-Glidden, who is a rare pearl and gem *at the same ding-dang time!* Thanks to Paul, for quietly approving and for surprising me with possibilities that I didn't think existed. Finally, thank you most of all to Mom, Dad, Olivia, and Elizabeth.

INDEX

ABOUT THE AUTHOR

KELLY WILLIAMS BROWN is an award-winning features reporter and columnist. In addition to this book, she is the author of *Gracious*. She is originally from Louisiana, now lives in Oregon, and is sometimes, but not always, an adult.